THE COMPLETE

VEGETARIAN

COOKBOOK

Cataloguing data available from Bibliothèque et Archives nationales du Québec.

08-17

© 2017, Juniper Publishing, a division of Sogides Group Inc., a subsidiary of Quebecor Media Inc. (Montreal, Quebec)

Legal deposit: 2017
Bibliothèque et Archives nationales du Québec
Library and Archives Canada

ISBN 978-1-988002-75-0

Printed in Canada

**EXCLUSIVE DISTRIBUTOR
FOR CANADA & USA**

Simon & Schuster Canada
166 King Street East, Suite 300
Toronto ON M5A 1J3

Tel: 647-427-8882
Toll Free: 800-387-0446
Fax: 647-430-9446

simonandschuster.ca
canadianliving.com/books

Government of Quebec – Tax credit for book publishing – Administered by SODEC. **sodec.gouv.qc.ca**

This publisher gratefully acknowledges the support of the Société de développement des enterprises culturelles du Québec.

Canada Council   Conseil des arts
for the Arts   du Canada

We gratefully acknowledge the support of the Canada Council for the Arts for its publishing program.

We acknowledge the financial support of our publishing activity by the Government of Canada through the Canada Book Fund for our publishing activities.

ART DIRECTOR	EDITOR	COPY EDITOR	INDEXER
Colin Elliott	Martin Zibauer	Ruth Hanley	Lisa Fielding

Canadian Living

THE COMPLETE
VEGETARIAN
COOKBOOK

BY THE CANADIAN LIVING TEST KITCHEN

JUNIPER
PUBLISHING
A Quebecor Media Corporation

FROM OUR KITCHEN

Vegetarian food everyone will love!

Whether motivated by health and wellness, ethical choices or sustainability, many of us are embracing a more veggie-forward, plant-based diet. And why not? We're enamoured with the rainbow hues and rich tones of flavourful fruits and vegetables, and we find soothing comfort and satisfaction in the sometimes chewy, sometimes velvety textures of grains and pulses. Vegetarianism is no longer just about going meatless, it's about cooking and eating great food, period. Whether you're introducing your family to new dishes or simply looking for ways to expand your repertoire of go-to favourites, we're here to help. Bringing you deliciously healthy, trustworthy recipes is the top priority for us in the Canadian Living Test Kitchen.

WHAT DOES TESTED TILL PERFECT MEAN?

Every year, the food specialists in the Canadian Living Test Kitchen work together to produce approximately 500 Tested-Till-Perfect recipes. So what does Tested Till Perfect mean? It means we follow a rigorous process to ensure you'll get the same results in your kitchen as we do in ours.

HERE'S WHAT WE DO:

- In the Test Kitchen, we use the same everyday ingredients and equipment commonly found in kitchens across Canada.

- We start by researching ideas and brainstorming as a team.

- We write up the recipe and go straight into the kitchen to try it out.

- We taste, evaluate and tweak the recipe until we really love it.

- Once developed, each recipe gets handed off to other food editors for more testing and another tasting session.

- We meticulously test and retest each recipe as many times as it takes to make sure it turns out as perfectly in your kitchen as it does in ours.

- We carefully weigh and measure all ingredients, record the data and send the recipe for nutritional analysis.

- The recipe is then edited and rechecked to ensure all the information is correct and it's ready for you to cook.

Complete Contents

Healthy & Delicious..............6

Breakfasts...........................12
Breads.................................36
Basics.................................46
Appetizers & Snacks..........70
Soups.................................94
Salads................................112
Mains.................................148
Sides..................................234
Desserts.............................276

Index..................................293

ONE-POT QUINOA CHILI
P 188

**CURRIED CAULIFLOWER &
SPINACH WRAPS**
P 154

Complete Healthy & Delicious | 1

The produce section of any grocery store is a
creative playground for family cooks, with
a rainbow of colours and an incredible variety
of flavours and textures, as well as new choices
of healthy, nutritious fruits and vegetables with
each season. To make the most of this vegetarian
abundance, all you need are outstanding recipes
and cooking tips that make easy, quick and
delicious meals. Here they are.

Many of us trying to go meatless worry about getting enough protein, but it's easier than you may think. And with the health and environmental benefits of switching to fruits, vegetables, grains, nuts and other plant-based foods, it's good to know that we can get all of our protein needs from these sources.

Protein helps build muscle and repair tissues. According to Health Canada, the average adult needs about 0.8 grams of protein daily for every kilogram of body weight. That means a 154-pound (70-kilogram) adult needs about 56 grams of protein a day. If you're very active or recovering from an illness or injury, you may need more.

In the past, vegetarians carefully paired foods in each meal to get a full complement of amino acids, the building blocks of protein. Current research has shown that protein combining within a single meal isn't necessary; as long as you eat a variety of plant-based foods through the course of the day and the week, your body will combine amino acids to form complete proteins.

Here are some of the foods you should be eating to help meet your body's protein needs and how much protein each contains.

Soy products

Long used by vegans and vegetarians in healthful meals, soy products are loaded with protein.

TOFU (firm, ½ cup): 20 g
TEMPEH (½ cup): 16 g
EDAMAME (½ cup): 9 g
SOY MILK (½ cup): 4 g

Legumes

Legumes—including beans, lentils, and peanuts—are some of the most healthful protein sources around.

LENTILS (cooked, ½ cup): 9 g
BLACK BEANS (cooked, ½ cup): 8 g
CHICKPEAS (cooked, ½ cup): 8 g
KIDNEY BEANS (cooked, ½ cup): 8 g
PEANUTS (¼ cup): 9 g

MENUS
Special occasion meals for family and friends

SUMMER BARBECUE

- *Grilled Black Bean Tostadas With Mango Avocado Salad*, **page 156**
- *Halloumi and Quinoa Salad With Sumac-Lime Dressing*, **page 137**
- *Grilled Parmesan Corn*, **page 265**
- *Rosé Snow Cones*, **page 280**

VEGAN BIRTHDAY PARTY

- *Fried Tofu With Spicy Sesame Dipping Sauce*, **page 76**
- *Shaved Beet and Celery Root Salad*, **page 146**
- *Spinach and Avocado Green Goddess Pasta*, **page 174**
- *Roasted Grape Tomatoes*, **page 155**
- *Dark and Delicious Vegan Chocolate Cake*, **page 290**

Protein power!

Grains

Grains in their whole form have a significant amount of protein. Check for "whole grain" on the label when you buy flours, and try these grains in salads or as the basis for protein-rich breakfasts.

STEEL-CUT OATS (dry, ¼ cup): 7 g
QUINOA (cooked, ½ cup): 4 g
SPROUTED BREAD (1 slice): 4 g
BUCKWHEAT (cooked, ½ cup): 3 g
MILLET (cooked, ½ cup): 3 g
BARLEY (cooked, ½ cup): 2 g

Nuts

Like seeds, nuts can be sprinkled on almost anything (think salads, noodle dishes and desserts), but they can also be eaten plain as a snack. And don't forget about nut butters, which are delicious spread on crackers or used in sauces.

ALMONDS (¼ cup): 8 g
ALMOND BUTTER (2 tbsp): 4 g
PISTACHIOS (¼ cup): 7 g
WALNUTS (¼ cup): 4 g

Vegetables

Other vegetables contain protein too, though often not in the amounts found in grains and legumes. But it all adds up—along with the many health benefits these foods offer.

MUSHROOM (sliced, ½ cup): 1 g
BROCCOLI (chopped, ½ cup): 1 g
KALE (1 cup): 2 g
SPINACH (1 cup): 1 g

Seeds

Seeds can serve as an easy and natural protein addition to just about any meal. Sprinkle them on a salad, over a stir-fry or into a smoothie. Many also contain healthy fats and fibre.

HEMP HEARTS (3 tbsp): 10 g
SUNFLOWER SEEDS (¼ cup): 7 g
CHIA SEEDS (1 tbsp): 3 g
TAHINI (1 tbsp): 3 g
FLAXSEED (1 tbsp): 2 g

FINE DINING

- *Apple and Blue Cheese Tartlets With Ice Wine Glaze,* **page 89**
- *Tomato Soup With Pesto Drizzle,* **page 96**
- *Spinach and Roasted Squash Lasagna,* **page 182**
- *Blood Orange and Fennel Salad,* **page 117**
- *Dairy-Free Chocolate Fondue,* **page 285**

SUNDAY BRUNCH

- *Clementine Turmeric Smoothie,* **page 14**
- *Easy No-Knead Whole Wheat Sandwich Bread,* **page 39**
- *Huevos Rancheros Casserole,* **page 20**
- *Gingery Fruit Salad,* **page 32**
- *Kale and Fennel Salad,* **page 118**

What flavour of vegetarian are you?

Whether you simply want to eat meat less often or are fully committed to a plants-only diet, there's a vegetarian style for you.

VEGAN OR PURE VEGETARIAN:

Avoids all foods of animal origin, including eggs, dairy, gelatin and honey. Many avoid other animal products, such as leather.

LACTO-OVO VEGETARIAN:

Does not eat meat but does include eggs and dairy products. The majority of vegetarians in North America are this type.

LACTO-VEGETARIAN:

Includes dairy products.

OVO-VEGETARIAN:

Includes eggs.

PESCO-VEGETARIAN:

Includes fish and seafood.

SEMI-VEGETARIAN:

Follows a vegetarian diet for most meals, but includes chicken, fish or seafood from time to time.

FLEXITARIAN:

Eats meatless meals most often, but will include red meat, chicken, fish or seafood on occasion.

"Eat food. Not too much.

THE VEGAN TOP 5

It's not hard to maintain a vegan diet that's healthy and packed with protein, but you need to pay attention to other nutrients too.

B12 **Vitamin B12** is important for healthy red blood cells and the proper functioning of the nervous system, especially in pregnant and lactating women. B12 comes primarily from animal-derived foods, and the only reliable vegan sources are foods that are fortified, including some brands of **soy** and **rice milk**, **cereal** and **nutritional yeast.**

Look for a daily supplement with at least 3 micrograms of B12 to meet requirements.

Omega-3 Fatty Acids are essential fats that nonvegetarians often get from **fish.** Vegans can get them from foods such as **walnuts, ground flaxseed** and **flaxseed oil.**

 Iron helps red blood cells carry oxygen to tissues and muscles, prevents anemia and supports the immune system. Good sources include **dried fruits, dried beans, spinach, chard, tofu** and iron-fortified foods, such as **cereals.**

To improve iron absorption, eat iron-rich foods along with foods containing vitamin C, such as **oranges, peppers, baked potatoes** or **fruit juice.**

Calcium maintains strong bones and teeth and regulates muscle function. Vegans may find it difficult to get as much as they need every day, so it is important to plan carefully.

Good calcium sources include **tofu, fortified soy milk, fortified orange juice, almonds, collard greens, broccoli** and **kale.**

D **Vitamin D** aids in calcium absorption. Sunlight enables us to make our own vitamin D, however, during Canadian winters, a dietary source, such as **fortified soy** or **rice milk**, is important.

Mostly plants." — MICHAEL POLLAN, *IN DEFENSE OF FOOD*

GOOD HOSTS, HAPPY VEGANS

Even for lacto-ovo vegetarians, hosting vegan guests for a holiday dinner can be challenging. Festive mains and side dishes for lacto-ovo diets often include dairy products and eggs, and many desserts, especially baked goods, aren't vegan-friendly. But that doesn't mean your vegan friends and family should get left out of the fun and feasting. Here are a few tips to make entertaining easy:

- **Choose simple, unprocessed, fresh ingredients.** Fruits, vegetables, nuts and seeds require little prep work and present beautifully for vegans and nonvegans alike. Try a crudité platter with bean dip for an appetizer; a fresh fruit platter for dessert.

- **Read ingredient lists on processed foods carefully.** Processed foods may use ingredients from animal sources including gelatin, rennet, whey, and casein. Along with honey, there are a few less common ingredients derived from insects, which vegans may or may not consider acceptable – to be sure, ask your guest.

- **Choose a meat-free centrepiece.** During the holidays, natural food stores carry meatless turkey products, which closely mimic the texture and flavour of the real bird.

- **Browse the natural food aisles.** Vegetarian and vegan products are mainstream now, and many are available in supermarkets. Look for nondairy ice cream, soy eggnog and vegetable pâtés to replace some of your holiday staples (but always be sure to read ingredient lists).

- **Let your vegan guests know that you are happy to accommodate their dietary preferences.** Ask that they send you their favourite holiday recipes ahead of time.

We've included more than 50 vegan recipes in this book, indicated by this symbol: `VEGAN`

WINE PAIRING FOR MEATLESS MEALS

Vegetarian dishes are usually lighter than meat-based meals, so they match well with leaner, greener wines from cool-climate regions, such as Ontario and New Zealand, as well as the Loire Valley, Burgundy and Alsace in France.

Some grapes go particularly well with vegetables. For whites, try Grüner Veltliner, Sauvignon Blanc, dry Muscat or Pinot Grigio. For reds, try Pinot Noir, Barbera, Gamay, Cabernet Franc or Tempranillo. Older, more mature reds or lighter vintages, which are softer and less tannic, won't overpower dishes with subtle flavours.

Since vegetarian dishes lack animal protein and fat, choose carefully if you want to pair them with heavier whites and tannic reds. Meals with cheese, mushrooms, tomato-based sauces and whole grains usually have enough heft to balance these wines.

PEANUT BUTTER & BANANA
FRENCH TOAST SANDWICHES
P 26

Complete Breakfasts | 2

No matter how rushed the morning, a healthy breakfast sets up the day for success. Pressed for time? Take a few minutes to blend a smoothie or cook scrambled eggs. On a relaxed weekend, treat yourself to a special poached eggs dish or decadent French toast. And if you're coaxing your family to try meatless meals more often, breakfast is the easiest way to start.

SWISS CHARD & MANGO SMOOTHIE

HANDS-ON TIME 5 minutes
TOTAL TIME 5 minutes
MAKES 2 servings

INGREDIENTS

2 cups	lightly packed chopped Swiss chard leaves
½ cup	chopped Swiss chard stems
1 cup	frozen mango chunks
1	banana, halved
1 cup	coconut milk beverage
½ cup	ice cubes
1 tbsp	liquid honey

DIRECTIONS

In blender, purée together Swiss chard leaves, Swiss chard stems, mango, banana, coconut milk beverage, ice cubes and honey until smooth and frothy.

NUTRITIONAL INFORMATION, PER SERVING: about 188 cal, 2 g pro, 3 g total fat (3 g sat. fat), 42 g carb (3 g dietary fibre, 32 g sugar), 0 mg chol, 177 mg sodium, 530 mg potassium. % RDI: 3% calcium, 9% iron, 23% vit A, 72% vit C, 14% folate.

CLEMENTINE YOGURT SMOOTHIE

HANDS-ON TIME 5 minutes
TOTAL TIME 5 minutes
MAKES 2 servings

INGREDIENTS

2	clementines, peeled, segmented and frozen
1	banana, sliced and frozen
1 cup	2% plain Balkan-style yogurt
¼ cup	frozen cranberries
2 tbsp	liquid honey
¼ tsp	turmeric

DIRECTIONS

In blender, purée together clementines, banana, yogurt, cranberries, honey and turmeric until smooth.

NUTRITIONAL INFORMATION, PER SERVING: about 226 cal, 7 g pro, 3 g total fat (2 g sat. fat), 47 g carb (3 g dietary fibre, 36 g sugar), 10 mg chol, 56 mg sodium, 651 mg potassium. % RDI: 17% calcium, 4% iron, 4% vit A, 72% vit C, 20% folate.

CLEMENTINE YOGURT SMOOTHIE

PORTOBELLO & EGG BREAKFAST SANDWICHES

HANDS-ON TIME
15 minutes

TOTAL TIME
15 minutes

MAKES
2 servings

INGREDIENTS

2	portobello mushrooms, stems and gills removed
2 tsp	olive oil
2	eggs
pinch	each salt and pepper
2 tbsp	soft herb-and-garlic cheese (such as Boursin)
2	English muffins, split and toasted

DIRECTIONS

Brush tops of mushrooms with half of the oil. Place, stem sides down, on baking sheet. Bake in 450°F oven until tender, about 7 minutes.

Meanwhile, in nonstick skillet, heat remaining oil over medium heat; crack eggs into pan. Cook, breaking yolks, until whites are set but yolks are still soft, about 3 minutes, or until desired doneness. Sprinkle with salt and pepper.

Spread herb-and-garlic cheese over cut sides of muffins; divide mushrooms and eggs between 2 halves. Sandwich with remaining halves.

NUTRITIONAL INFORMATION, PER SERVING: about 332 cal, 14 g pro, 17 g total fat (7 g sat. fat), 32 g carb (3 g dietary fibre, 4 g sugar), 195 mg chol, 405 mg sodium, 494 mg potassium. % RDI: 13% calcium, 26% iron, 14% vit A, 2% vit C, 46% folate.

Tip from the Test Kitchen

The gills of portobello mushrooms become mushy and dark when cooked; remove them before cooking by scraping gently with a spoon.

HANDS-ON TIME
10 minutes
TOTAL TIME
10 minutes
MAKES
2 servings

FETA & DILL SCRAMBLED EGGS

INGREDIENTS

4	eggs, lightly beaten
¼ cup	crumbled feta cheese
2 tbsp	chopped fresh dill
¼ tsp	pepper
pinch	salt
2 tsp	olive oil
1	pita, warmed and cut in wedges

DIRECTIONS

Whisk together eggs, feta, dill, pepper and salt.

In nonstick skillet, heat oil over medium-low heat; cook egg mixture, stirring, until creamy and just set, about 5 minutes. Serve with pita.

NUTRITIONAL INFORMATION, PER SERVING: about 318 cal, 17 g pro, 19 g total fat (7 g sat. fat), 19 g carb (1 g dietary fibre, 2 g sugar), 383 mg chol, 496 mg sodium. % RDI: 15% calcium, 17% iron, 22% vit A, 0% vit C.

HANDS-ON TIME
15 minutes
TOTAL TIME
25 minutes
MAKES
4 servings

POACHED EGGS & ASPARAGUS
WITH HERBED MUSTARD

INGREDIENTS

HERBED MUSTARD

¼ cup	chopped fresh basil
3 tbsp	light mayonnaise
2 tbsp	Dijon mustard

POACHED EGGS & ASPARAGUS

1 tsp	vinegar
8	eggs
16	asparagus spears (about 150 g total)
8	slices whole wheat bread, toasted
¼ tsp	each salt and pepper
¼ cup	shaved Parmesan cheese

DIRECTIONS

HERBED MUSTARD Stir together basil, mayonnaise and mustard; set aside.

POACHED EGGS & ASPARAGUS In large saucepan or deep skillet, heat 2 to 3 inches of water with vinegar over medium heat until simmering. Cooking eggs in batches of 2 to 4, crack eggs, 1 at a time, into small bowl; gently slide into simmering water. Poach until whites are set but yolks are still runny, about 3 minutes.

Using slotted spoon, transfer poached eggs to bowl of warm water; keep warm while cooking remaining batches. Using slotted spoon, transfer eggs to paper towel–lined tray; blot dry.

Meanwhile, in pot of boiling lightly salted water, cook asparagus just until tender, about 2 minutes. Drain; diagonally slice crosswise.

Spread 1 side of each toast with herbed mustard. Top with asparagus, poached eggs, salt, pepper and Parmesan. Serve immediately.

NUTRITIONAL INFORMATION, PER SERVING: about 384 cal, 22 g pro, 19 g total fat (5 g sat. fat), 35 g carb (6 g dietary fibre, 15 g sugar), 373 mg chol, 973 mg sodium, 395 mg potassium. % RDI: 16% calcium, 31% iron, 25% vit A, 5% vit C, 60% folate.

Tip from the Test Kitchen
The fresher the egg, the better it is for poaching, so check the best-before date on the carton.

HUEVOS RANCHEROS CASSEROLE

HANDS-ON TIME
35 minutes
TOTAL TIME
1 hour
MAKES
8 servings

INGREDIENTS

RED SAUCE

2 tsp	light-tasting olive oil
1	onion, finely chopped
3	cloves garlic, finely grated or pressed
2 tsp	chili powder
1 tsp	ground cumin
2 cups	bottled strained tomatoes (passata)
1	chipotle chili in adobo sauce, seeded and finely chopped
1 tsp	granulated sugar
½ tsp	dried oregano
¼ tsp	pepper
pinch	salt

CASSEROLE

6	soft corn or flour tortillas (6 inches)
1	can (540 mL) pinto or black beans, drained and rinsed
3 cups	shredded Monterey Jack cheese
8	eggs
3	green onions, finely chopped
pinch	salt
3 tbsp	coarsely chopped fresh cilantro

DIRECTIONS

RED SAUCE In saucepan, heat oil over medium heat; cook onion, stirring often, until softened, about 5 minutes. Add garlic, chili powder and cumin; cook until fragrant, about 1 minute. Stir in strained tomatoes, chipotle chili, sugar, oregano, pepper, salt and 1 cup water; bring to boil. Reduce heat and simmer, stirring occasionally, until slightly thickened, about 20 minutes.

CASSEROLE Halve 2 of the tortillas. Spoon 1 cup of the sauce into 13- × 9-inch baking dish, spreading to coat bottom. Layer 2 of the remaining tortillas in opposite corners of dish; arrange 2 of the tortilla halves, flat edges facing out, in remaining opposite corners to cover bottom of dish. Top with beans, spreading evenly. Spoon half of the remaining sauce over top. Sprinkle with 2 cups of the Monterey Jack. Repeat layers with remaining tortillas, sauce and Monterey Jack. *(Make-ahead: Cover with plastic wrap; refrigerate for up to 12 hours. Remove wrap and continue with recipe as directed, adding 14 minutes to bake time.)*

Using back of spoon, make 8 shallow wells in top of casserole; crack 1 egg into each. Sprinkle with green onions and salt. Bake in 350°F oven, rotating dish halfway through, until egg whites are set but yolks are still runny, 22 to 26 minutes. Sprinkle with cilantro.

NUTRITIONAL INFORMATION, PER SERVING: about 391 cal, 23 g pro, 21 g total fat (10 g sat. fat), 26 g carb (5 g dietary fibre, 4 g sugar), 230 mg chol, 591 mg sodium, 331 mg potassium. % RDI: 37% calcium, 20% iron, 22% vit A, 12% vit C, 32% folate.

Tip from the Test Kitchen

Freeze leftover chipotle chilies in recipe-friendly amounts. Spoon chilies, leaving space between each, onto a length of plastic wrap; fold wrap over to enclose chilies, and twist between each. Freeze in an airtight container for up to three months. Snip off chilies with scissors as needed.

TROPICAL MINT OATMEAL

OVERNIGHT STEEL-CUT OATMEAL

HANDS-ON TIME 5 minutes
TOTAL TIME 9½ hours
MAKES about 4 cups

INGREDIENTS

1 tsp	butter
1 cup	steel-cut oats
¼ tsp	salt

DIRECTIONS

In saucepan, melt butter over medium heat; cook oats, stirring, until fragrant, about 2 minutes.

Add 3½ cups water and the salt; bring to boil. Turn off heat; cover and let stand until cooled to room temperature, 1½ to 2 hours.

Refrigerate in airtight container for 8 hours. *(Make-ahead: Refrigerate for up to 4 days.)* Microwave on high for 2 minutes before serving.

NUTRITIONAL INFORMATION, PER 1 CUP: about 139 cal, 4 g pro, 3 g total fat (1 g sat. fat), 23 g carb (3 g dietary fibre, trace sugar), 3 mg chol, 158 mg sodium, 132 mg potassium. % RDI: 2% calcium, 9% iron, 1% vit A, 5% folate.

TROPICAL MINT OATMEAL

HANDS-ON TIME 5 minutes
TOTAL TIME 5 minutes
MAKES 1 serving

INGREDIENTS

1 cup	Overnight Steel-Cut Oatmeal (see recipe, left)
¼ cup	coconut milk
half	mango, peeled, pitted and chopped
2 tbsp	chopped fresh mint
2 tbsp	toasted macadamia nuts, roughly chopped

DIRECTIONS

In bowl, mix oatmeal with coconut milk; microwave on high for 2 minutes. Stir well. Stir mango with mint; spoon over oatmeal. Sprinkle with macadamia nuts.

NUTRITIONAL INFORMATION, PER SERVING: about 505 cal, 10 g pro, 29 g total fat (13 g sat. fat), 57 g carb (9 g dietary fibre, 18 g sugar), 0 mg chol, 16 mg sodium, 598 mg potassium. % RDI: 8% calcium, 43% iron, 13% vit A, 52% vit C, 29% folate.

COZY APPLE PIE OATMEAL

HANDS-ON TIME 5 minutes
TOTAL TIME 5 minutes
MAKES 1 serving

INGREDIENTS

1 cup	Overnight Steel-Cut Oatmeal (see recipe, page 23)
1 tbsp	butter
1	Gala apple, cored and chopped
¾ tsp	cinnamon
pinch	salt
2 tbsp	chopped toasted walnuts
1 tbsp	maple syrup

DIRECTIONS

In bowl, mix oatmeal with ¼ cup water; microwave on high for 2 minutes. Stir well.

Meanwhile, in nonstick skillet, melt butter over medium heat; cook apple, stirring, until softened, 2 to 3 minutes. Stir in cinnamon and salt; cook for 1 minute.

Spoon apple mixture over oatmeal. Top with walnuts; drizzle with maple syrup.

NUTRITIONAL INFORMATION, PER SERVING: about 527 cal, 10 g pro, 25 g total fat (9 g sat. fat), 70 g carb (9 g dietary fibre, 27 g sugar), 31 mg chol, 90 mg sodium, 465 mg potassium. % RDI: 8% calcium, 25% iron, 11% vit A, 8% vit C, 20% folate.

SWEET & SPICY THAI OATMEAL

HANDS-ON TIME 5 minutes
TOTAL TIME 5 minutes
MAKES 1 serving

INGREDIENTS

1 cup	Overnight Steel-Cut Oatmeal (see recipe, page 23)
¼ cup	coconut milk
3 tbsp	smooth or chunky peanut butter
2 tbsp	toasted coconut chips
1 tbsp	thinly sliced seeded red finger chili pepper

DIRECTIONS

In bowl, mix oatmeal with coconut milk; microwave on high for 2 minutes. Stir in peanut butter. Sprinkle with coconut chips and chili pepper.

NUTRITIONAL INFORMATION, PER SERVING: about 647 cal, 21 g pro, 43 g total fat (19 g sat. fat), 52 g carb (9 g dietary fibre, 10 g sugar), 0 mg chol, 233 mg sodium, 717 mg potassium. % RDI: 6% calcium, 36% iron, 9% vit A, 35% vit C, 33% folate.

COCONUT DATE BREAKFAST COOKIES

HANDS-ON TIME
20 minutes
TOTAL TIME
40 minutes
MAKES
about 15 cookies

INGREDIENTS

¼ cup	dates, pitted and chopped
3 tbsp	coconut oil
3 tbsp	maple syrup
2 tbsp	coconut sugar
1	egg
1 tsp	vanilla
¾ cup	whole wheat flour
¼ cup	all-purpose flour
¼ cup	large-flake rolled oats
½ tsp	each baking powder and baking soda
½ tsp	cinnamon
¼ tsp	each salt and nutmeg
½ cup	dried cranberries

DIRECTIONS

In food processor, purée dates into smooth paste. Add coconut oil, maple syrup, coconut sugar, egg and vanilla; purée until smooth. Scrape into large bowl.

In separate bowl, whisk together whole wheat flour, all-purpose flour, oats, baking powder, baking soda, cinnamon, salt and nutmeg; stir into date mixture until combined. Stir in cranberries.

Roll by 2 tbsp into balls. Arrange, 3 inches apart, on parchment paper–lined rimless baking sheets; flatten to ½-inch thickness.

Bake in top and bottom thirds of 350°F oven, switching and rotating pans halfway through, until cookies are firm and no longer shiny, 13 to 15 minutes. Let cool on pans for 5 minutes; transfer to racks to cool completely. (*Make-ahead: Store in airtight container for up to 3 days.*)

NUTRITIONAL INFORMATION, PER COOKIE: about 106 cal, 2 g pro, 4 g total fat (3 g sat. fat), 17 g carb (1 g dietary fibre, 9 g sugar), 13 mg chol, 96 mg sodium, 84 mg potassium. % RDI: 1% calcium, 4% iron, 1% vit A, 4% folate.

Tip from the Test Kitchen

Dates are a source of protein and iron and, when puréed, add natural sweetness and moisture to baked goods. Use soft dates for the paste—they purée more easily and add more moisture to the dough. To soften dried dates, place in a bowl; pour boiling water over top. Let stand 5 minutes; drain.

PEANUT BUTTER & BANANA FRENCH TOAST SANDWICHES

HANDS-ON TIME
15 minutes

TOTAL TIME
15 minutes

MAKES
2 servings

INGREDIENTS

2	eggs
¼ cup	milk
dash	vanilla
2 tbsp	crunchy peanut butter
4	slices (¾-inch thick) cinnamon-raisin bread
1	banana, cut in ¼-inch thick slices
1 tsp	butter

DIRECTIONS

In shallow dish, whisk together eggs, milk and vanilla; set aside.

Spread peanut butter over 1 side of 2 of the bread slices; arrange banana slices evenly over peanut butter. Sandwich with remaining bread. Dip sandwiches into egg mixture, turning to coat; discard any remaining egg mixture.

In nonstick skillet, melt butter over medium heat; cook sandwiches, turning once, until light golden and peanut butter is runny, about 4 minutes per side.

NUTRITIONAL INFORMATION, PER SERVING: about 456 cal, 16 g pro, 18 g total fat (5 g sat. fat), 63 g carb (6 g dietary fibre, 15 g sugar), 134 mg chol, 475 mg sodium, 592 mg potassium. % RDI: 10% calcium, 24% iron, 10% vit A, 7% vit C, 53% folate.

P 12

GLUTEN-FREE, DAIRY-FREE BANANA PANCAKES

HANDS-ON TIME
15 minutes

TOTAL TIME
15 minutes

MAKES
about 8 pancakes

INGREDIENTS

2	ripe bananas
2 tbsp	liquid honey
pinch	baking powder
2	eggs, beaten
1 tbsp	vegetable oil
2 tbsp	chopped shelled pistachios

DIRECTIONS

In bowl, mash 1 of the bananas until smooth. Stir in 2 tsp of the honey, the baking powder and ¼ tsp salt. Stir in eggs until well combined.

Heat nonstick skillet or griddle over medium heat; lightly brush with some of the oil. Working in batches, drop batter by 2 tbsp into skillet; sprinkle ½ tsp of the pistachios over each pancake. Cook until bottoms are golden, about 2 minutes. Turn pancakes; cook until bottoms are golden, about 1 minute. Transfer to plate. Repeat with remaining oil, batter and all but 2 tsp of the pistachios. *(Make-ahead: Wrap in plastic wrap and refrigerate for up to 3 days or overwrap in foil and freeze for up to 3 weeks; reheat in microwave.)*

Slice remaining banana; arrange over pancakes. Sprinkle with remaining pistachios; drizzle with remaining honey.

NUTRITIONAL INFORMATION, PER PANCAKE: about 87 cal, 2 g pro, 4 g total fat (1 g sat. fat), 12 g carb (1 g dietary fibre, 8 g sugar), 48 mg chol, 158 mg sodium, 132 mg potassium. % RDI: 2% calcium, 9% iron, 1% vit A, 5% folate.

Tip from the Test Kitchen

Flourless pancakes can be challenging to flip, but here's a trick: Use a thin spatula, lightly misting it with cooking spray before turning the pancakes.

THE PERFECT DUTCH BABY PANCAKE

HANDS-ON TIME
10 minutes

TOTAL TIME
20 minutes

MAKES
6 servings

INGREDIENTS

3	eggs
⅔ cup	milk
⅔ cup	all-purpose flour
2 tbsp	granulated sugar
pinch	salt
3 tbsp	butter

DIRECTIONS

In blender or large spouted bowl with whisk, mix together eggs, milk, flour, sugar and salt until smooth.

Heat 10-inch cast-iron or ovenproof skillet over medium-high heat; add butter, swirling pan until melted. Pour in batter. Transfer to 475°F oven; bake until puffed and browned, about 13 minutes. Using spatula, gently loosen pancake from pan.

NUTRITIONAL INFORMATION, PER SERVING: about 202 cal, 6 g pro, 7 g total fat (5 g sat. fat), 24 g carb (3 g dietary fibre, 11 g sugar), 114 mg chol, 87 mg sodium, 161 mg potassium. % RDI: 5% calcium, 9% iron, 13% vit A, 29% vit C, 21% folate.

Tip from the Test Kitchen

Dutch baby pancakes are traditionally served with fruit dusted with powdered sugar or other sweet toppings, but they also lend themselves to savoury flavours, such as sautéed asparagus, mushrooms or peppers.

HANDS-ON TIME
15 minutes

TOTAL TIME
1 hour

MAKES
6 servings

GRANOLA BOWLS

INGREDIENTS

3 tbsp	packed brown sugar
3 tbsp	vegetable oil
3 tbsp	liquid honey
2 tsp	vanilla
1¾ cups	large-flake rolled oats
¾ cup	sliced natural (skin-on) almonds
¾ tsp	cinnamon
¼ tsp	salt

DIRECTIONS

In small saucepan, cook brown sugar, oil and honey over medium-high heat, stirring often, until sugar is dissolved, about 2 minutes. Stir in vanilla.

In food processor, pulse together oats, almonds, cinnamon, salt and brown sugar mixture until combined but still chunky, about 5 or 6 times. Press scant ½ cup into bottom and up side of each well of greased 6-count jumbo muffin pan.

Bake in 300°F oven until golden, 25 to 30 minutes. Let cool in pan for 20 minutes. Gently twist granola bowls to loosen from pan; transfer to rack to cool completely. *(Make-ahead: Store in airtight container for up to 5 days.)*

NUTRITIONAL INFORMATION, PER SERVING: about 292 cal, 7 g pro, 14 g total fat (1 g sat. fat), 37 g carb (4 g dietary fibre, 17 g sugar), 0 mg chol, 101 mg sodium, 196 mg potassium. % RDI: 4% calcium, 14% iron, 4% folate.

VARIATION
TOASTED ALMOND GRANOLA

Follow first paragraph as directed. In large bowl, toss brown sugar mixture together with oats, almonds, cinnamon and salt to coat. Spread onto parchment paper–lined rimmed baking sheet. Bake in 300°F oven, stirring once, until golden, about 30 minutes.

HANDS-ON TIME
20 minutes
TOTAL TIME
30 minutes
MAKES
8 servings

VEGAN

GINGERY FRUIT SALAD

INGREDIENTS

¼ cup	sweetened shredded coconut
2	large ruby red grapefruit
2	large oranges
2 tbsp	granulated sugar
4	slices fresh ginger
2 cups	pineapple wedges
2	kiwifruit, peeled and cut into wedges
1 cup	green grapes, halved
1 cup	blueberries
1 cup	strawberries, halved
2	bananas, sliced

DIRECTIONS

In small skillet, toast coconut over medium heat, stirring, until golden, about 3 minutes. Set aside. *(Make-ahead: Set aside in airtight container for up to 24 hours.)*

Cut off zest and pith from grapefruit and oranges. Working over large sieve set over bowl, cut between membrane and pulp to release sections into sieve. Squeeze membranes to extract juice. Pour ¾ cup juice into saucepan, reserving any remaining juice for another use.

Add sugar and ginger to saucepan; bring to boil over medium-high heat. Boil, stirring, until sugar is dissolved; reduce heat and simmer, stirring occasionally, for 2 minutes. Let cool. Discard ginger.

In large bowl, combine grapefruit mixture, pineapple, kiwifruit, grapes and blueberries. *(Make-ahead: Cover and refrigerate juice mixture and fruit separately for up to 12 hours.)* Pour in juice mixture, tossing gently to coat; cover and let stand for 1 hour.

Add strawberries and bananas; stir to combine. Sprinkle with coconut.

NUTRITIONAL INFORMATION, PER SERVING: about 161 cal, 2 g pro, 2 g total fat (1 g sat. fat), 39 g carb (5 g dietary fibre), 0 mg chol, 10 mg sodium. % RDI: 4% calcium, 4% iron, 4% vit A, 177% vit C, 21% folate.

EASY CRANBERRY YOGURT PARFAITS

HANDS-ON TIME
10 minutes

TOTAL TIME
10 minutes

MAKES
4 servings

INGREDIENTS

3 cups 2% plain Greek yogurt

1 cup whole berry cranberry sauce

½ cup granola

DIRECTIONS

In 4 glasses or bowls, layer half each of the yogurt, cranberry sauce, and granola. Repeat layers with remaining ingredients. Serve immediately.

NUTRITIONAL INFORMATION, PER SERVING: about 284 cal, 19 g pro, 6 g total fat (4 g sat. fat), 42 g carb (1 g dietary fibre, 37 g sugar), 11 mg chol, 138 mg sodium, 295 mg potassium. % RDI: 17% calcium, 5% iron, 2% vit A, 2% vit C, 2% folate.

HANDS-ON TIME
15 minutes
TOTAL TIME
15 minutes
MAKES
4 servings

TROPICAL YOGURT PARFAIT

INGREDIENTS

½ cup	natural (skin-on) almonds
¼ cup	sweetened shredded coconut
1 cup	chopped pitted peeled mango
1 cup	chopped cored peeled pineapple
1⅔ cups	coconut- or vanilla-flavoured 2% Greek yogurt

DIRECTIONS

In dry skillet, toast almonds and coconut over medium heat, stirring often, until golden, 3 to 4 minutes; set aside.

In small bowl, stir together mango and pineapple; set aside.

In 4 glasses or bowls, layer half each of the yogurt and the fruit mixture; sprinkle with half of the almond mixture. Repeat layers with remaining ingredients. Serve immediately.

NUTRITIONAL INFORMATION, PER SERVING: about 342 cal, 17 g pro, 17 g total fat (7 g sat. fat), 34 g carb (5 g dietary fibre, 29 g sugar), 8 mg chol, 76 mg sodium, 255 mg potassium. % RDI: 21% calcium, 8% iron, 6% vit A, 53% vit C, 8% folate.

EASY NO-KNEAD WHITE SANDWICH BREAD
P 38

Complete Breads | 3

Baking your own breads is a satisfying experience, and not just because of the amazing aroma in your kitchen. We've included several no-knead, vegan-friendly bread recipes that take a lot less effort (but more time) than a traditional kneaded loaf. When you need fresh bread quickly, you can make a traditional Irish soda bread in less than an hour. And for a special treat, try our Tested-Till-Perfect recipes for homemade crackers and crispbreads.

HANDS-ON TIME
15 minutes

TOTAL TIME
14¾ hours
(includes rising)

MAKES
2 loaves,
each 16 slices

VEGAN

EASY NO-KNEAD WHITE SANDWICH BREAD

INGREDIENTS

6 cups	white bread flour (approx)
2 tsp	salt
1 tsp	quick-rising (instant) dry yeast
2½ cups	lukewarm water

DIRECTIONS

In large bowl, whisk together 5 cups of the flour, the salt and yeast. Stir in lukewarm water until well combined. Cover with plastic wrap; let rise (in warm draft-free place) until bubbly and doubled in size, about 12 hours. *(Make-ahead: Let rise for up to 18 hours.)*

Sprinkle work surface with ⅓ cup of the remaining flour. Scrape dough onto work surface; sprinkle ¼ cup of the remaining flour over top. Cover with tea towel; let stand for 15 minutes.

Using floured hands, gently press dough into ½-inch thick rectangle, sprinkling with up to ¼ cup of the remaining flour if dough is too sticky.

Cut in half crosswise. Roll each half into scant 8- × 4-inch cylinder; place, seam side down, in greased nonstick 8- × 4-inch loaf pan. Cover loosely with lightly greased plastic wrap; let rise (in warm draft-free place) until almost doubled in size, about 1½ hours.

Bake in 425°F oven for 10 minutes. Decrease heat to 375°F; bake until light golden and loaves sound hollow when tapped, about 30 minutes.

Transfer to racks; serve warm or let cool. *(Make-ahead: Let cool completely. Slice loaves; wrap in plastic wrap and freeze in resealable freezer bag for up to 3 weeks. Thaw in bag at room temperature.)*

NUTRITIONAL INFORMATION, PER SLICE: about 95 cal, 4 g pro, 1 g total fat (trace sat. fat), 18 g carb (2 g dietary fibre, trace sugar), 0 mg chol, 146 mg sodium, 23 mg potassium. % RDI: 1% calcium, 8% iron, 10% folate.

HANDS-ON TIME
15 minutes

TOTAL TIME
14¾ hours
(includes rising)

MAKES
2 loaves,
each 16 slices

VEGAN

EASY NO-KNEAD WHOLE WHEAT SANDWICH BREAD

INGREDIENTS

2 tbsp	sesame seeds
1 tbsp	poppy seeds
¼ tsp	flaxseeds (optional)
3 cups	whole wheat bread flour
3 cups	white bread flour (approx)
2 tsp	salt
1 tsp	quick-rising (instant) dry yeast
2½ cups	lukewarm water

DIRECTIONS

Stir ¼ tsp of the sesame seeds with ¼ tsp of the poppy seeds; stir in flaxseeds (if using). Set aside. In large bowl, whisk together whole wheat flour, 2 cups of the white bread flour, the remaining sesame seeds and poppy seeds, the salt and yeast. Stir in lukewarm water until well combined. Cover with plastic wrap; let rise (in warm draft-free place) until bubbly and doubled in size, about 12 hours. *(Make-ahead: Let rise for up to 18 hours.)*

Sprinkle work surface with ⅓ cup of the remaining white bread flour. Scrape dough onto work surface; sprinkle ¼ cup of the remaining white bread flour over top. Cover with tea towel; let stand for 15 minutes.

Using floured hands, gently press out dough into ½-inch thick rectangle, sprinkling with up to ¼ cup of the remaining white bread flour if dough is too sticky.

Cut in half crosswise. Roll each half into scant 8- × 4-inch cylinder; place, seam side down, in greased nonstick 8- × 4-inch loaf pan. Sprinkle loaves with reserved sesame seed mixture. Cover loosely with lightly greased plastic wrap; let rise (in warm draft-free place) until almost doubled in size, about 1½ hours.

Bake in 425°F oven for 10 minutes. Decrease heat to 375°F; bake until light golden and loaves sound hollow when tapped, about 30 minutes.

Transfer to racks; serve warm or let cool. *(Make-ahead: Let cool completely. Slice loaves; wrap in plastic wrap and freeze in resealable freezer bag for up to 3 weeks. Thaw in bag at room temperature.)*

NUTRITIONAL INFORMATION, PER SLICE: about 95 cal, 4 g pro, 1 g total fat (trace sat. fat), 18 g carb (2 g dietary fibre, trace sugar), 0 mg chol, 146 mg sodium, 23 mg potassium. % RDI: 1% calcium, 8% iron, 10% folate.

📷
P 36

HANDS-ON TIME
15 minutes
TOTAL TIME
14¾ hours
(includes rising)
MAKES
2 loaves,
each 16 slices

VEGAN

EASY NO-KNEAD CINNAMON RAISIN BREAD

INGREDIENTS

2 tbsp	sesame seeds
1 tbsp	poppy seeds
¼ tsp	flaxseeds (optional)
3 cups	whole wheat bread flour
3 cups	white bread flour (approx)
2 tsp	salt
1 tsp	quick-rising (instant) dry yeast
2½ cups	lukewarm water
1½ cups	raisins
1 tbsp	cinnamon

DIRECTIONS

Stir ¼ tsp of the sesame seeds with ¼ tsp of the poppy seeds; stir in flaxseeds (if using). Set aside. In large bowl, whisk together whole wheat flour, 2 cups of the white bread flour, the remaining sesame seeds and poppy seeds, the salt and yeast. Stir in lukewarm water until well combined. Cover with plastic wrap; let rise (in warm draft-free place) until bubbly and doubled in size, about 12 hours. *(Make-ahead: Let rise for up to 18 hours.)*

Sprinkle work surface with ⅓ cup of the remaining white bread flour. Scrape dough onto work surface; sprinkle ¼ cup of the remaining white bread flour over top. Cover with tea towel; let stand for 15 minutes.

Using floured hands, gently press out dough into ½-inch thick rectangle, sprinkling with up to ¼ cup of the remaining flour if dough is too sticky. Sprinkle with raisins and cinnamon. Knead until well combined, adding up to ¼ cup more white bread flour if dough is too sticky.

Reshape into rectangle; cut in half crosswise. Roll each half into scant 8- × 4-inch cylinder; place, seam side down, in greased nonstick 8- × 4-inch loaf pan. Sprinkle loaves with reserved sesame seed mixture. Cover loosely with lightly greased plastic wrap; let rise (in warm draft-free place) until almost doubled in size, about 1½ hours.

Bake in 425°F oven for 10 minutes. Decrease heat to 375°F; bake until light golden and loaves sound hollow when tapped, about 30 minutes.

Transfer to racks; serve warm or let cool. *(Make-ahead: Let cool completely. Slice loaves; wrap in plastic wrap and freeze in resealable freezer bag for up to 3 weeks. Thaw in bag at room temperature.)*

NUTRITIONAL INFORMATION, PER SLICE: about 112 cal, 4 g pro, 1 g total fat (trace sat. fat), 25 g carb (2 g dietary fibre, 4 G sugar), 0 mg chol, 147 mg sodium, 90 mg potassium. % RDI: 2% calcium, 8% iron, 10% folate.

HANDS-ON TIME
15 minutes
TOTAL TIME
3¼ hours
MAKES
1 large loaf,
20 slices

MALT & YOGURT RYE BREAD

INGREDIENTS

2½ tsp	active dry yeast
¼ tsp	granulated sugar
1 cup	fat-free plain yogurt
¼ cup	malt syrup
1½ tsp	salt
2⅓ cups	whole rye flour (dark)
2 cups	white bread flour (approx)
1½ tsp	butter, melted
2 tsp	caraway seeds

DIRECTIONS

In large bowl, sprinkle yeast over ¾ cup warm water and the sugar; let stand in warm place until frothy, 5 to 10 minutes.

Stir in yogurt, malt syrup and salt until combined. Stir in rye flour and 2 cups white bread flour to make shaggy dough.

Turn out onto lightly floured surface; knead, adding up to ½ cup more white bread flour as necessary, to make soft, smooth dough. Place in greased bowl, turning to grease all over; cover and let rise (in warm draft-free place) until doubled in size, about 1½ hours.

Gently punch down dough to deflate. On lightly floured surface, knead gently; shape into smooth ball by pulling down edge and pinching together underneath. Cover with tea towel; let rest for 10 minutes. Flatten into 1-inch thick oval, long side facing you. Fold top and bottom thirds over centre to form long, torpedo-shaped loaf; pinch seam to seal.

Place, seam side down, on rye-floured or parchment paper–lined peel or baking sheet. Cover with tea towel; let rise (in warm draft-free place) until doubled in size, ¾ to 1¼ hours.

Brush top with butter; sprinkle with caraway seeds. With razor blade or serrated knife, cut three or four ½-inch deep slits in loaf.

Bake on preheated baking stone or on baking sheet in 400°F convection oven or 425°F conventional oven for 20 minutes, sprinkling bottom of oven with a few handfuls of water when putting loaf in oven and again after 3 minutes of baking.

Reduce heat to 375°F (convection or conventional oven); bake until crust is hard and bread sounds hollow when tapped on bottom, about 20 minutes for convection or 25 minutes for conventional oven. Let cool on rack.

NUTRITIONAL INFORMATION, PER SLICE: about 115 cal, 5 g pro, 1 g total fat (trace sat. fat), 23 g carb, 1 mg chol, 184 mg sodium, 170 mg potassium. % RDI: 3% calcium, 12% iron, 15% folate.

CARAWAY & THYME IRISH SODA BREAD

HANDS-ON TIME
15 minutes
TOTAL TIME
50 minutes
MAKES
12 servings

INGREDIENTS

4 cups	all-purpose flour
4 tsp	chopped fresh thyme
1 tbsp	caraway seeds
1 tbsp	granulated sugar
1 tsp	each baking soda and salt
2 cups	buttermilk

DIRECTIONS

In large bowl, whisk together flour, thyme, caraway seeds, sugar, baking soda and salt. Make well in centre; add buttermilk all at once.

Using hands, mix buttermilk into flour mixture to form soft sticky dough. Turn dough out onto lightly floured work surface. Lightly knead a few times to form smooth ball.

Place dough on parchment paper–lined or greased rimless baking sheet. Using sharp knife, cut large X in top of dough. Bake in 425°F oven until bottom is browned and loaf sounds hollow when tapped, about 35 minutes. Serve warm.

NUTRITIONAL INFORMATION, PER SERVING: about 174 cal, 7 g pro, 2 g total fat (trace sat. fat), 33 g carb (1 g dietary fibre, 3 g sugar), 2 mg chol, 339 mg sodium, 112 mg potassium. % RDI: 5% calcium, 16% iron, 1% vit A, 2% vit C, 29% folate.

Tip from the Test Kitchen

You can replace half of the all-purpose flour with whole wheat flour for a more rustic texture and a fibre boost.

HANDS-ON TIME
15 minutes
TOTAL TIME
1½ hours
MAKES
about 40 pieces

VEGAN

WHOLE WHEAT SESAME CRISPBREAD

INGREDIENTS

½ cup	warm water
1½ tsp	granulated sugar
1 tsp	active dry yeast
1¼ cups	whole wheat bread flour (approx)
½ cup	sesame seeds
2 tbsp	sesame oil
½ tsp	salt

DIRECTIONS

In small bowl, mix warm water with sugar. Sprinkle in yeast; let stand in warm place until frothy, 10 minutes.

In separate bowl, whisk together 1¼ cups of flour, the sesame seeds, oil and salt until crumbly. Mix in yeast mixture until clumped together, adding up to ¼ cup more flour, if necessary, to make stiff dough.

Turn out onto lightly floured surface; knead just until smooth. Cover with plastic wrap and let rise (in warm draft-free) place until slightly risen and no longer springy, about 1 hour. *(Make-ahead: let rise in refrigerator overnight; let come to room temperature, about 2 hours, before proceeding.)*

Divide dough in half. On lightly floured surface, roll out each to ⅛-inch thickness. Let rest for 5 minutes. On unfloured surface, roll out again, making two 13- × 8-inch ovals. Transfer to 2 ungreased baking sheets.

Bake in 375°F oven until golden and crisp, 15 to 20 minutes. Transfer to rack; let cool. Break into pieces. *(Make-ahead: Store in airtight container for up to 1 week.)*

NUTRITIONAL INFORMATION, PER PIECE: about 31 cal, 1 g pro, 2 g total fat (trace sat. fat), 3 g carb (1 g dietary fibre), 0 mg chol, 30 mg sodium, 25 mg potassium. % RDI: 2% iron, 2% folate.

VARIATION

YEASTLESS WHOLE WHEAT SESAME THINS

For a thinner cracker, omit warm water, sugar, yeast and standing time. Whisk ½ tsp baking powder into flour, sesame seeds, oil and salt; stir in ½ cup water. Let dough rest in refrigerator for 10 minutes before dividing dough in half and rolling.

OLIVE & PARMESAN CRACKERS

HANDS-ON TIME
20 minutes

TOTAL TIME
50 minutes

MAKES
about 60 pieces

INGREDIENTS

1 cup	grated Parmesan cheese (125 g)
¾ cup	all-purpose flour
¼ cup	cornmeal
½ tsp	crushed fennel seeds
¼ tsp	baking powder
pinch	cayenne pepper
¼ cup	cold salted butter, cubed
¼ cup	cold water
3 tbsp	pitted, drained oil-cured black olives, finely chopped
1	egg white, beaten

DIRECTIONS

In food processor, mix together Parmesan, flour, cornmeal, fennel seeds, baking powder and cayenne pepper. Add butter; pulse until mixture resembles coarse crumbs. Add water; pulse just until dough starts to come together.

Turn out onto lightly floured surface; sprinkle with olives and knead to form smooth dough. Cut in half; shape into discs. Cover with clean tea towel and let rest for 20 minutes.

On lightly floured surface, roll out each disc into 12-inch circle. Using 2½-inch round, star or other cookie cutter, cut out shapes, rerolling and cutting scraps. Transfer shapes to greased or parchment paper–lined baking sheets. Brush lightly with egg white.

Bake in 400°F oven until golden, 8 to 10 minutes. Transfer to racks and let cool. *(Make-ahead: Store in airtight container for up to 1 week or freeze for up to 1 month.)*

NUTRITIONAL INFORMATION, PER PIECE: about 23 cal, 1 g pro, 1 g total fat (1 g sat. fat), 2 g carb, trace dietary fibre, 3 mg chol, 45 mg sodium, 6 mg potassium. % RDI: 2% calcium, 1% iron, 1% vit A, 2% folate.

CLASSIC CHILI SAUCE
P 48

Complete Basics | 4

Every cook needs go-to recipes that become foundations for a variety of easy meals—sauces and pestos that turn pasta into a quick, tasty weeknight dinner; stocks that add depth and flavour to soups and stews; and spreads and condiments that brighten up sandwiches, steamed or blanched vegetables and so much more.

HANDS-ON TIME
1½ hours
TOTAL TIME
25¾ hours
MAKES
about 6 cups

VEGAN

CLASSIC CHILI SAUCE

INGREDIENTS

8 cups	chopped peeled tomatoes (about 1.5 kg)
1½ cups	chopped onions
1½ cups	chopped sweet red peppers
1½ cups	white vinegar
1 cup	chopped sweet green peppers
1 cup	chopped celery
¾ cup	granulated sugar (approx)
1 tbsp	finely chopped red finger chili pepper
1	clove garlic, minced
1 tsp	salt
1 tsp	mustard seeds
½ tsp	each celery seeds, ground cloves and cinnamon
¼ tsp	each ground ginger and pepper
pinch	cayenne pepper (approx)

DIRECTIONS

In large heavy-bottomed saucepan, combine tomatoes, onions, red peppers, vinegar, green peppers, celery, sugar, chili pepper, garlic, salt, mustard seeds, celery seeds, cloves, cinnamon, ginger, pepper and cayenne pepper. Bring to boil, stirring often; reduce heat and simmer briskly, stirring often, until thickened and saucy and mixture is reduced to just over 6 cups, about 1 hour. Add up to ¼ cup more sugar and increase cayenne pepper to taste, if desired.

Pack into 6 hot (sterilized) 1-cup canning jars with tight-fitting lids, leaving ¼ inch headspace. Scrape down sides of jars with nonmetallic utensil to remove any air bubbles. Cover with lids. Screw on bands until resistance is met; increase to fingertip tight.

Transfer to boiling water canner; boil for 10 minutes. Turn off heat. Uncover and let jars stand in canner for 5 minutes. Lift up rack. Using canning tongs, transfer jars to cooling rack; let cool for 24 hours.

NUTRITIONAL INFORMATION, PER 1 TBSP: about 12 cal, trace pro, trace total fat (trace sat. fat), 3 g carb (trace dietary fibre, 2 g sugar), 0 mg chol, 26 mg sodium, 50 mg potassium. % RDI: 1% iron, 2% vit A, 12% vit C, 1% folate.

Tip from the Test Kitchen

Tomatoes vary in their sweetness; to strike the perfect balance between sweet and spicy, you may want to add more sugar.

P 46

HANDS-ON TIME
30 minutes
TOTAL TIME
2 hours
MAKES
about 11 cups

VEGAN

FRESH TOMATO SAUCE

INGREDIENTS

4 kg	plum tomatoes (about 40)
2	onions, chopped
½ cup	olive oil
3	cloves garlic, minced
1	can (156 mL) tomato paste
1¼ tsp	salt
½ tsp	pepper

DIRECTIONS

Score an X in bottom of each tomato. In large saucepan of boiling water, cook tomatoes until skins begin to loosen, about 1 minute. Using slotted spoon, transfer to bowl of ice water and chill for 20 seconds; drain.

Working over fine-mesh sieve set over bowl, peel off tomato skins; discard. Core tomatoes and remove seeds to sieve; press seeds to extract juices, reserving 3 cups. Set juices aside. Discard seeds and cores.

In food processor, working in batches, purée tomato flesh until smooth. (Purée should yield about 10 cups.) Scrape into bowl. Set aside.

In food processor, purée onions until smooth.

In Dutch oven or large heavy-bottomed saucepan, heat oil over medium heat; cook onions, stirring occasionally, until golden and liquid has evaporated, about 12 minutes. Stir in garlic; cook, stirring, until fragrant, about 1 minute. Stir in tomato purée, reserved tomato juice, tomato paste, salt and pepper. Bring to boil; reduce heat and simmer, uncovered, stirring occasionally, until sauce has reduced to about 11 cups, about 1½ hours. *(Make-ahead: Let cool; refrigerate in airtight container for up to 1 week or freeze for up to 2 months.)*

NUTRITIONAL INFORMATION, PER ½ CUP: about 80 cal, 2 g pro, 5 g total fat (1 g sat. fat), 8 g carb (2 g dietary fibre, 5 g sugar), 0 mg chol, 146 mg sodium, 429 mg potassium. % RDI: 2% calcium, 5% iron, 12% vit A, 32% vit C, 8% folate.

VARIATION

PRESSURE COOKER FRESH TOMATO SAUCE

Follow first 4 paragraphs as directed. In pressure cooker, heat oil over medium heat; cook onions and garlic as directed. Stir in tomato purée, 2 cups of the reserved tomato juice, the tomato paste, salt and pepper. (Reserve remaining tomato juice for another use.) Secure lid; bring to high pressure over high heat. Reduce heat while maintaining high pressure; cook for 20 minutes. Remove from heat; let pressure release completely, about 2 minutes.

HANDS-ON TIME
10 minutes
TOTAL TIME
35 minutes
MAKES
about 3 cups

VEGAN

EASY MARINARA SAUCE

INGREDIENTS

1 tbsp	olive oil
1	onion, diced
1	clove garlic, chopped
1	can (796 mL) whole tomatoes
1 tbsp	balsamic vinegar
¼ tsp	granulated sugar
¼ cup	thinly sliced fresh basil leaves (optional)

DIRECTIONS

In saucepan, heat oil over medium heat; cook onion, stirring occasionally, until golden, about 3 minutes. Add garlic; cook until fragrant, about 1 minute.

Stir in tomatoes, vinegar and sugar, breaking up tomatoes with back of spoon. Bring to boil; reduce heat and simmer, stirring occasionally, until thickened, about 30 minutes. Purée until smooth. Stir in basil (if using). *(Make-ahead: Refrigerate in airtight container for up to 3 days.)*

NUTRITIONAL INFORMATION, PER ¼ CUP: about 27 cal, 1 g pro, 1 g total fat (trace sat. fat), 4 g carb (1 g dietary fibre, 2 g sugar), 0 mg chol, 86 mg sodium, 142 mg potassium. % RDI: 2% calcium, 5% iron, 1% vit A, 15% vit C, 2% folate.

Tip from the Test Kitchen

You can double or triple this recipe and freeze 1-cup portions in airtight containers to use instead of store-bought pasta sauce.

VEGAN
LIGHT VEGETABLE STOCK

HANDS-ON TIME 10 minutes
TOTAL TIME 1½ hours
MAKES about 8 cups

INGREDIENTS

3	plum tomatoes, halved
3	carrots (unpeeled), coarsely chopped
3	onions (unpeeled), coarsely chopped
3	ribs celery with leaves, coarsely chopped
1	head garlic (unpeeled), broken into cloves
2	bay leaves
6	sprigs fresh parsley
5	sprigs fresh thyme
10	black peppercorns
½ tsp	salt

DIRECTIONS

In stockpot, add tomatoes, carrots, onions, celery, garlic, bay leaves, parsley, thyme, peppercorns and 10 cups water.

Bring to boil; reduce heat and simmer until liquid is flavourful, about 1 hour.

Strain through fine-mesh sieve, gently pressing vegetables to extract liquid. Stir in salt (if using). *(Make-ahead: Refrigerate in airtight container for up to 3 days or freeze for up to 4 months.)*

NUTRITIONAL INFORMATION, PER ½ CUP: about 1 cal, 0 g pro, 1 g total fat (0 g sat. fat), trace carb (0 g dietary fibre), 0 mg chol, 0 mg sodium. % RDI: 1% folate.

VEGAN
ROASTED VEGETABLE STOCK

HANDS-ON TIME 25 minutes
TOTAL TIME 2 hours
MAKES about 5 cups

INGREDIENTS

3	carrots, coarsely chopped
3	onions, coarsely chopped
3	ribs celery, coarsely chopped
1 cup	sliced mushroom caps and/or stems
3	cloves garlic
2 tsp	vegetable oil
10	sprigs fresh parsley
10	black peppercorns, cracked
2	bay leaves
½ tsp	salt (optional)

DIRECTIONS

In large roasting pan, stir together carrots, onions, celery, mushrooms, garlic and oil to coat. Roast in 450°F oven, stirring once, until softened and browned, about 40 minutes. Transfer to stockpot.

Pour 1 cup of water into roasting pan, stirring and scraping up brown bits from bottom of pan, over heat if necessary. Scrape into stockpot. Add parsley, peppercorns, bay leaves and 7 cups water. Bring to boil; skim off any foam. Reduce heat to medium; simmer until liquid is flavourful, about 1 hour.

Strain through fine-mesh sieve, gently pressing vegetables to extract liquid. Stir in salt (if using). *(Make-ahead: Refrigerate in airtight container for up to 3 days or freeze for up to 4 months.)*

NUTRITIONAL INFORMATION, PER ½ CUP: about 33 cal, 1 g pro, 1 g total fat (0 g sat. fat), 5 g carb (0 g dietary fibre), 0 mg sodium. % RDI: 2% calcium, 4% iron, 57% vit A, 13% vit C, 8% folate.

HANDS-ON TIME
15 minutes
TOTAL TIME
35 minutes
MAKES
1 batch dough
(for 4 servings)

FRESH PASTA DOUGH

INGREDIENTS

2 cups	all-purpose flour
3	eggs
¼ tsp	salt

DIRECTIONS

Mound flour on work surface; make well in centre. Crack eggs into well; sprinkle with salt. Using fork, beat eggs. Starting at inside edge and working around well, gradually stir flour into egg mixture until soft dough forms. Sift flour remaining on work surface; discard any bits of dough.

On lightly floured work surface, knead dough, dusting with some of the reserved flour, until dough is smooth, elastic and no longer sticky, about 10 minutes. Shape into disc; wrap in plastic wrap. Let stand for 20 minutes.

Cut dough into thirds; roll or press each into 5-inch wide sheet. Dust with reserved flour. Cover with damp towel to prevent drying out.

Tip from the Test Kitchen

Homemade fresh pasta is best cooked as soon as made, but you can store it in the refrigerator for up to 2 days. Or dry at room temperature and store in the refrigerator for up to 1 week.

WILD MUSHROOM CREAM SAUCE

HANDS-ON TIME
20 minutes

TOTAL TIME
20 minutes

MAKES
1¼ cups

INGREDIENTS

1 tbsp	butter
1	shallot, diced
2	cloves garlic, minced
2 cups	mixed sliced wild mushrooms (such as cremini, shiitake and oyster)
½ cup	white wine
½ cup	whipping cream (35%)
pinch	each salt and pepper
1 tbsp	chopped fresh parsley

DIRECTIONS

In skillet, melt butter over medium heat; cook shallot until softened, about 2 minutes. Add garlic; cook for 1 minute.

Add mushrooms; cook over medium-high heat until softened and no liquid remains, about 5 minutes. Add wine; reduce heat and simmer for 4 minutes.

Add cream, salt and pepper; simmer until thick enough to coat back of spoon, about 2 minutes. Stir in parsley.

NUTRITIONAL INFORMATION, PER ¼ CUP: about 94 cal, 1 g pro, 8 g total fat (5 g sat. fat), 3 g carb (1 g dietary fibre, 1 g sugar), 26 mg chol, 27 mg sodium, 159 mg potassium. % RDI: 2% calcium, 3% iron, 8% vit A, 2% vit C, 3% folate.

SUN-DRIED TOMATO & ROASTED RED PEPPER CREAM SAUCE

HANDS-ON TIME
15 minutes

TOTAL TIME
15 minutes

MAKES
about 1 cup

INGREDIENTS

1 tbsp	olive oil
3	cloves garlic, minced
¼ cup	chopped drained oil-packed sun-dried tomatoes
¼ cup	chopped roasted red pepper
¼ tsp	hot pepper flakes
1 cup	whipping cream (35%)
2 tbsp	sliced fresh basil

DIRECTIONS

In saucepan, heat oil over medium heat; cook garlic until slightly golden, about 1 minute. Add tomatoes, red pepper and hot pepper flakes; cook, stirring occasionally, until fragrant, about 2 minutes.

Stir in cream; simmer until thick enough to coat back of spoon, about 5 minutes. Stir in basil.

NUTRITIONAL INFORMATION, PER ¼ CUP: about 246 cal, 2 g pro, 25 g total fat (14 g sat. fat), 5 g carb (1 g dietary fibre, 2 g sugar), 76 mg chol, 86 mg sodium, 193 mg potassium. % RDI: 5% calcium, 3% iron, 25% vit A, 47% vit C, 3% folate.

CLASSIC PESTO

HANDS-ON TIME 5 minutes
TOTAL TIME 5 minutes
MAKES ¾ cup

INGREDIENTS

½ **cup**	grated Parmesan cheese
⅓ **cup**	pine nuts
2	cloves garlic, chopped
2½ **cups**	packed fresh basil
¼ **tsp**	each salt and pepper
⅓ **cup**	extra-virgin olive oil

DIRECTIONS

In food processor, pulse together Parmesan, pine nuts and garlic until coarsely ground. Add basil, salt and pepper; pulse 6 times.

With motor running, add oil in thin steady stream until smooth. *(Make-ahead: Refrigerate in airtight container for up to 3 days or freeze for up to 6 months.)*

NUTRITIONAL INFORMATION, PER 1 TBSP: about 99 cal, 2 g pro, 10 g total fat (2 g sat. fat), 1 g carb (trace dietary fibre, trace sugar), 4 mg chol, 112 mg sodium, 60 mg potassium. % RDI: 5% calcium, 4% iron, 4% vit A, 2% vit C, 3% folate.

VEGAN

SPICY CILANTRO PESTO

HANDS-ON TIME 5 minutes
TOTAL TIME 5 minutes
MAKES 1 cup

INGREDIENTS

1	hot red pepper, seeded and chopped
½ **cup**	unsalted roasted sunflower seeds
3	cloves garlic, chopped
1 **cup**	fresh cilantro leaves
½ **tsp**	grated lime zest
pinch	salt
⅓ **cup**	extra-virgin olive oil

DIRECTIONS

In food processor, pulse together hot pepper, sunflower seeds and garlic until coarsely ground. Add cilantro, lime zest and salt; pulse 6 times.

With motor running, add oil in thin steady stream until smooth. *(Make-ahead: Refrigerate in airtight container for up to 3 days or freeze for up to 6 months.)*

NUTRITIONAL INFORMATION, PER 1 TBSP: about 66 cal, 1 g pro, 7 g total fat (1 g sat. fat), 1 g carb (trace dietary fibre, trace sugar), 0 mg chol, 1 mg sodium, 30 mg potassium. % RDI: 1% calcium, 1% iron, 1% vit A, 3% vit C, 5% folate.

VEGAN

SUN-DRIED TOMATO & ALMOND PESTO

HANDS-ON TIME 5 minutes
TOTAL TIME 5 minutes
MAKES 1 cup

INGREDIENTS

½ cup	slivered almonds
2	cloves garlic, chopped
1 cup	drained oil-packed sun-dried tomatoes
¼ tsp	each salt and pepper
⅓ cup	extra-virgin olive oil

DIRECTIONS

In food processor, pulse almonds with garlic until coarsely ground. Add tomatoes, salt and pepper; pulse until finely chopped.

With motor running, add oil in thin steady stream until smooth. *(Make-ahead: Refrigerate in airtight container for up to 3 days or freeze for up to 6 months.)*

NUTRITIONAL INFORMATION, PER 1 TBSP: about 75 cal, 1 g pro, 7 g total fat (1 g sat. fat), 2 g carb (1 g dietary fibre, 1 g sugar), 0 mg chol, 55 mg sodium, 133 mg potassium. % RDI: 1% calcium, 3% iron, 1% vit A, 12% vit C, 1% folate.

VEGAN

WATERCRESS & WALNUT PESTO

HANDS-ON TIME 5 minutes
TOTAL TIME 5 minutes
MAKES ¾ cup

INGREDIENTS

½ cup	walnuts, toasted
1	clove garlic, chopped
2 cups	loosely packed trimmed watercress
½ cup	tightly packed fresh flat-leaf parsley leaves
¼ tsp	each salt and pepper
⅓ cup	extra-virgin olive oil

DIRECTIONS

In food processor, pulse walnuts with garlic until coarsely ground. Add watercress, parsley, salt and pepper; pulse 6 times.

With motor running, add oil in thin steady stream until smooth. *(Make-ahead: Refrigerate in airtight container for up to 3 days or freeze for up to 6 months.)*

NUTRITIONAL INFORMATION, PER 1 TBSP: about 87 cal, 1 g pro, 9 g total fat (1 g sat. fat), 1 g carb (1 g dietary fibre, trace sugar), 0 mg chol, 52 mg sodium, 56 mg potassium. % RDI: 1% calcium, 3% iron, 4% vit A, 10% vit C, 4% folate.

TOMATO & BASIL MAYONNAISE

HANDS-ON TIME 5 minutes
TOTAL TIME 5 minutes
MAKES about ¾ cup

INGREDIENTS

⅔ cup	mayonnaise
⅓ cup	fresh basil, chopped
¼ cup	minced drained oil-packed sun-dried tomatoes
¼ cup	grated Pecorino-Romano cheese
1	small clove garlic, pressed or finely grated

DIRECTIONS

In small bowl, stir together mayonnaise, basil, sun-dried tomatoes, Pecorino-Romano and garlic. *(Make-ahead: Refrigerate in airtight container for up to 5 days.)*

NUTRITIONAL INFORMATION, PER 1 TBSP: about 105 cal, 1 g pro, 11 g total fat (2 g sat. fat), 1 g carb (trace dietary fibre, 1 g sugar), 7 mg chol, 125 mg sodium, 61 mg potassium. % RDI: 1% calcium, 1% iron, 2% vit A, 7% vit C, 1% folate.

TARRAGON CHIVE MAYONNAISE

HANDS-ON TIME 5 minutes
TOTAL TIME 5 minutes
MAKES about ¾ cup

INGREDIENTS

⅔ cup	mayonnaise
2 tbsp	finely chopped fresh chives
1 tbsp	finely chopped fresh tarragon
1 tbsp	grainy mustard
2 tsp	capers, drained, rinsed and chopped

DIRECTIONS

In small bowl, stir together mayonnaise, chives, tarragon, mustard and capers. *(Make-ahead: Refrigerate in airtight container for up to 5 days.)*

NUTRITIONAL INFORMATION, PER 1 TBSP: about 89 cal, trace pro, 10 g total fat (1 g sat. fat), 1 g carb (trace dietary fibre, trace sugar), 5 mg chol, 100 mg sodium, 6 mg potassium. % RDI: 1% iron, 1% vit A.

FROM LEFT
CILANTRO-JALAPEÑO SAUCE P 48,
TOMATO & BASIL MAYONNAISE AND
TARRAGON CHIVE MAYONNAISE

CLASSIC AIOLI

CLASSIC AIOLI

HANDS-ON TIME
15 minutes

TOTAL TIME
15 minutes

MAKES
about 2½ cups

INGREDIENTS

4	cloves garlic, pressed or finely grated
5	egg yolks
1 tsp	Dijon mustard
pinch	salt
1½ cups	vegetable oil
½ cup	extra-virgin olive oil
1 tsp	white wine vinegar

DIRECTIONS

In large bowl, whisk together garlic, egg yolks, mustard and salt. Gradually whisk in vegetable oil until pale yellow and thickened. Gradually whisk in olive oil. Stir in vinegar. *(Make-ahead: Refrigerate in airtight container for up to 5 days.)*

NUTRITIONAL INFORMATION, PER 1 TBSP: about 102 cal, trace pro, 11 g total fat (1 g sat. fat), trace carb (trace dietary fibre, trace sugar), 14 mg chol, 4 mg sodium, 4 mg potassium. % RDI: 1% iron, 1% vit A, 1% folate.

HANDS-ON TIME
10 minutes

TOTAL TIME
10 minutes

MAKES
about ¾ cup

VEGAN
CILANTRO-JALAPEÑO SAUCE

INGREDIENTS

¼ cup	blanched almonds, toasted
1 cup	lightly packed fresh cilantro
½ cup	chopped fresh chives
2 tbsp	minced seeded jalapeño pepper
1 tsp	grated lemon zest
3 tbsp	lemon juice
¼ tsp	each salt and pepper
⅓ cup	extra-virgin olive oil

DIRECTIONS

In food processor, pulse almonds until coarsely ground. Add cilantro, chives, jalapeño pepper, lemon zest, lemon juice, salt and pepper; pulse, scraping down side, until in coarse paste. With motor running, add oil and 2 tbsp water in thin steady stream until smooth. *(Make-ahead: Refrigerate in airtight container for up to 3 days; whisk before using.)*

NUTRITIONAL INFORMATION, PER 1 TBSP: about 73 cal, 1 g pro, 8 g total fat (1 g sat. fat), 1 g carb (trace dietary fibre, trace sugar), 5 mg chol, 70 mg sodium, 13 mg potassium. % RDI: 1% iron, 2% vit A, 3% vit C, 1% folate.

HANDS-ON TIME
10 minutes
TOTAL TIME
45 minutes
MAKES
about ½ cup

GREEN ONION & GINGER BUTTER

INGREDIENTS

½ **cup**	butter, softened
4	cloves garlic, pressed or finely grated
2 tsp	grated fresh ginger
2	green onions, finely chopped

DIRECTIONS

In small nonstick skillet, melt 1 tbsp of the butter over medium heat; cook garlic and ginger, stirring often, until very fragrant, 2 to 3 minutes. Add green onions; cook, stirring often, until softened, about 2 minutes. Scrape into bowl; refrigerate until chilled.

Stir remaining butter into garlic mixture. Scrape onto piece of plastic wrap and shape into 1-inch thick log; wrap tightly. Refrigerate until firm, about 30 minutes. *(Make-ahead: Refrigerate for up to 3 days. Or freeze in resealable plastic bag for up to 2 weeks; thaw in refrigerator for 12 hours before using.)*

NUTRITIONAL INFORMATION, PER 1 TBSP: about 106 cal, trace pro, 12 g total fat (7 g sat. fat), 1 g carb (trace dietary fibre, trace sugar), 31 mg chol, 83 mg sodium, 24 mg potassium. % RDI: 1% calcium, 1% iron, 10% vit A, 2% vit C, 1% folate.

Tip from the Test Kitchen

Try this compound butter on grilled corn, baked potatoes or roasted cauliflower.

HANDS-ON TIME
8 minutes each
TOTAL TIME
8 minutes each
MAKES
4 servings each

MAKE-AHEAD BUTTER SAUCES

SHERRIED SHALLOT BUTTER

In small skillet, heat 1 tsp butter over medium-high heat. Add 2 shallots, minced; ¼ tsp paprika; and pinch salt. Cook, stirring, until shallots are softened and light golden, about 3 minutes. Stir in 1 tbsp dry sherry; cook until no liquid remains, about 1 minute. Let cool for 3 minutes. In bowl, mash together shallot mixture; ⅓ cup butter, softened; and 1 tsp chopped fresh parsley. Melt in saucepan over low heat.

Tip from the Test Kitchen

These sauces are an easy way to dress up steamed vegetables, and you can make all of them ahead: After combining the ingredients, cover and refrigerate for up to 3 days or freeze in airtight container for up to 2 months. Just before serving, melt in saucepan over low heat.

GINGER, HOT PEPPER & LIME BUTTER

In bowl, mash together ⅓ cup butter, softened; 2 tsp grated fresh ginger; 1 tsp minced seeded red or green hot peppers; ¼ tsp grated lime zest; ½ tsp lime juice; and pinch salt. Melt in saucepan over low heat.

ORANGE TARRAGON GARLIC BUTTER

In bowl, mash together ⅓ cup butter, softened; 1 clove garlic, grated; 1 tsp each chopped fresh tarragon and parsley; ½ tsp grated orange zest; and pinch salt. Melt in saucepan over low heat.

VEGAN

THAI GREEN CURRY PASTE

HANDS-ON TIME 20 minutes
TOTAL TIME 20 minutes
MAKES ¾ cup

INGREDIENTS

5	green chilies, seeded and chopped
2	stalks lemongrass, finely chopped (or 2 tsp lemongrass paste)
1 cup	packed fresh cilantro (with roots and stems)
¼ cup	chopped shallots
2 tbsp	each minced garlic and fresh ginger
2 tsp	grated lime zest
½ tsp	each ground coriander, ground cumin, and turmeric

DIRECTIONS

In blender, purée together chilies, lemongrass, cilantro, shallots, garlic, ginger, lime zest, coriander, cumin and turmeric, adding up to ¼ cup water, if necessary, to make smooth paste. *(Make-ahead: Refrigerate in airtight container for up to 2 weeks.)*

NUTRITIONAL INFORMATION, PER 1 TBSP: about 13 cal, trace pro, trace total fat (0 g sat. fat), 3 g carb (trace dietary fibre), 0 mg chol, 2 mg sodium. % RDI: 1% calcium, 4% iron, 2% vit A, 5% vit C, 2% folate.

VEGAN

SESAME GARLIC CHILI OIL

HANDS-ON TIME 10 minutes
TOTAL TIME 1¼ hours
MAKES about 1 cup

INGREDIENTS

1 cup	vegetable oil
4	cloves garlic, finely grated or pressed
1 tbsp	thinly sliced Thai bird's-eye peppers (about 4)
4 tsp	sesame oil

DIRECTIONS

In saucepan, heat 3 tbsp of the vegetable oil over medium heat; cook garlic and Thai peppers, stirring, until garlic is fragrant and peppers are softened, about 2 minutes. Add remaining vegetable oil and the sesame oil; cook until oil is warm but not hot. Let cool completely, about 1 hour.

Strain oil through fine-mesh sieve; discard solids. *(Make-ahead: Refrigerate in airtight container for up to 2 weeks.)*

NUTRITIONAL INFORMATION, PER 1 TSP: about 131 cal, 0 g pro, 15 g total fat (1 g sat. fat), 0 g carb (0 g dietary fibre, 0 g sugar), 10 mg chol, 0 mg sodium.

VEGAN

SWEET & SOUR KETCHUP

HANDS-ON TIME
15 minutes

TOTAL TIME
25 minutes

MAKES
⅔ cup

INGREDIENTS

2 tsp	vegetable oil
1	onion, finely diced
2	cloves garlic, minced
⅔ cup	bottled strained tomatoes (passata)
1	canned chipotle pepper in adobo sauce, chopped
2 tbsp	tomato paste
1 tbsp	red wine vinegar
2 tsp	packed brown sugar
pinch	salt

DIRECTIONS

In small saucepan, heat oil over medium heat; cook onion and garlic, stirring occasionally, until softened and light golden, about 5 minutes.

Stir in strained tomatoes, chipotle pepper, tomato paste, vinegar, sugar and salt; bring to boil. Reduce heat and simmer until thickened, 10 to 12 minutes. Let cool slightly. Using immersion blender, purée until smooth. *(Make-ahead: Refrigerate in airtight container for up to 1 week.)*

NUTRITIONAL INFORMATION, PER 1 TBSP: about 21 cal, trace pro, 1 g total fat (trace sat. fat), 3 g carb (trace dietary fibre, 2 g sugar), 0 mg chol, 41 mg sodium, 71 mg potassium. % RDI: 1% calcium, 3% iron, 1% vit A, 2% vit C, 1% folate.

VEGAN

ZESTY TOMATO JAM

HANDS-ON TIME
40 minutes

TOTAL TIME
2¾ hours

MAKES
2 cups

INGREDIENTS

1.125 kg	ripe tomatoes
1 tbsp	olive oil
1	onion, finely diced
3	cloves garlic, minced
1½ tsp	pickling spice
¼ cup	balsamic vinegar
3 tbsp	packed brown sugar
½ tsp	each salt and pepper

DIRECTIONS

Score an X in bottom of each tomato; plunge into saucepan of boiling water until skins loosen, about 12 seconds. Using slotted spoon, transfer to bowl of ice water; chill for 20 seconds. Peel off skins; core and chop to make 4½ cups. Set aside.

In large shallow saucepan, heat oil over medium heat; cook onion, garlic and pickling spice, stirring often, until onion is tender, about 3 minutes.

Add tomatoes, vinegar, sugar, salt and pepper; cook, stirring occasionally, until thickened and reduced to about 2 cups, about 30 minutes. Let cool. *(Make-ahead: Refrigerate in airtight containers for up to 3 weeks or freeze for up to 3 months.)*

NUTRITIONAL INFORMATION, PER 1 TBSP: about 17 cal, trace pro, 1 g total fat (trace sat. fat), 3 g carb (trace dietary fibre, 2 g sugar), 0 mg chol, 38 mg sodium, 70 mg potassium. % RDI: 1% calcium, 1% iron, 2% vit A, 5% vit C, 1% folate.

HONEY KETCHUP

HANDS-ON TIME 25 minutes
TOTAL TIME 50 minutes
MAKES about 1 cup

INGREDIENTS

1 tbsp	olive oil
1	small onion, diced
1	rib celery, diced
565 g	plum tomatoes (about 5), coarsely chopped
3 tbsp	red wine vinegar
2 tbsp	liquid honey
1 tsp	each dry mustard and garlic powder
¼ tsp	each salt and pepper
pinch	ground cloves

DIRECTIONS

In saucepan, heat oil over medium heat; cook onion and celery, stirring occasionally, until softened and light golden, about 6 minutes.

Stir in tomatoes, vinegar, honey, dry mustard, garlic powder, salt, pepper and cloves; bring to boil. Reduce heat, cover and simmer for 10 minutes. Uncover and simmer until thickened and almost no liquid remains, 25 to 30 minutes.

In blender or using immersion blender, purée until smooth; press through fine sieve. Serve warm or at room temperature. *(Make-ahead: Refrigerate in airtight container for up to 1 week.)*

NUTRITIONAL INFORMATION, PER 1 TBSP: about 22 cal, trace pro, 1 g total fat (trace sat. fat), 3 g carb (trace dietary fibre, 3 g sugar), 0 mg chol, 39 mg sodium, 61 mg potassium. % RDI: 1% iron, 2% vit A, 5% vit C, 1% folate.

VEGAN

TOMATO PEAR KETCHUP

HANDS-ON TIME 25 minutes
TOTAL TIME 1¼ hours
MAKES about 1½ cups

INGREDIENTS

1 cup	chopped seeded peeled tomatoes
1	pear, peeled, cored and diced
1	green hot pepper
1	clove garlic, minced
¼ cup	golden raisins
3 tbsp	cider vinegar
2 tbsp	packed brown sugar
1 tbsp	tomato paste
1	cinnamon stick
¼ tsp	each salt and pepper

DIRECTIONS

In saucepan, combine tomatoes, pear, hot pepper, garlic, raisins, vinegar, brown sugar, tomato paste, cinnamon stick, salt, pepper and ⅓ cup water; bring to boil. Reduce heat, cover and simmer, stirring occasionally, for 45 minutes.

Discard cinnamon stick and hot pepper; uncover and simmer, breaking up some of the pear, until thickened, about 20 minutes. Let cool. *(Make-ahead: Refrigerate in airtight container for up to 1 week.)*

NUTRITIONAL INFORMATION, PER 1 TBSP: about 15 cal, trace pro, 0 g total fat (0 g sat. fat), 4 g carb (trace dietary fibre, 3 g sugar), 0 mg chol, 26 mg sodium, 46 mg potassium. % RDI: 1% iron, 1% vit A, 2% vit C.

FROM TOP
TOMATO PEAR KETCHUP,
ZESTY TOMATO JAM P 63,
HONEY KETCHUP AND
SWEET & SOUR KETCHUP P 63

HANDS-ON TIME
25 minutes
TOTAL TIME
2 hours
MAKES
3 cups

VEGAN

SPICED PEACH CHUTNEY

INGREDIENTS

4	firm ripe peaches
2 tsp	vegetable oil
1	onion, chopped
1 tbsp	minced seeded jalapeño pepper
2 tsp	minced fresh ginger
¼ tsp	ground coriander
pinch	cinnamon
6 tbsp	granulated sugar
3 tbsp	cider vinegar
½ tsp	each salt and pepper
1 tsp	cornstarch

DIRECTIONS

Score X in bottom of each peach; plunge into saucepan of boiling water until skin starts to loosen, about 30 seconds. Using slotted spoon, transfer to bowl of ice water; chill for 20 seconds. Peel off skins; halve peaches and remove pits. Chop into ½-inch chunks to make about 3 cups; set aside.

In saucepan, heat oil over medium heat; cook onion, jalapeño pepper, ginger, coriander and cinnamon, stirring often, until onion is golden, about 10 minutes.

Stir in peaches, sugar, vinegar, 2 tbsp water, the salt and pepper; cook, stirring, until peaches are tender but still hold their shape, about 5 minutes.

Stir cornstarch with 1 tbsp water; stir into peach mixture and cook, stirring, until thickened, about 1 minute. Let cool. *(Make-ahead: Refrigerate in airtight containers for up to 3 weeks or freeze for up to 2 months.)*

NUTRITIONAL INFORMATION, PER 1 TBSP: about 13 cal, trace pro, trace total fat (0 g sat. fat), 3 g carb (trace dietary fibre, 3 g sugar), 0 mg chol, 24 mg sodium, 25 mg potassium. % RDI: 2% vit C.

HANDS-ON TIME
10 minutes
TOTAL TIME
10 minutes
MAKES
1 cup

VEGAN

CILANTRO GINGER CHUTNEY

INGREDIENTS

1 tbsp	lemon juice
1	shallot, chopped
1	piece (1 inch) ginger, peeled and sliced
1	red or green chili pepper, halved lengthwise and seeded
½ tsp	cumin seeds
½ tsp	pepper
¼ tsp	salt
1	large bunch cilantro, chopped

DIRECTIONS

In blender, purée together ½ cup water, lemon juice, shallot, ginger, chili pepper, cumin seeds, pepper and salt.

Add cilantro, ½ cup at a time, puréeing until smooth and scraping down side as needed. *(Make-ahead: Refrigerate in airtight container for up to 2 weeks or freeze for up to 3 months.)*

NUTRITIONAL INFORMATION, PER 1 TBSP: about 3 cal, trace pro, trace total fat (0 g sat. fat), 1 g carb (trace dietary fibre, 0 g sugar), 0 mg chol, 40 mg sodium, 46 mg potassium. % RDI: 1% calcium, 1% iron, 6% vit A, 7% vit C, 2% folate.

HANDS-ON TIME
30 minutes

TOTAL TIME
30 minutes

MAKES
2 cups

VEGAN

GREEN TOMATO CHOW CHOW

INGREDIENTS

1 tbsp	vegetable oil
1	large onion, chopped
2 tsp	mustard seeds
½ tsp	each celery seeds and dry mustard
¼ tsp	turmeric
2 cups	diced green tomatoes or tomatillos
1	sweet yellow pepper, diced
½ cup	water
2 tbsp	granulated sugar
2 tbsp	vinegar
½ tsp	each salt and pepper

DIRECTIONS

In saucepan, heat oil over medium heat; cook onion, mustard seeds, celery seeds, dry mustard and turmeric, stirring, until onion is softened, about 5 minutes.

Add tomatoes, yellow pepper, water, sugar, vinegar, salt and pepper; cook, stirring occasionally, until thickened and pepper is tender, about 15 minutes. Let cool. *(Make-ahead: Refrigerate in airtight container for up to 3 weeks or freeze for up to 2 months.)*

NUTRITIONAL INFORMATION, PER 1 TBSP: about 13 cal, trace pro, 1 g total fat (0 g sat. fat), 2 g carb (trace dietary fibre, 1 g sugar), 0 mg chol, 37 mg sodium, 36 mg potassium. % RDI: 1% iron, 1% vit A, 13% vit C, 1% folate.

Tip from the Test Kitchen

If you grow your own tomatoes, this relish is a good way to use any that haven't ripened before the first frost.

SWEET POTATO &
TWO-CHEESE TARTE TATIN
P 91

Complete Appetizers & Snacks | 5

You can serve these vegetarian appetizers before an elaborate dinner or as a snack on their own, or try making a few for party nibbles or a tapas-style meal. You can even batch up many of these recipes to make main courses and side dishes.

HANDS-ON TIME
20 minutes
TOTAL TIME
30 minutes
MAKES
4 servings

JALAPEÑO BEAN CAKES
WITH LIME MAYO

INGREDIENTS

1	clove garlic
4	green onions, chopped
1	jalapeño pepper, seeded and chopped
1	can (540 mL) white kidney beans, drained and rinsed
¾ cup	fresh bread crumbs
¼ cup	chopped fresh parsley
¼ tsp	pepper
pinch	salt
1	egg
¼ cup	cornmeal
1 tbsp	olive oil
⅓ cup	light mayonnaise
1 tsp	lime juice

DIRECTIONS

In food processor, pulse together garlic, green onions and jalapeño pepper until finely chopped. Add beans, bread crumbs, parsley, pepper, salt and egg; pulse until combined, leaving pieces of beans. Form into eight 2-inch round patties. Gently dredge in cornmeal; refrigerate in single layer for 10 minutes.

In large nonstick skillet, heat oil over medium heat; cook patties, turning once, until golden, 8 to 10 minutes. Meanwhile, stir mayonnaise with lime juice. Serve with bean cakes.

NUTRITIONAL INFORMATION, PER SERVING: about 273 cal, 10 g pro, 13 g total fat (2 g sat. fat), 32 g carb (9 g dietary fibre, 4 g sugar), 54 mg chol, 504 mg sodium, 367 mg potassium. % RDI: 6% calcium, 16% iron, 7% vit A, 15% vit C, 35% folate.

VARIATION

CHIPOTLE BEAN CAKES WITH LIME MAYO

Replace jalapeño pepper with 1 canned whole chipotle pepper and 1 tsp adobo sauce; replace fresh parsley with fresh cilantro.

SMOKED CHEDDAR PANCAKES
WITH PICKLED BEETS

HANDS-ON TIME
30 minutes
TOTAL TIME
30 minutes
MAKES
about 30 pancakes

INGREDIENTS

¾ cup	all-purpose flour
½ tsp	each baking powder and baking soda
pinch	salt
¾ cup	buttermilk
1	egg
2 tbsp	butter, melted
½ cup	shredded smoked Cheddar cheese
3	green onions, sliced
⅓ cup	crème fraîche or sour cream
1 tbsp	finely chopped fresh chives
¼ cup	pickled beets, julienned (about 2)

DIRECTIONS

In large bowl, whisk together flour, baking powder, baking soda and salt. In separate bowl, whisk together buttermilk, egg and half of the butter; pour over flour mixture. Whisk until combined but still lumpy. Fold in Cheddar and green onions.

Lightly brush large nonstick skillet or griddle with some of the remaining butter; heat over medium heat. Working in batches and brushing skillet with remaining butter as necessary, drop batter by 1 tbsp, spreading slightly to form 1¾-inch rounds; cook until bubbles form on tops, about 2 minutes. Turn pancakes; cook until bottoms are golden, about 1½ minutes. Transfer to warmed plate.

Mix crème fraîche with 2 tsp of the chives; dollop scant ½ tsp onto each pancake. Top with beets; sprinkle with remaining chives.

NUTRITIONAL INFORMATION, PER PANCAKE: about 43 cal, 1 g pro, 3 g total fat (2 g sat. fat), 3 g carb (trace dietary fibre, 1 g sugar), 15 mg chol, 55 mg sodium, 24 mg potassium. % RDI: 2% calcium, 1% iron, 4% vit A, 3% folate.

Tip from the Test Kitchen
For the best texture, make sure not to overstir the pancake batter; it should still be a bit lumpy before you fold in the cheese and green onions.

HANDS-ON TIME
35 minutes

TOTAL TIME
1 hour

MAKES
about 30 pieces

VEGAN

FRIED TOFU
WITH SPICY SESAME DIPPING SAUCE

INGREDIENTS

FRIED TOFU

1	pkg (454 g) firm tofu
¼ cup	vegetable oil

SPICY SESAME DIPPING SAUCE

¼ cup	soy sauce
2 tbsp	minced green onion
2 tbsp	rice vinegar
2	cloves garlic, minced
2 tsp	sesame seeds, toasted
2 tsp	sesame oil
1 tsp	hot pepper flakes
½ tsp	granulated sugar

DIRECTIONS

FRIED TOFU Cut tofu into 1-inch cubes. Let stand on plate for 30 minutes; discard liquid. Using paper towels, pat cubes dry.

In skillet, heat oil over medium-high heat; working in batches, cook tofu, turning often, until golden brown, 5 to 7 minutes. Transfer to paper towel–lined plate to drain. *(Make-ahead: Cover and refrigerate for up to 24 hours. Bring to room temperature before serving.)*

SPICY SESAME DIPPING SAUCE Meanwhile, in bowl, mix together soy sauce, green onion, vinegar, garlic, sesame seeds, sesame oil, hot pepper flakes and sugar. Serve with tofu.

NUTRITIONAL INFORMATION, PER PIECE WITH SAUCE: about 25 cal, 2 g pro, 2 g total fat (trace sat. fat), 1 g carb (trace dietary fibre), 0 mg chol, 140 mg sodium. % RDI: 3% calcium, 2% iron, 2% vit A, 3% vit C, 3% folate.

BAKED SPRING ROLLS
WITH CHILI GARLIC DIPPING SAUCE

HANDS-ON TIME
25 minutes
TOTAL TIME
45 minutes
MAKES
12 pieces

INGREDIENTS

SPRING ROLLS

2 tbsp	vegetable oil
1 cup	thinly sliced shiitake mushrooms
2	green onions, thinly sliced
2	cloves garlic, minced
1 tsp	grated fresh ginger
2 cups	shredded Savoy cabbage
1	carrot, shredded
half	sweet red pepper, thinly sliced
pinch	each salt and pepper
½ cup	water
1 tbsp	cornstarch
1 tbsp	hoisin sauce
12	spring roll wrappers
½ tsp	sesame oil

CHILI GARLIC SAUCE

2 tbsp	rice vinegar
1 tbsp	liquid honey
1 tbsp	water
2 tsp	sodium-reduced soy sauce
1	clove garlic, minced
½ tsp	sambal oelek

DIRECTIONS

SPRING ROLLS In large skillet, heat half of the vegetable oil over medium-high heat; cook mushrooms, green onions, garlic and ginger, stirring, until mushrooms are slightly softened, about 2 minutes.

Stir in cabbage, carrot, red pepper, salt and pepper; cook, stirring, until tender-crisp, about 4 minutes.

Whisk together water, cornstarch and hoisin sauce; pour over cabbage mixture, stirring to combine. Transfer to bowl and let cool.

Lay 1 spring roll wrapper on work surface with point facing up; place 2 tbsp cabbage mixture on bottom third of wrapper. Fold bottom point of wrapper over filling. Fold in sides and roll up until 2-inch triangle of wrapper remains at top.

Lightly brush triangle with a little water and roll up to seal. Repeat with remaining filling and wrappers. Place on greased baking sheet. *(Make-ahead: Cover and refrigerate for up to 8 hours.)*

Combine sesame oil with remaining vegetable oil; brush all over spring rolls. Bake in 425°F oven, turning once, until crisp and golden, about 20 minutes.

CHILI GARLIC SAUCE Meanwhile, in small bowl, whisk together vinegar, honey, water, soy sauce, garlic and sambal oelek until honey is dissolved. Serve with spring rolls.

NUTRITIONAL INFORMATION, PER PIECE WITH SAUCE: about 84 cal, 2 g pro, 3 g total fat (trace sat. fat), 13 g carb (1 g dietary fibre, 3 g sugar), 1 mg chol, 139 mg sodium, 92 mg potassium. % RDI: 2% calcium, 5% iron, 14% vit A, 18% vit C, 10% folate.

Tip from the Test Kitchen

Look for spring roll wrappers in the freezer section of many grocery stores. Thaw according to package directions before using. If you can't find sambal oelek, any hot pepper sauce will work.

HANDS-ON TIME
20 minutes
TOTAL TIME
1½ hours
MAKES
about 2 cups

HOMEMADE RICOTTA

INGREDIENTS
8 cups homogenized milk
½ tsp salt
⅓ cup white vinegar

DIRECTIONS
In large heavy-bottomed saucepan, heat milk with salt over low heat, stirring often, until instant-read thermometer reads 203°F, about 40 minutes.

Add vinegar; slowly stir 3 times. Remove from heat. Let stand for 20 minutes. Line fine-mesh sieve with 2 layers of damp cheesecloth. Using slotted spoon, gently skim off curds and place in sieve. Let drain for 30 minutes. Transfer to serving bowl.

NUTRITIONAL INFORMATION, PER 1 TBSP: about 25 cal, 2 g pro, 2 g total fat (1 g sat. fat), 1 g carb (trace dietary fibre), 7 mg chol, 19 mg sodium, 18 mg potassium. % RDI: 5% calcium, 1% vit A, 1% folate.

Tip from the Test Kitchen
Ricotta spread on crostini makes a creamy base for your favourite toppings. Try roasted cherry tomatoes with balsamic vinegar and basil; fresh figs with arugula and cracked pepper; or roasted crushed hazelnuts drizzled with honey.

FROM TOP
EDAMAME GUACAMOLE P 82,
CREAMY DILL DIP P 82, AND
CAULIFLOWER & WHITE BEAN DIP

CAULIFLOWER & WHITE BEAN DIP

HANDS-ON TIME
15 minutes
TOTAL TIME
35 minutes
MAKES
about 2 cups

INGREDIENTS

5 cups	cauliflower florets (about 1 small head)
1 tbsp	olive oil
1 cup	canned no-salt-added cannellini beans, drained and rinsed
⅓ cup	light mayonnaise
¼ cup	fat-free plain yogurt
1 tsp	grated lemon zest
2 tbsp	lemon juice
1	clove garlic, minced
½ tsp	ground sumac
½ tsp	each salt and pepper

DIRECTIONS

Toss cauliflower florets with oil. Arrange in single layer on lightly greased rimmed baking sheet. Bake in 425°F oven, turning once, until tender and light golden, about 20 minutes. In food processor, purée together cauliflower, cannellini beans, mayonnaise, yogurt, lemon zest, lemon juice, garlic, sumac, salt, pepper and ¼ cup warm water until smooth.

NUTRITIONAL INFORMATION, PER 1 TBSP: about 23 cal, 1 g pro, 1 g total fat, 2 g carb (1 g dietary fibre), 1 mg chol, 61 mg sodium, 45 mg potassium. % RDI: 1% calcium, 1% iron, 0% vit A, 12% vit C.

Tip from the Test Kitchen

Roasting the cauliflower before puréeing dehydrates it slightly, removing excess water and concentrating its flavour.

VEGAN

EDAMAME GUACAMOLE

HANDS-ON TIME 10 minutes

TOTAL TIME 10 minutes

MAKES 1½ cups

INGREDIENTS

1 cup	frozen shelled edamame
1	avocado, peeled, pitted and chopped
1	green onion, sliced
1 tbsp	lime juice
1	small clove garlic, minced
½ tsp	salt
¼ tsp	pepper
1 tbsp	chopped fresh cilantro

DIRECTIONS

In saucepan of boiling salted water, cook edamame for 1 minute. Drain and let cool to room temperature.

In food processor, purée together edamame, avocado, green onion, lime juice, garlic, salt, pepper and 1 tbsp water until smooth. Stir in cilantro.

NUTRITIONAL INFORMATION, PER 1 TBSP: about 20 cal, 1 g pro, 2 g total fat, 1 g carb (1 g dietary fibre), 0 mg chol, 61 mg sodium, 66 mg potassium. % RDI: 0% calcium, 1% iron, 0% vit A, 2% vit C, 10% folate.

CREAMY DILL DIP

HANDS-ON TIME 10 minutes

TOTAL TIME 10 minutes

MAKES about 1¼ cups

INGREDIENTS

⅔ cups	light mayonnaise
½ cup	sour cream
¼ cup	chopped fresh dill
1 tsp	liquid honey
1	clove garlic, pressed or finely grated

DIRECTIONS

In bowl, stir together mayonnaise, sour cream, dill, honey and garlic. *(Make-ahead: Cover and refrigerate for up to 5 days.)*

NUTRITIONAL INFORMATION, PER 2 TBSP: about 70 cal, 1 g pro, 6 g total fat (2 g sat. fat), 3 g carb (1 g dietary fibre), 10 mg chol, 108 mg sodium, 32 mg potassium. % RDI: 2% calcium, 0% iron, 2% vit A, 0% vit C, 0% folate.

HANDS-ON TIME
20 minutes
TOTAL TIME
9 hours
MAKES
10 to 12 servings

VEGAN

EGGPLANT WALNUT DIP
WITH ZA'ATAR PITA CHIPS

INGREDIENTS

EGGPLANT WALNUT DIP

1½ cups	whole walnuts
2	large eggplants
1	head garlic
1	can (540 mL) chickpeas, drained and rinsed
¼ cup	lemon juice
3 tbsp	tahini
1 tsp	za'atar
½ tsp	each salt and pepper
¼ tsp	cayenne pepper
½ cup	chopped fresh parsley

ZA'ATAR PITA CHIPS

6	white or whole wheat pitas
1 tbsp	vegetable oil
1 tsp	za'atar

DIRECTIONS

EGGPLANT WALNUT DIP In bowl, soak walnuts in water for 8 hours; drain and pat dry. Spread on baking sheet; toast in 350°F oven, turning once, until crisp, about 15 minutes.

Using fork, prick eggplants all over; place on lightly greased baking sheet. Set aside.

Remove 1 clove garlic from head; peel, mince and set aside. Slice off top third of remaining garlic head to expose cloves; wrap in foil and add to baking sheet with eggplant. Bake in 375°F oven, turning eggplants once, until softened, 40 to 45 minutes. Let stand until eggplants are cool enough to handle.

Cut eggplants in half lengthwise; using spoon, scoop flesh into food processor. Squeeze cloves of roasted garlic from skins into food processor. Add chickpeas; pulse until combined.

Add walnuts, lemon juice, tahini, za'atar, reserved minced garlic, salt, pepper and cayenne pepper; pulse until walnuts are finely chopped. Stir in parsley. Cover and refrigerate for 1 hour. Serve with pita chips. *(Make-ahead: Cover and refrigerate for up to 2 days.)*

ZA'ATAR PITA CHIPS While walnuts are toasting, brush 1 side of each pita with some of the oil; sprinkle with some of the za'atar. Cut each into 8 wedges; arrange on baking sheet. Working in batches, bake in 350°F oven until crisp, about 8 minutes. *(Make-ahead: Let cool; store in airtight container for up to 2 days.)*

NUTRITIONAL INFORMATION, PER EACH OF 12 SERVINGS: about 278 cal, 8 g pro, 12 g total fat (1 g sat. fat), 37 g carb (6 g dietary fibre, 5 g sugar), 0 mg chol, 357 mg sodium, 305 mg potassium. % RDI: 8% calcium, 18% iron, 3% vit A, 13% vit C, 34% folate.

HANDS-ON TIME
50 minutes

TOTAL TIME
1¼ hours

MAKES
about 40 pieces

POTATO & ZUCCHINI MINI LATKES

INGREDIENTS

2	small zucchini (about 250 g total)
½ tsp	salt
3	yellow-fleshed potatoes, peeled (about 450 g total)
half	onion, grated
1	egg, lightly whisked
3 tbsp	all-purpose flour
	vegetable oil for frying

DIRECTIONS

Using grater or food processor with shredder blade, coarsely grate zucchini. Transfer to colander; sprinkle with half of the salt. Let stand for 30 minutes. Using tea towel or potato ricer, squeeze out and discard liquid. Transfer zucchini to large bowl.

Using grater or food processor with shredder blade, coarsely grate potatoes. Using tea towel or potato ricer, squeeze out and discard liquid. Add potatoes to bowl with zucchini. With fork, mix in onion, egg, flour and remaining salt.

In large skillet, add enough oil to cover bottom of pan; heat over medium-high heat. Shape zucchini mixture by rounded 1 tbsp; working in batches, add to skillet, flattening slightly and leaving 1 inch between each. Cook, turning halfway through and adding more oil as needed, until golden and edges are crisp, about 5 minutes. Transfer to paper towel–lined racks to drain. *(Make-ahead: Remove paper towels; let stand on racks for up to 4 hours or cover and refrigerate on racks for up to 24 hours. Reheat on racks on baking sheets in 425°F oven for 6 to 8 minutes.)*

NUTRITIONAL INFORMATION, PER PIECE: about 36 cal, trace pro, 2 g total fat (trace sat. fat), 4 g carb (trace dietary fibre), 0 mg chol, 16 mg sodium, 60 mg potassium. % RDI: 1% iron, 1% vit A, 2% vit C, 2% folate.

HANDS-ON TIME
10 minutes
TOTAL TIME
30 minutes
MAKES
4 cups

VEGAN

MUSTARD-SPICED NUTS

INGREDIENTS

1 cup	natural (skin-on) almonds
1 cup	raw cashews
1 cup	shelled pistachios
1 cup	walnut halves
1 tbsp	extra-virgin olive oil
1 tbsp	Dijon mustard
2 tbsp	packed brown sugar
1 tbsp	dry mustard
1½ tsp	ground coriander
1 tsp	salt
½ tsp	cayenne pepper
¼ tsp	pepper

DIRECTIONS

In bowl, stir together almonds, cashews, pistachios, walnuts, oil and Dijon mustard. In a separate bowl, mix together brown sugar, dry mustard, coriander, salt, cayenne pepper and pepper; toss with nut mixture to coat.

Spread on parchment paper–lined baking sheet; bake in 350°F oven, stirring once, until fragrant and lightly toasted, about 20 minutes. *(Make-ahead: Store in airtight container for up to 1 week.)*

NUTRITIONAL INFORMATION, PER 2 TBSP: about 101 cal, 3 g pro, 8 g total fat (1 g sat. fat), 5 g carb (1 g dietary fibre), 0 mg chol, 79 mg sodium, 120 mg potassium. % RDI: 2% calcium, 6% iron, 4% folate.

Tip from the Test Kitchen
You can switch up the nuts according to your taste and what you have on hand—just keep the total amount at 4 cups.

HANDS-ON TIME
10 minutes
TOTAL TIME
30 minutes
MAKES
4 to 6 servings

ZUCCHINI, CHÈVRE & WALNUT TART

INGREDIENTS

1	zucchini
1	sheet (half 450 g pkg) frozen butter puff pastry, thawed
5 tsp	extra-virgin olive oil
50 g	soft goat cheese (chèvre), crumbled
¼ cup	chopped walnuts
2 tsp	chopped fresh rosemary
¼ tsp	kosher salt
pinch	pepper

DIRECTIONS

Using vegetable peeler, slice zucchini lengthwise into paper-thin strips.

On rimless baking sheet, gently unroll pastry; lightly brush with 2 tsp of the oil. Top with zucchini. Sprinkle with goat cheese, walnuts, rosemary, salt and pepper. Bake in 400°F oven until pastry is golden, about 20 minutes.

Drizzle with remaining oil. Cut diagonally into wedges.

NUTRITIONAL INFORMATION, PER EACH OF 6 SERVINGS: about 252 cal, 6 g pro, 19 g total fat (7 g sat. fat), 16 g carb (2 g dietary fibre, 2 g sugar), 19 mg chol, 215 mg sodium, 134 mg potassium. % RDI: 2% calcium, 9% iron, 11% vit A, 8% vit C, 8% folate.

APPLE & BLUE CHEESE TARTLETS
WITH ICEWINE GLAZE

HANDS-ON TIME
20 minutes

TOTAL TIME
35 minutes

MAKES
16 tartlets

INGREDIENTS

2 tbsp	Dijon mustard
2 tsp	chopped fresh thyme
1	sheet (half 450 g pkg) frozen butter puff pastry, thawed
1	sweet-tart apple (such as Empire), cored and thinly sliced
1	egg
¼ cup	crumbled blue cheese (such as Bleu Bénédictin)
¼ cup	red or white icewine
4 tsp	granulated sugar
1	shallot, sliced
1 tsp	mixed peppercorns
2 tbsp	fresh tarragon leaves, chopped

DIRECTIONS

In small bowl, mix mustard with thyme. Set aside.

On lightly floured work surface, gently roll out pastry into 12-inch square; prick all over with fork. Cut into 16 squares; transfer to parchment paper–lined rimmed baking sheets. Brush tops of pastry with mustard mixture, leaving ½-inch border. Arrange 3 apple slices in centre of each. *(Make-ahead: Freeze until firm. Layer between waxed paper in airtight container; freeze for up to 2 weeks. Add 2 minutes to baking time.)*

Whisk egg with 1 tsp water; generously brush over pastry edges. Bake, 1 sheet at a time, in 400°F oven until pastry is crisp and golden, 15 to 17 minutes. Sprinkle with blue cheese.

While tartlets are baking, in small saucepan, bring icewine, sugar, shallot and peppercorns to boil. Reduce heat to medium; simmer, stirring occasionally, until thickened and syrupy, about 6 minutes.

Strain syrup through fine-mesh sieve, pressing on solids with back of spoon; discard solids. Drizzle syrup over tartlets. Sprinkle with tarragon.

NUTRITIONAL INFORMATION, PER TARTLET: about 83 cal, 2 g pro, 5 g total fat (2 g sat. fat), 8 g carb (1 g dietary fibre, 3 g sugar), 10 mg chol, 101 mg sodium, 25 mg potassium. % RDI: 1% calcium, 3% iron, 2% vit A, 1% folate.

Tip from the Test Kitchen

As soon as the tartlets come out of the oven, sprinkle the cheese over top so that it will melt slightly.

SPINACH & ARTICHOKE PISSALADIÈRE

HANDS-ON TIME
35 minutes
TOTAL TIME
1¼ hours
MAKES
32 pieces

INGREDIENTS

1 tbsp	butter
1	sweet onion, thinly sliced
1 tbsp	red wine vinegar
pinch	each salt and pepper
2	sheets (450 g pkg) frozen butter puff pastry, thawed
3 cups	lightly packed baby spinach, thinly sliced
½ cup	water-packed artichoke hearts (about 2), drained, chopped and patted dry
¼ cup	thinly sliced drained oil-packed sun-dried tomatoes

DIRECTIONS

In skillet, melt butter over medium heat; cook onion, stirring occasionally, until softened and golden, about 20 minutes. Stir in vinegar, salt and pepper.

On parchment paper–lined rimless baking sheet, gently unroll 1 sheet of the pastry. Top with half each of the spinach, onion mixture, artichokes and sun-dried tomatoes. On separate baking sheet, repeat with remaining pastry, onion mixture, artichokes, sun-dried tomatoes and spinach. Bake, 1 sheet at a time, in 425°F oven until edges are golden, 18 to 20 minutes. Cut each sheet into 16 squares.

NUTRITIONAL INFORMATION, PER PIECE: about 71 cal, 1 g pro, 4 g total fat (2 g sat. fat), 7 g carb (1 g dietary fibre, 1 g sugar), 7 mg chol, 63 mg sodium, 61 mg potassium. % RDI: 1% calcium, 4% iron, 5% vit A, 5% vit C, 4% folate.

Tip from the Test Kitchen

If the onion begins to stick to the skillet, add up to a tablespoon of water, a little at a time.

SWEET POTATO & TWO-CHEESE TARTE TATIN

HANDS-ON TIME
15 minutes

TOTAL TIME
1¼ hours

MAKES
8 servings

INGREDIENTS

600 g	sweet potatoes (about 2), peeled and sliced in generous ¼-inch rounds
2 tsp	olive oil
¼ tsp	each salt and pepper
⅓ cup	granulated sugar
2 tsp	balsamic vinegar
6	fresh sage leaves, chopped
2 tsp	chopped fresh thyme
¾ cup	shredded Gruyère cheese
30 g	soft goat cheese (chèvre), crumbled
1	sheet (half 450 g pkg) frozen butter puff pastry, thawed
4 tsp	Dijon mustard
	arugula (optional)

DIRECTIONS

In bowl, drizzle sweet potatoes with oil. Sprinkle with salt and pepper; toss to coat. Arrange in single layer on parchment paper–lined rimmed baking sheet. Bake in 400°F oven until tender, about 25 minutes. Let cool slightly. *(Make-ahead: Cover and refrigerate for up to 24 hours.)*

While sweet potatoes are cooling, in tall saucepan, cook sugar and 2 tbsp water over medium heat, swirling pan occasionally, until sugar is dissolved and mixture bubbles and becomes light amber, about 7 minutes. Remove from heat. Standing back and averting face, stir in vinegar and 1 tsp water. Immediately pour into lightly greased 9-inch square cake pan, swirling to coat.

Arrange sweet potatoes in rows over top of sugar mixture, overlapping slightly (do not touch hot sugar mixture). Sprinkle with sage, thyme and Gruyère; dot with goat cheese.

Gently unroll puff pastry; brush 1 side with mustard. Place over sweet potatoes, mustard side down, tucking edges between pan and sweet potatoes. Cut 4 steam vents in centre of pastry.

Bake on rimmed baking sheet in 400°F oven until crust is golden, about 35 minutes. Wearing oven mitts, carefully invert onto heatproof platter. Let cool for 5 minutes and garnish with arugula (if using) before serving.

NUTRITIONAL INFORMATION, PER SERVING: about 270 cal, 8 g pro, 14 g total fat (6 g sat. fat), 32 g carb (3 g dietary fibre, 14 g sugar), 24 mg chol, 260 mg sodium, 179 mg potassium. % RDI: 12% calcium, 9% iron, 119% vit A, 15% vit C, 3% folate.

P 70

HANDS-ON TIME
30 minutes
TOTAL TIME
4½ hours
MAKES
6 pieces

SMOKED TOMATO BRUSCHETTA
WITH GOUDA

INGREDIENTS

18	cocktail tomatoes, halved crosswise
2 tbsp	olive oil
6	slices (¾-inch thick) crusty Italian bread or French bread
1½ cups	shredded Gouda cheese
pinch	each salt and pepper
¼ cup	torn fresh basil leaves

DIRECTIONS

Soak 3 cups wood chips in water for 1 hour; drain.

For gas barbecue: Heat 1 burner of 2-burner barbecue or 2 burners of 3-burner barbecue to medium heat (if using 3-burner barbecue, keep centre burner unlit). Remove rack above 1 lit burner. Seal wood chips in double layer of heavy-duty foil to make packet; poke several holes in top. Place packet directly on lit burner without rack; close lid and let smoke fill barbecue. (For charcoal barbecue: Omit foil and place wood chips directly on coals.)

In bowl, gently toss tomatoes with 2 tsp of the oil. Arrange, cut sides up, on rimmed baking sheet. Place baking sheet on rack over unlit burner; close lid and cook on low heat (about 275°F) until tomatoes are shrivelled and appear dry but still plump, about 3 hours.

Remove from grill; set aside. Remove wood chips and return rack to lit burner. Leaving 1 burner unlit, heat remaining burner(s) to medium-high.

Brush both sides of bread slices with remaining oil. Place on greased grill; close lid and grill, turning occasionally, until crisp and grill-marked, about 4 minutes. Sprinkle with Gouda and transfer to rack over unlit burner; close lid and cook until cheese is melted, 4 to 6 minutes. Top with tomatoes; sprinkle with salt, pepper and basil.

NUTRITIONAL INFORMATION, PER PIECE: about 267 cal, 12 g pro, 14 g total fat (6 g sat. fat), 25 g carb (3 g dietary fibre, 6 g sugar), 33 mg chol, 442 mg sodium, 506 mg potassium. % RDI: 23% calcium, 12% iron, 21% vit A, 37% vit C, 33% folate.

Tip from the Test Kitchen

Gentle roasting gives tomatoes the best flavour and texture. Use an oven thermometer to monitor the temperature; adjust the heat to the keep the grill at 275°F.

MEXICAN TORTILLA SOUP
P 107

Complete Soups | 6

Soups are a mainstay of every cook's repertoire, from simple, pure expressions of a main ingredient's unique flavour to complex medleys of vegetables and grains. Some are light starters to a dinner, and others make a hearty meal all by themselves. Best of all, soups are easy to prepare.

CREAMY TOMATO SOUP
WITH PESTO DRIZZLE

HANDS-ON TIME
30 minutes
TOTAL TIME
1¼ hours
MAKES
6 to 8 servings

INGREDIENTS

SOUP

2 tbsp	butter
2	onions, thinly sliced
2	cloves garlic, minced
2	cans (each 796 mL) good-quality whole tomatoes
2 cups	sodium-reduced vegetable broth
¼ cup	tomato paste
1 tbsp	granulated sugar
½ tsp	hot pepper flakes
¼ tsp	pepper
⅓ cup	whipping cream (35%)

ALMOND & BASIL PESTO

½ cup	grated Parmesan cheese
⅓ cup	slivered almonds, toasted
2	cloves garlic
2 cups	fresh basil leaves
¼ tsp	each salt and pepper
⅓ cup	extra-virgin olive oil

DIRECTIONS

SOUP In Dutch oven or large heavy-bottomed saucepan, melt butter over medium heat; cook onions, stirring occasionally, until golden, about 7 minutes. Add garlic; cook, stirring, until fragrant, about 1 minute.

Stir in tomatoes, broth, tomato paste, sugar, hot pepper flakes and pepper; bring to boil. Reduce heat, partially cover and simmer, stirring occasionally, until flavours are well blended, 50 to 55 minutes. Stir in cream. In blender, working in batches, purée soup until smooth. Divide among serving bowls.

ALMOND & BASIL PESTO While soup is simmering, in food processor, pulse together Parmesan, almonds and garlic until coarsely ground. Add basil, salt and pepper; pulse 6 times. With motor running, add oil in thin steady stream until smooth. *(Make-ahead: Refrigerate in airtight container for up to 3 days.)* Drizzle over soup.

NUTRITIONAL INFORMATION, PER EACH OF 8 SERVINGS: about 258 cal, 6 g pro, 20 g total fat (7 g sat. fat), 17 g carb (3 g dietary fibre, 10 g sugar), 26 mg chol, 600 mg sodium, 628 mg potassium. % RDI: 16% calcium, 21% iron, 17% vit A, 57% vit C, 11% folate.

Tip from the Test Kitchen

When blending a hot soup, work in small batches and remove the vent from your blender lid to relieve any pressure caused by escaping steam; cover the hole with a folded tea towel to avoid scalding yourself with hot liquid.

TOMATO & VEGETABLE SOUP
WITH HALLOUMI

HANDS-ON TIME
30 minutes

TOTAL TIME
30 minutes

MAKES
4 servings

INGREDIENTS

4 tsp	olive oil
2	carrots, sliced
1	rib celery, diced
1	onion, diced
4	cloves garlic, minced
1 tsp	each ground cumin, ground coriander and curry powder
pinch	each cinnamon and hot pepper flakes
1	can (796 mL) diced tomatoes
2 cups	sodium-reduced vegetable broth
1	zucchini, diced
3 cups	lightly packed baby spinach
¼ cup	chopped fresh cilantro (optional)
1 tbsp	lemon juice
4	slices (about ¼-inch thick) baguette
½ tsp	za'atar
half	pkg (250 g pkg) halloumi cheese, cut crosswise in 4 slices

DIRECTIONS

In Dutch oven or large heavy-bottomed saucepan, heat 3½ tsp of the oil over medium heat; cook carrots, celery and onion, stirring, until softened, about 5 minutes. Add garlic, cumin, coriander, curry powder, cinnamon and hot pepper flakes; cook, stirring, for 1 minute.

Stir in tomatoes, broth and 2 cups water; bring to boil. Reduce heat; simmer for 15 minutes. Stir in zucchini; cook until tender-crisp, about 2 minutes. Remove from heat; stir in spinach, cilantro (if using) and lemon juice.

Meanwhile, arrange baguette slices on rimmed baking sheet; drizzle with remaining oil and sprinkle with za'atar. Bake in 400°F oven until crisp and light golden, about 6 minutes.

Meanwhile, in nonstick skillet, cook halloumi over medium heat, turning once, until golden, about 4 minutes. Top each bowl of soup with a slice of halloumi and baguette.

NUTRITIONAL INFORMATION, PER SERVING: about 261 cal, 11 g pro, 14 g total fat (6 g sat. fat), 26 g carb (5 g dietary fibre, 12 g sugar), 31 mg chol, 996 mg sodium, 930 mg potassium. % RDI: 31% calcium, 31% iron, 110% vit A, 77% vit C, 40% folate.

Tip from the Test Kitchen

Za'atar is a Middle Eastern spice blend that usually includes sesame seeds, thyme, sumac, marjoram and oregano.

HANDS-ON TIME
15 minutes
TOTAL TIME
35 minutes
MAKES
6 to 8 servings

VEGAN

EDAMAME VEGETABLE SOUP

INGREDIENTS

1 tbsp	olive oil
2	carrots, thinly sliced
2	ribs celery, thinly sliced
1	onion, diced
2	cloves garlic, minced
¼ tsp	pepper
3 cups	vegetable broth
1	zucchini, thinly sliced
half	sweet red pepper, diced
2 tbsp	sodium-reduced soy sauce
1½ tsp	grated fresh ginger
½ tsp	sesame oil
half	pkg (450 g pkg) medium or firm tofu, drained
1 cup	frozen shelled edamame, thawed

DIRECTIONS

In Dutch oven or large heavy-bottomed saucepan, heat olive oil over medium heat; cook carrots, celery, onion, garlic and pepper, stirring occasionally, until softened, about 8 minutes.

Add broth, 3 cups water, the zucchini, red pepper, soy sauce, ginger and sesame oil; bring to boil. Reduce heat and simmer until carrots are tender, about 8 minutes.

Cut tofu into ½-inch cubes. Add to soup along with edamame; simmer for 3 minutes.

NUTRITIONAL INFORMATION, PER EACH OF 8 SERVINGS: about 105 cal, 5 g pro, 6 g total fat (2 g sat. fat), 9 g carb (2 g dietary fibre), 5 mg chol, 392 mg sodium, 325 mg potassium. % RDI: 10% calcium, 9% iron, 41% vit A, 30% vit C, 31% folate.

HANDS-ON TIME
25 minutes
TOTAL TIME
25 minutes
MAKES
4 servings

VEGAN

VEGETABLE QUINOA SOUP

INGREDIENTS

2 tsp	olive oil
1	onion, diced
2	cloves garlic, minced
1 cup	thinly sliced cremini mushrooms (about 115 g)
1	sweet potato (about 340 g), peeled and diced
2 cups	sodium-reduced vegetable broth
½ cup	quinoa
½ tsp	pepper
¼ tsp	salt
2 cups	stemmed kale, thinly sliced
1 tbsp	red wine vinegar

DIRECTIONS

In large saucepan, heat oil over medium heat; cook onion and garlic, stirring occasionally, until softened, about 5 minutes.

Add mushrooms; cook, stirring occasionally, until beginning to soften, about 4 minutes. Stir in sweet potato, 3 cups water, broth, quinoa, pepper and salt; bring to boil. Reduce heat to medium; cook until quinoa is tender, 10 to 12 minutes.

Stir in kale; cook until tender, about 4 minutes. Stir in vinegar.

NUTRITIONAL INFORMATION, PER SERVING: about 195 cal, 6 g pro, 5 g total fat (1 g sat. fat), 36 g carb (5 g dietary fibre, 7 g sugar), 0 mg chol, 194 mg sodium, 668 mg potassium. % RDI: 9% calcium, 24% iron, 164% vit A, 77% vit C, 15% folate.

HANDS-ON TIME
30 minutes
TOTAL TIME
30 minutes
MAKES
4 servings

RAMEN NOODLE SOUP

INGREDIENTS

2 tsp	sesame oil
3	cloves garlic, minced
1	pkg (900 mL) vegetable broth
225 g	shiitake mushrooms, stemmed and thinly sliced
4 tsp	miso paste
2 tsp	sodium-reduced soy sauce
280 g	fresh ramen noodles
4	hard-cooked eggs, peeled and halved lengthwise
6	green onions, thinly sliced
1	strip (2 inches wide) roasted seaweed, cut crosswise in 8 strips

DIRECTIONS

In saucepan, heat oil over medium-high heat; cook garlic until fragrant, 2 minutes.

Add broth and 3 cups water; bring to boil. Add mushrooms; reduce heat and simmer for 5 minutes. Stir in miso paste and soy sauce.

Meanwhile, in pot of boiling water, cook noodles according to package directions; drain and divide among 4 large soup bowls. Top each with 2 egg halves. Ladle soup over top. Sprinkle with green onions and seaweed.

NUTRITIONAL INFORMATION, PER SERVING: about 284 cal, 15 g pro, 9 g total fat (3 g sat. fat), 39 g carb (3 g dietary fibre, 6 g sugar), 222 mg chol, 1,110 mg sodium, 287 mg potassium. % RDI: 6% calcium, 16% iron, 17% vit A, 7% vit C, 22% folate.

Tip from the Test Kitchen

You'll find fresh ramen noodles in the refrigerated Asian section of many grocery stores, but you can also use rice stick vermicelli.

BROCCOLI SOUP
WITH CHEDDAR CROUTONS

HANDS-ON TIME
35 minutes

TOTAL TIME
40 minutes

MAKES
6 to 8 servings

INGREDIENTS

BROCCOLI SOUP

1	large head broccoli
1 tbsp	butter
3	leeks (white and light green parts only), sliced
2	yellow-fleshed potatoes (about 450 g total), peeled and cut in ½-inch cubes
4	cloves garlic, sliced
1 tsp	dry mustard
¾ tsp	dried savory
1	pkg (900 mL) sodium-reduced vegetable broth
1 cup	shredded extra-old white Cheddar cheese
¼ cup	chopped fresh parsley
½ cup	sour cream
½ tsp	each salt and pepper

CHEDDAR CROUTONS

3 cups	cubed (½ inch) baguette (about one-third baguette)
2 tsp	olive oil
½ cup	shredded extra-old white Cheddar cheese

DIRECTIONS

BROCCOLI SOUP Cut stem from broccoli head; cut head into florets to yield 5 cups. Trim bottom end from stem; peel outer layer. Slice stem to yield ¾ cup. Set aside.

In Dutch oven or large heavy-bottomed saucepan, melt butter over medium heat; cook leeks, potatoes and broccoli stems, stirring occasionally, until leeks are softened, about 12 minutes. Add garlic, mustard and savory; cook, stirring, until fragrant, about 1 minute.

Stir in broth and 2 cups water; bring to boil. Reduce heat and simmer for 5 minutes. Stir in broccoli florets; simmer until broccoli stems and potatoes are tender, about 8 minutes. Stir in Cheddar until melted; stir in parsley.

Working in batches, purée soup in blender until smooth. Pour into clean Dutch oven or large saucepan; heat over medium-low. Whisk in sour cream, salt and pepper; cook until heated through. *(Make-ahead: Refrigerate in airtight container for up to 2 days or freeze for up to 2 weeks.)*

CHEDDAR CROUTONS While soup is simmering, in bowl, toss baguette with oil to coat. Arrange in single layer on parchment paper–lined baking sheet; sprinkle with Cheddar. Bake in 400°F oven, turning once, until baguette is golden and cheese is melted, about 10 minutes. Break apart croutons; serve over soup and garnish with freshly ground pepper.

NUTRITIONAL INFORMATION, PER EACH OF 8 SERVINGS: about 279 cal, 11 g pro, 13 g total fat (7 g sat. fat), 32 g carb (4 g dietary fibre, 5 g sugar), 31 mg chol, 31 mg sodium, 550 mg potassium. % RDI: 24% calcium, 21% iron, 36% vit A, 72% vit C, 43% folate.

HANDS-ON TIME
25 minutes
TOTAL TIME
8½ hours
MAKES
8 to 10 servings

SLOW COOKER FRENCH LEEK SOUP

INGREDIENTS

6	leeks (white and light green parts only), halved lengthwise and thinly sliced crosswise
¼ cup	butter, melted
2 tbsp	chopped fresh thyme
1 tbsp	sodium-reduced soy sauce
1 tbsp	white wine vinegar
1 tbsp	vegetarian Worcestershire sauce
½ tsp	each salt and pepper
1	pkg (900 mL) sodium-reduced vegetable broth
16	slices (½ inch thick) baguette
½ cup	shredded Gruyère cheese
1 tbsp	chopped fresh parsley

DIRECTIONS

In slow cooker, combine leeks, butter, thyme, soy sauce, vinegar, Worcestershire sauce, salt and pepper; stir in broth and 3 cups water. Cover and cook on low for 8 hours.

Arrange baguette slices on baking sheet; broil, turning once, until golden brown, about 2 minutes.

Combine Gruyère with parsley. Place ovenproof soup bowls on baking sheet; ladle soup into bowls. Top each bowl with 2 baguette slices; sprinkle cheese mixture over top. Broil until cheese is bubbly and golden, about 2 minutes.

NUTRITIONAL INFORMATION, PER EACH OF 10 SERVINGS: about 147 cal, 6 g pro, 7 g total fat (4 g sat. fat), 17 g carb (2 g dietary fibre, 3 g sugar), 18 mg chol, 575 mg sodium, 145 mg potassium. % RDI: 9% calcium, 14% iron, 14% vit A, 12% vit C, 22% folate.

Tip from the Test Kitchen

Worcestershire sauce traditionally contains anchovies, but vegetarian versions are available. As well, many brown steak sauces, including HP and A1, are actually vegan-friendly (check the label to be sure).

HANDS-ON TIME
20 minutes
TOTAL TIME
30 minutes
MAKES
4 servings

VEGAN

MEXICAN TORTILLA SOUP

INGREDIENTS

4 tsp	olive oil
1	onion, diced
3	cloves garlic, minced
1	jalapeño pepper, halved, seeded and thinly sliced
¾ tsp	each ground cumin and dried oregano
¾ tsp	salt
½ tsp	ground coriander
½ tsp	pepper
4 cups	diced tomatoes (about 4 large)
2 cups	vegetable broth
2	corn tortillas (6 inches)
1	avocado, peeled, pitted and cubed
2	radishes, quartered and thinly sliced
2 tbsp	chopped fresh cilantro
4	lime wedges

DIRECTIONS

In Dutch oven or large heavy-bottomed saucepan, heat 1 tbsp of the oil over medium heat; cook onion, garlic and jalapeño pepper, stirring occasionally, until softened, about 4 minutes. Add cumin, oregano, salt, coriander and pepper; cook, stirring, for 1 minute. Stir in tomatoes, 4 cups water and the stock; bring to boil. Reduce heat and simmer for 20 minutes.

Meanwhile, halve tortillas; cut crosswise into ½-inch thick strips. Toss with remaining oil. Bake on rimmed baking sheet in 425°F oven, turning once, until crisp and golden, 6 to 8 minutes.

Ladle soup into bowls; top with avocado, radishes, cilantro and tortilla strips. Serve with lime wedges.

NUTRITIONAL INFORMATION, PER SERVING: about 202 cal, 5 g pro, 13 g total fat (2 g sat. fat), 23 g carb (7 g dietary fibre, 8 g sugar), 2 mg chol, 838 mg sodium, 784 mg potassium. % RDI: 6% calcium, 11% iron, 18% vit A, 55% vit C, 30% folate.

Tip from the Test Kitchen

Corn tortillas give this dish authentic Mexican flavour, but flour tortillas will work just as well.

P 94

HANDS-ON TIME
15 minutes
TOTAL TIME
1¼ hours
MAKES
4 servings

HUNGARIAN POTATO SOUP

INGREDIENTS

8	whole black peppercorns
2	bay leaves
1 tbsp	vegetable oil
2	ribs celery, diced
1	onion, diced
½ tsp	salt
4	russet potatoes (about 750 g total), peeled and diced
2 cups	sodium-reduced vegetable broth
3 tbsp	white vinegar
⅓ cup	sour cream
2 tbsp	chopped fresh parsley

DIRECTIONS

In cheesecloth square, tie together peppercorns and bay leaves with string; set aside.

In large saucepan, heat oil over medium heat; cook celery, onion and salt, stirring occasionally, until tender but not browned, about 8 minutes.

Add potatoes to pan; cook, stirring, for 2 minutes. Add 3 cups water, the vegetable broth, vinegar and spice bag; bring to boil. Reduce heat, cover and simmer until potatoes are tender, about 45 minutes. Discard spice bag.

Using immersion blender, purée soup until smooth. *(Make-ahead: Let cool for 30 minutes; refrigerate in airtight container for up to 2 days.)* Whisk in sour cream and parsley. Heat through over medium heat, stirring occasionally.

NUTRITIONAL INFORMATION, PER SERVING: about 201 cal, 5 g pro, 6 g total fat (2 g sat. fat), 33 g carb (3 g dietary fibre), 8 mg chol, 626 mg sodium. % RDI: 5% calcium, 5% iron, 5% vit A, 23% vit C, 11% folate.

CAULIFLOWER CORN CHOWDER

HANDS-ON TIME
30 minutes

TOTAL TIME
30 minutes

MAKES
6 servings

INGREDIENTS

2 tbsp	olive oil
1	onion, diced
4	cloves garlic, minced
1 tbsp	chopped fresh thyme
3	corn cobs, husked and kernels removed
1	small head cauliflower, cut in bite-size florets (about 6 cups)
3 cups	sodium-reduced vegetable broth
¼ tsp	each salt and pepper
1½ cups	milk
3 tbsp	all-purpose flour
1	sweet red pepper, diced
2 tbsp	lemon juice

DIRECTIONS

In Dutch oven or large heavy-bottomed saucepan, heat oil over medium-high heat; sauté onion, garlic and 2 tsp of the thyme until onion is softened, about 3 minutes. Stir in corn kernels, cauliflower, broth, salt, pepper and ½ cup water; bring to boil. Reduce heat, cover and simmer until cauliflower is tender, about 8 minutes.

In blender, working in batches, purée 4 cups of the soup until smooth; return to pot. Whisk milk with flour; stir into soup. Add red pepper; bring to boil. Reduce heat; simmer, uncovered and stirring occasionally, just until red pepper is tender and soup is slightly thickened, about 2 minutes. Stir in lemon juice. Sprinkle with remaining thyme.

NUTRITIONAL INFORMATION, PER SERVING: about 198 cal, 7 g pro, 7 g total fat (1 g sat. fat), 31 g carb (6 g dietary fibre, 9 g sugar), 5 mg chol, 221 mg sodium, 446 mg potassium. % RDI: 10% calcium, 10% iron, 11% vit A, 133% vit C, 38% folate.

HANDS-ON TIME
35 minutes
TOTAL TIME
1¼ hours
MAKES
10 to 12 servings

VEGAN

BEET BORSCHT

INGREDIENTS

2 tbsp	vegetable oil
1	onion, diced
3	cloves garlic, minced
½ tsp	caraway seeds
5 cups	diced green cabbage
675 g	beets, peeled and diced
2	small white potatoes (about 280 g total), peeled and cubed
2	ribs celery, diced
1	carrot, diced
2	bay leaves
1¾ tsp	salt
½ tsp	pepper
1	can (156 mL) tomato paste
1 tbsp	packed brown sugar
3 tbsp	vinegar

DIRECTIONS

In Dutch oven or large heavy-bottomed saucepan, heat oil over medium-high heat; cook onion, garlic and caraway seeds, stirring occasionally, until onion is softened and light golden, about 4 minutes.

Stir in cabbage, beets, potatoes, celery, carrot, bay leaves, salt and pepper; cook over medium heat, stirring often, until beets are starting to soften, about 10 minutes.

Stir in tomato paste and brown sugar; cook, stirring, for 2 minutes. Stir in 10 cups water; bring to boil. Reduce heat and simmer, stirring occasionally, until beets are tender, about 40 minutes. Stir in vinegar; discard bay leaves. *(Make-ahead: Freeze in airtight container for up to 2 weeks.)*

NUTRITIONAL INFORMATION, PER EACH OF 12 SERVINGS: about 85 cal, 2 g pro, 3 g total fat (trace sat. fat), 15 g carb (3 g dietary fibre, 7 g sugar), 0 mg chol, 398 mg sodium, 425 mg potassium. % RDI: 3% calcium, 8% iron, 14% vit A, 23% vit C, 20% folate.

Tip from the Test Kitchen

This borscht is vegan on its own, but for a traditional topping, add a dollop of sour cream (vegan versions are available) and a sprinkle of chopped fresh dill to each serving bowl.

GREEK HALLOUMI SALAD
WITH HERBED PITA CHIPS
P 119

Complete Salads | 7

Bright colours, contrasting textures and fresh flavour—salads bring out the best in vegetables, and they're easily adapted to the seasonal ingredients you have on hand. Whether you try a different dressing, toss in some nuts or cheese for added protein or add fresh herbs from your garden, it's all good.

HANDS-ON TIME
10 minutes
TOTAL TIME
10 minutes
MAKES
4 servings

SWISS CHARD, STRAWBERRY & FETA SALAD

INGREDIENTS

HONEY DRESSING

3 tbsp	extra-virgin olive oil
2 tbsp	lemon juice
1 tsp	liquid honey
¼ tsp	each salt and pepper

SALAD

6 cups	thinly sliced stemmed Swiss chard (about 1 small bunch)
1 cup	strawberries, hulled and cut in 8 wedges
½ cup	crumbled feta cheese
2 tbsp	pepitas, toasted

DIRECTIONS

HONEY DRESSING In large bowl, whisk together oil, lemon juice, honey, salt and pepper.

SALAD Add Swiss chard, strawberries, feta and pepitas to dressing; toss to coat. *(Make-ahead: Refrigerate in airtight container for up to 12 hours.)*

NUTRITIONAL INFORMATION, PER SERVING: about 187 cal, 5 g pro, 16 g total fat (5 g sat. fat), 7 g carb (2 g dietary fibre, 4 g sugar), 17 mg chol, 418 mg sodium, 224 mg potassium. % RDI: 11% calcium, 11% iron, 12% vit A, 53% vit C, 10% folate.

Tip from the Test Kitchen

Swiss chard's sturdy leaves resist wilting when dressed with vinaigrette, making it a great choice for a make-ahead salad.

BLOOD ORANGE & FENNEL SALAD

HANDS-ON TIME
15 minutes

TOTAL TIME
15 minutes

MAKES
12 servings

INGREDIENTS

3	small blood oranges or Cara Cara navel oranges
3 tbsp	red wine vinegar
1 tbsp	Dijon mustard
2 tsp	liquid honey
1	clove garlic, pressed or finely grated
¼ tsp	each salt and pepper
½ cup	extra-virgin olive oil
12 cups	torn red or green leaf lettuce
1	small bulb fennel, trimmed, cored and thinly sliced
¾ cup	thinly sliced red onion

DIRECTIONS

Finely grate orange zest to make 1 tsp. Remove remaining peel and pith from oranges; cut oranges crosswise into generous ¼-inch thick slices. Set aside.

In small bowl, whisk together vinegar, mustard, honey, orange zest, garlic, salt and pepper. Gradually whisk in oil in thin steady stream until well combined. *(Make-ahead: Refrigerate in airtight container for up to 5 days.)*

In large bowl, combine lettuce, fennel, red onion and oranges. Drizzle with vinaigrette; toss to coat. Serve immediately.

NUTRITIONAL INFORMATION, PER SERVING: about 113 cal, 1 g pro, 9 g total fat (1 g sat. fat), 7 g carb (2 g dietary fibre, 5 g sugar), 0 mg chol, 82 mg sodium, 195 mg potassium. % RDI: 3% calcium, 4% iron, 35% vit A, 37% vit C, 12% folate.

Tip from the Test Kitchen

At the grocery store, choose blood oranges that feel heavy for their size, and store them in your refrigerator or in a cool, dry place. They'll keep for up to a week.

HANDS-ON TIME
15 minutes
TOTAL TIME
15 minutes
MAKES
10 to 12 servings

KALE & FENNEL SALAD
WITH LEMON DILL DRESSING

INGREDIENTS

LEMON DILL DRESSING

⅓ cup	extra-virgin olive oil
3 tbsp	lemon juice
1 tbsp	Dijon mustard
1 tbsp	liquid honey
¼ tsp	pepper
pinch	salt

SALAD

12 cups	packed baby kale
2 cups	shaved fennel
½ cup	shaved Parmesan cheese
2 tbsp	chopped fresh dill
½ cup	pepitas, toasted

DIRECTIONS

LEMON DILL DRESSING In large bowl, whisk together oil, lemon juice, mustard, honey, pepper and salt. *(Make-ahead: Refrigerate in airtight container for up to 3 days; whisk before using.)*

SALAD Add kale, fennel, Parmesan and dill to dressing; toss to coat. Sprinkle with pepitas.

NUTRITIONAL INFORMATION, PER EACH OF 12 SERVINGS: about 118 cal, 4 g pro, 10 g total fat (2 g sat. fat), 6 g carb (1 g dietary fibre, 3 g sugar), 2 mg chol, 79 mg sodium, 220 mg potassium. % RDI: 7% calcium, 10% iron, 25% vit A, 52% vit C, 19% folate.

Tip from the Test Kitchen

If baby kale isn't in season, you can substitute with baby spinach.

GREEK HALLOUMI SALAD
WITH HERBED PITA CHIPS

HANDS-ON TIME
15 minutes
TOTAL TIME
15 minutes
MAKES
4 servings

INGREDIENTS

HERBED PITA CHIPS

1	Greek pita
1 tsp	olive oil
¼ tsp	each dried basil and dried oregano

SALAD

half	pkg (250 g pkg) halloumi cheese, cut crosswise in scant ¼-inch thick slices
2 tbsp	extra-virgin olive oil
1 tbsp	red wine vinegar
1	clove garlic, minced
¼ tsp	dried oregano
pinch	pepper
5 cups	mixed baby greens
1	sweet green pepper, chopped
1	pkg (250 g) cherry tomatoes or grape tomatoes, halved
half	English cucumber, chopped
half	red onion, thinly sliced
½ cup	pitted Kalamata olives

DIRECTIONS

HERBED PITA CHIPS Brush pita with oil; sprinkle with basil and oregano. Cut into 8 wedges; arrange in single layer on rimmed baking sheet. Bake in 350°F oven until crisp and light golden, about 8 minutes. *(Make-ahead: Let cool completely; store in airtight container for up to 2 days.)*

SALAD While pita is baking, in nonstick skillet, cook halloumi over medium heat, turning once, until light golden, about 3 minutes.

Meanwhile, in large bowl, whisk together oil, vinegar, garlic, oregano and pepper. Add baby greens, green pepper, tomatoes, cucumber, red onion and olives; toss to coat. Divide among serving plates; top with halloumi. Serve with pita chips.

NUTRITIONAL INFORMATION, PER SERVING: about 296 cal, 10 g pro, 21 g total fat (7 g sat. fat), 19 g carb (3 g dietary fibre, 5 g sugar), 31 mg chol, 743 mg sodium, 453 mg potassium. % RDI: 21% calcium, 11% iron, 42% vit A, 82% vit C, 24% folate.

Tip from the Test Kitchen

To pit olives quickly, spread them on a cutting board and press with the bottom of a saucepan. This exposes the pits, making them easy to remove.

P 112

HANDS-ON TIME
20 minutes
TOTAL TIME
20 minutes
MAKES
4 servings

CILANTRO-JALAPEÑO GRILLED TOFU SALAD

INGREDIENTS

1	pkg (about 450 g) firm tofu, drained
½ tsp	salt
¼ cup	lime juice
4 tsp	liquid honey
half	jalapeño pepper, seeded and minced
2	cloves garlic, minced
½ tsp	chili powder
½ tsp	pepper
¼ cup	chopped fresh cilantro
2	green onions, minced
¼ cup	extra-virgin olive oil
6 cups	lightly packed mixed baby greens
1 cup	cherry tomatoes, halved
1	small carrot, shredded

DIRECTIONS

Cut tofu into 12 scant ½-inch thick slices. Sprinkle with a pinch of the salt; set aside.

In large bowl, whisk together lime juice, honey, jalapeño, garlic, chili powder, pepper and remaining salt. Stir in cilantro, green onions and oil.

Brush tofu all over with ¼ cup of the dressing. Place on greased grill over medium-high heat; close lid and grill, turning once, until golden and heated through, 6 to 8 minutes. Transfer to plate; top with ¼ cup of the dressing.

Toss together baby greens, cherry tomatoes, carrot and remaining dressing. Serve with tofu.

NUTRITIONAL INFORMATION, PER SERVING: about 323 cal, 18 g pro, 22 g total fat (3 g sat. fat), 17 g carb (3 g dietary fibre, 9 g sugar), 0 mg chol, 356 mg sodium, 658 mg potassium. % RDI: 24% calcium, 25% iron, 102% vit A, 37% vit C, 58% folate.

Tip from the Test Kitchen

Jalapeños, and other hot peppers, can vary in spiciness. It's always a good idea to taste a tiny bit before adding to a dish.

HANDS-ON TIME
10 minutes
TOTAL TIME
10 minutes
MAKES
2 servings

VEGAN

CRUNCHY PEANUT VEGGIE NOODLE SALAD

INGREDIENTS

3 tbsp	smooth peanut butter
4 tsp	rice vinegar
1 tbsp	sodium-reduced soy sauce
2 tsp	sesame oil
⅓ cup	hot water
2 cups	cooked linguine or other long pasta
1 cup	frozen peas, cooked and cooled
2	green onions, thinly sliced
1 cup	grated zucchini (peel-on)
1 cup	julienned carrots
2 tbsp	roasted salted peanuts, chopped

DIRECTIONS

In large bowl, whisk together peanut butter, vinegar, soy sauce and sesame oil; gradually whisk in hot water until smooth. Add pasta, peas, green onions, zucchini and carrots; toss to coat. *(Make-ahead: Refrigerate in airtight container for up to 6 hours; stir in hot water, ½ tsp at a time, until sauce reaches desired consistency.)* Sprinkle with peanuts.

NUTRITIONAL INFORMATION, PER SERVING: about 518 cal, 21 g pro, 24 g total fat (4 g sat. fat), 60 g carb (8 g dietary fibre, 10 g sugar), 0 mg chol, 694 mg sodium, 671 mg potassium. % RDI: 7% calcium, 27% iron, 81% vit A, 33% vit C, 95% folate.

Tip from the Test Kitchen

Toss leftover cooked pasta with vegetable oil before storing it in the fridge. That way, the noodles won't stick together.

HANDS-ON TIME
30 minutes
TOTAL TIME
30 minutes
MAKES
8 servings

VEGAN

HEIRLOOM TOMATO TABBOULEH SALAD

INGREDIENTS

¾ cup	whole grain coarse bulgur
¼ cup	red quinoa, rinsed
4	large heirloom tomatoes, cut in wedges or sliced
1	shallot, thinly sliced
1 tsp	salt
¼ cup	olive oil
2 tbsp	lemon juice
2 tbsp	pomegranate molasses or balsamic glaze
½ cup	coarsely chopped fresh parsley
½ cup	coarsely chopped fresh mint
quarter	English cucumber, thinly sliced
¼ cup	pine nuts, toasted

DIRECTIONS

In saucepan, bring 2 cups water to boil. Stir in bulgur and quinoa; return to boil. Reduce heat to low and simmer, covered, until no liquid remains, 15 to 18 minutes. Fluff with fork; let cool.

Meanwhile, in large bowl, gently toss together tomatoes, shallot and ½ tsp of the salt. Let stand.

In small bowl, whisk together oil, lemon juice, molasses and remaining salt. Pour over bulgur mixture. Add parsley, mint and cucumber; toss to mix. Spoon onto platter; top with tomato mixture. Sprinkle with pine nuts. *(Make-ahead: Stir together bulgur, quinoa and dressing; refrigerate in airtight container for up to 24 hours. Before serving, toss with tomatoes, shallot, parsley, mint and cucumber; sprinkle with pine nuts.)*

NUTRITIONAL INFORMATION, PER SERVING: about 203 cal, 5 g pro, 10 g total fat (1 g sat. fat), 25 g carb (5 g dietary fibre, 6 g sugar), 0 mg chol, 300 mg sodium, 438 mg potassium. % RDI: 4% calcium, 17% iron, 15% vit A, 33% vit C, 17% folate.

Tip from the Test Kitchen

Red quinoa has the same nutritional value and nutty, earthy flavour as white quinoa; it also adds vibrant colour to dishes.

WHEAT BERRY & CHICKPEA SALAD
WITH GARAM MASALA DRESSING

HANDS-ON TIME
15 minutes

TOTAL TIME
1¼ hours

MAKES
4 to 6 servings

INGREDIENTS

1 cup	wheat berries
4 cups	broccoli florets (about 1 small head)
3 tbsp	extra-virgin olive oil
2 tbsp	lime juice
1 tsp	garam masala
1 tsp	liquid honey
¼ tsp	salt
pinch	pepper
1	can (540 mL) chickpeas, drained, rinsed and patted dry
⅓ cup	diced red onion
¼ cup	torn fresh cilantro

DIRECTIONS

In large saucepan of boiling salted water, cook wheat berries, covered, until chewy on the outside with a soft centre, about 1 hour; let cool.

Meanwhile, place broccoli in steamer over boiling water; cover and steam until tender-crisp, about 3 minutes; set aside and let cool.

In large bowl, whisk together oil, lime juice, garam masala, honey, salt and pepper. Stir in wheat berries, broccoli, chickpeas, red onion and cilantro; toss to combine.

NUTRITIONAL INFORMATION, PER EACH OF 6 SERVINGS: about 271 cal, 9 g pro, 8 g total fat (1 g sat. fat), 44 g carb (6 g dietary fibre, 5 g sugar), 0 mg chol, 847 mg sodium, 399 mg potassium. % RDI: 5% calcium, 18% iron, 14% vit A, 50% vit C, 34% folate.

Tip from the Test Kitchen

Wheat berries are whole, unprocessed wheat kernels. They have a pleasant, slightly chewy texture when cooked. To save prep time, you can cook the wheat berries ahead of time and refrigerate in an airtight container for up to 3 days.

BROWN RICE & BABY KALE SALAD
WITH CURRY DRESSING

HANDS-ON TIME
10 minutes
TOTAL TIME
10 minutes
MAKES
2 servings

INGREDIENTS

CURRY DRESSING

4 tsp	extra-virgin olive oil
1 tbsp	lemon juice
¾ tsp	curry powder
½ tsp	liquid honey
pinch	each salt and pepper

BROWN RICE SALAD

2 cups	lightly packed baby kale
1½ cups	cold cooked brown rice
½ cup	canned green lentils, drained and rinsed
½ cup	grated carrot
2 tbsp	dried currants

DIRECTIONS

CURRY DRESSING In small bowl, whisk together oil, lemon juice, curry powder, honey, salt and pepper. *(Make-ahead: Refrigerate in airtight container for up to 2 days.)*

BROWN RICE SALAD In separate bowl, combine kale, rice, lentils, carrot and currants. *(Make-ahead: Refrigerate in airtight container for up to 6 hours.)* Add dressing; toss to coat.

NUTRITIONAL INFORMATION, PER SERVING: about 351 cal, 9 g pro, 11 g total fat (2 g sat. fat), 57 g carb (6 g dietary fibre, 11 g sugar), 0 mg chol, 144 mg sodium, 525 mg potassium. % RDI: 7% calcium, 23% iron, 71% vit A, 58% vit C, 45% folate.

Tip from the Test Kitchen

To store leftover brown rice, refrigerate it in an airtight container for up to 2 days.

HANDS-ON TIME
20 minutes

TOTAL TIME
1¼ hours

MAKES
4 to 6 servings

VEGAN

RICE SALAD
WITH QUICK-PICKLED CARROT & DAIKON

INGREDIENTS

GINGER DRESSING

4 tsp	vegetable oil
1 tbsp	lime juice
2 tsp	grated ginger
1 tsp	sesame oil
¼ tsp	salt

SALAD

1	carrot, julienned
1 cup	julienned daikon
2 tsp	granulated sugar
¼ tsp	salt
¼ cup	unseasoned rice vinegar
1 cup	medium-grain rice
half	avocado, sliced
⅓ cup	chopped fresh cilantro
¼ cup	chopped unsalted roasted peanuts
half	hot red pepper, seeded and thinly sliced

DIRECTIONS

GINGER DRESSING In large bowl, whisk together vegetable oil, lime juice, ginger, sesame oil and salt. Set aside.

SALAD In separate bowl, toss together carrot, daikon and half each of the sugar and salt; let stand for 10 minutes. Rinse under cold water; drain and return to bowl.

Whisk together vinegar and remaining sugar and salt until sugar is dissolved. Pour over carrot mixture; cover and refrigerate, stirring once, for 1 hour. Drain well.

Meanwhile, in saucepan, cook rice according to package directions. Spread onto plate; cover and cool completely.

Add carrot mixture, rice, avocado and cilantro to ginger dressing; toss to combine. Sprinkle with peanuts and hot pepper.

NUTRITIONAL INFORMATION, PER EACH OF 6 SERVINGS: about 219 cal, 4 g pro, 9 g total fat (1 g sat. fat), 31 g carb (3 g dietary fibre, 2 g sugar), 0 mg chol, 158 mg sodium, 240 mg potassium. % RDI: 2% calcium, 4% iron, 21% vit A, 12% vit C, 14% folate.

Tip from the Test Kitchen

This Korean-style rice salad features daikon, a sweet and crisp Asian radish. You can also use quick-pickled daikon as a crunchy addition to sandwiches and vegetarian burgers.

HANDS-ON TIME
15 minutes

TOTAL TIME
15 minutes

MAKES
4 to 6 servings

VEGAN

MISO GINGER SOBA SALAD

INGREDIENTS

MISO DRESSING

½ cup	vegetable oil
¼ cup	lemon juice
3 tbsp	white or yellow miso paste
2 tbsp	maple syrup
2 tbsp	grated fresh ginger
1	clove garlic, minced
½ tsp	salt (optional)
¼ tsp	cayenne pepper

SALAD

225 g	soba noodles
1 cup	sugar snap peas, trimmed
1 cup	bite-size broccoli florets
1	sweet red pepper, thinly sliced
quarter	red onion, thinly sliced
quarter	English cucumber, halved lengthwise and sliced crosswise
½ cup	chopped fresh cilantro (with stems)
¼ cup	natural (skin-on) almonds, toasted and chopped

DIRECTIONS

MISO DRESSING In large bowl, whisk together oil, lemon juice, miso paste, maple syrup, ginger, garlic, salt (if using) and cayenne pepper. Set aside.

SALAD In saucepan of boiling water, cook noodles according to package directions. Drain and rinse under cold water; drain well. Set aside.

Meanwhile, in separate saucepan of boiling salted water, cook snap peas and broccoli until tender-crisp, about 2 minutes. Drain and transfer to bowl of ice water to chill; drain well.

Thinly slice snap peas; place in large bowl. Add broccoli, red pepper, red onion and cucumber; toss with half of the dressing. Add noodles and cilantro; gently toss with remaining dressing. Sprinkle with almonds.

NUTRITIONAL INFORMATION, PER EACH OF 6 SERVINGS: about 385 cal, 10 g pro, 22 g total fat (2 g sat. fat), 41 g carb (4 g dietary fibre, 7 g sugar), 0 mg chol, 407 mg sodium, 309 mg potassium. % RDI: 4% calcium, 13% iron, 13% vit A, 77% vit C, 17% folate.

Tip from the Test Kitchen

Avoiding gluten? Check the labels when you buy soba noodles and miso paste. Some brands are wheat-free; others are not.

HANDS-ON TIME
15 minutes
TOTAL TIME
30 minutes
MAKES
4 to 6 servings

WALNUT PESTO POTATO SALAD

INGREDIENTS

675 g	yellow-fleshed mini potatoes, scrubbed
1⅓ cups	lightly packed fresh basil leaves
⅓ cup	chopped walnuts, toasted
¼ cup	grated Parmesan cheese
¼ tsp	lemon zest
4 tsp	lemon juice
1	clove garlic, minced
¼ tsp	salt
pinch	pepper
3 tbsp	extra-virgin olive oil
1 tbsp	chopped fresh chives

DIRECTIONS

In large saucepan of boiling salted water, cook potatoes until tender, about 15 minutes; drain, reserving 2 tbsp cooking liquid. Let cool enough to handle; peel and set aside.

Meanwhile, in food processor, pulse together basil, all but 1 tbsp of the walnuts, the Parmesan, lemon zest, lemon juice, garlic, salt and pepper until mixture becomes coarse paste; scrape down side. With motor running, add oil and reserved cooking liquid in thin, steady stream until smooth.

Toss potatoes with pesto and half of the chives to coat. Top with remaining chives and reserved walnuts.

NUTRITIONAL INFORMATION, PER EACH OF 6 SERVINGS: about 184 cal, 4 g pro, 12 g total fat (2 g sat. fat), 16 g carb (2 g dietary fibre, 1 g sugar), 4 mg chol, 332 mg sodium, 346 mg potassium. % RDI: 7% calcium, 6% iron, 6% vit A, 22% vit C, 10% folate.

LENTIL & SWEET POTATO SALAD
WITH HALLOUMI

HANDS-ON TIME
20 minutes

TOTAL TIME
50 minutes .

MAKES
4 servings

INGREDIENTS

SHALLOT VINAIGRETTE

1	shallot, minced
2 tbsp	extra-virgin olive oil
4 tsp	lemon juice
1 tsp	Dijon mustard
pinch	each salt and pepper

SALAD

⅔ cup	dried green lentils, rinsed
4 cups	cubed peeled sweet potato
2 tsp	extra-virgin olive oil
1½ tsp	garlic powder
1 tsp	smoked paprika
¼ tsp	pepper
pinch	salt
4	slices halloumi cheese (about 100 g total)
¼ cup	chopped fresh cilantro

DIRECTIONS

SHALLOT VINAIGRETTE In small bowl, whisk together shallot, oil, lemon juice, mustard, salt and pepper. Set aside.

SALAD In saucepan, bring lentils and 3 cups water to boil. Reduce heat, cover and simmer until lentils are tender, 15 to 20 minutes; drain. Let cool slightly.

While lentils are cooking, in large bowl, toss together sweet potato, oil, garlic powder, paprika, pepper and salt. Arrange in single layer on greased rimmed baking sheet. Roast in 425°F oven, turning once, until tender, 15 to 18 minutes. Scrape onto plate; set aside. Wipe baking sheet clean.

Arrange halloumi in single layer on same sheet; broil until golden, about 3 minutes. Remove to cutting board; coarsely chop.

In clean large bowl, combine lentils, sweet potato, halloumi and cilantro. Drizzle with vinaigrette; toss to coat.

NUTRITIONAL INFORMATION, PER SERVING: about 382 cal, 16 g pro, 16 g total fat (6 g sat. fat), 45 g carb (8 g dietary fibre, 10 g sugar), 25 mg chol, 357 mg sodium, 701 mg potassium. % RDI: 18% calcium, 31% iron, 222% vit A, 35% vit C, 81% folate.

Tip from the Test Kitchen

Halloumi is a Test Kitchen favourite. This firm, intensely flavourful and salty cheese holds its shape when heated, making it ideal for broiling and grilling.

WARM ROASTED CAULIFLOWER SALAD
WITH GARLICKY TAHINI DRESSING

HANDS-ON TIME
25 minutes
TOTAL TIME
1½ hours
MAKES
6 servings

INGREDIENTS

TAHINI DRESSING

half	head garlic
1 tsp	olive oil
⅓ cup	tahini
5 tbsp	lemon juice
1 tbsp	liquid honey
1 tsp	salt
½ tsp	ground cumin
½ tsp	ground sumac
3 tbsp	chopped fresh parsley or cilantro

SALAD

16 cups	bite-size cauliflower florets (about 1 large head)
¼ cup	olive oil
3 tbsp	chopped fresh thyme
1 tbsp	coriander seeds, lightly crushed
1 tbsp	fennel seeds, lightly crushed
1 tsp	ground sumac
⅓ cup	pomegranate seeds
3 tbsp	chopped fresh parsley or cilantro

DIRECTIONS

TAHINI DRESSING Slice top third off half garlic head to expose cloves; discard. Drizzle cloves with oil; wrap in foil. Bake in 400°F oven until tender, about 30 minutes; let cool slightly. Squeeze cloves into blender.

In blender, purée together garlic, tahini, 6 tbsp water, the lemon juice, honey, salt, cumin and sumac. Add parsley; blend until combined. *(Make-ahead: Refrigerate in airtight container for up to 1 week.)*

SALAD In large bowl, toss together cauliflower, oil, thyme, coriander seeds, fennel seeds and sumac. Arrange in single layer on 2 parchment paper–lined rimmed baking sheets. Roast in 425°F oven, turning once, until tender and golden brown, 35 to 40 minutes. Scrape into same bowl; toss with dressing and half each of the pomegranate seeds and parsley. Transfer to large platter; sprinkle with the remaining pomegranate seeds and parsley.

NUTRITIONAL INFORMATION, PER SERVING: about 246 cal, 7 g pro, 18 g total fat (3 g sat. fat), 19 g carb (8 g dietary fibre, 7 g sugar), 0 mg chol, 458 mg sodium, 436 mg potassium. % RDI: 11% calcium, 21% iron, 4% vit A, 165% vit C, 49% folate.

Tip from the Test Kitchen

Tahini, a paste of ground sesame seeds, is a versatile pantry staple—spread it on toast with honey, mix it with Greek yogurt and lemon juice as a dip, or use it as a creamy, nutty base for salad dressings.

VEGETARIAN WATERMELON POKE BOWL

HANDS-ON TIME
30 minutes

TOTAL TIME
30 minutes

MAKES
4 servings

INGREDIENTS

DRESSING

¼ cup	cider vinegar
3 tbsp	white miso paste
2 tbsp	lemon juice
2 tbsp	chipotle mayonnaise
4 tsp	grated fresh ginger
1 tbsp	liquid honey or maple syrup
1	clove garlic, halved
¾ cup	vegetable oil

SALAD

1 cup	frozen shelled edamame
1	English cucumber
1 tbsp	chopped pickled jalapeño peppers (optional)
6 cups	diced seedless watermelon
4 cups	packed baby spinach
1	avocado, pitted, peeled and sliced
4 tsp	black sesame seeds

DIRECTIONS

DRESSING In blender, purée together vinegar, miso paste, lemon juice, mayonnaise, ginger, honey and garlic. With motor running, gradually add oil in thin steady stream until smooth; set aside. *(Make-ahead: Refrigerate in airtight container for up to 5 days.)*

SALAD In saucepan of boiling water, cook edamame for 2 minutes. Drain and rinse under cold water until cool; drain well. Toss with ¼ cup of the dressing.

Halve cucumber lengthwise; using spoon, scrape out and discard seeds. Thinly slice each half crosswise. Toss with jalapeño peppers (if using). Arrange watermelon, spinach, avocado, edamame and cucumber mixture in 4 bowls; sprinkle with sesame seeds. Drizzle each bowl with about ¼ cup of the remaining dressing. Reserve remaining dressing for another use.

NUTRITIONAL INFORMATION, PER SERVING: about 519 cal, 9 g pro, 40 g total fat (4 g sat. fat), 37 g carb (8 g dietary fibre, 21 g sugar), 2 mg chol, 428 mg sodium, 1,005 mg potassium. % RDI: 9% calcium, 23% iron, 43% vit A, 62% vit C, 93% folate.

Tip from the Test Kitchen

For a heartier dish, double the avocado and serve with brown rice, Buddha bowl–style.

HANDS-ON TIME
10 minutes
TOTAL TIME
20 minutes
MAKES
2 servings

HALLOUMI & QUINOA SALAD
WITH SUMAC-LIME DRESSING

INGREDIENTS

SUMAC-LIME DRESSING

3 tbsp	extra-virgin olive oil
2 tbsp	lime juice
1 tsp	ground sumac
½ tsp	liquid honey
pinch	each salt and pepper
1	clove garlic, smashed

QUINOA SALAD

3 cups	lightly packed baby spinach
1½ cups	cold cooked quinoa
2	plum tomatoes, chopped
⅓ cup	cubed halloumi cheese
16	mint leaves, torn

DIRECTIONS

SUMAC-LIME DRESSING In small bowl, whisk together oil, lime juice, sumac, honey, salt and pepper; stir in garlic. Let stand until fragrant, about 15 minutes; discard garlic. *(Make-ahead: Refrigerate in airtight container for up to 2 days.)*

QUINOA SALAD Meanwhile, in separate bowl, combine spinach, quinoa, tomatoes, halloumi and mint. *(Make-ahead: Layer in airtight container and refrigerate for up to 6 hours.)* Add dressing; toss to coat.

NUTRITIONAL INFORMATION, PER SERVING: about 431 cal, 12 g pro, 30 g total fat (8 g sat. fat), 31 g carb (5 g dietary fibre, 6 g sugar), 27 mg chol, 419 mg sodium, 655 mg potassium. % RDI: 20% calcium, 24% iron, 51% vit A, 42% vit C, 59% folate.

Tip from the Test Kitchen
Freeze cooled cooked quinoa in freezer-safe bags for up to one month and thaw it in portions as needed.

WARM KALE & QUINOA SALAD

HANDS-ON TIME
30 minutes
TOTAL TIME
30 minutes
MAKES
4 servings

INGREDIENTS

TARRAGON VINAIGRETTE

¼ cup	chopped fresh tarragon
2 tbsp	white wine vinegar
2 tsp	liquid honey
1	clove garlic, pressed or finely grated
½ tsp	each salt and pepper
½ cup	vegetable oil

SALAD

½ cup	quinoa
1 tbsp	olive oil
2	pkg (each 100 g) shiitake mushrooms, stemmed and sliced
1	pkg (227 g) cremini mushrooms, thinly sliced
1	shallot, minced
1	bunch asparagus, trimmed and cut in 1½-inch lengths
8 cups	packed baby kale
½ cup	shaved Parmesan cheese

DIRECTIONS

TARRAGON VINAIGRETTE In small bowl, whisk together tarragon, vinegar, honey, garlic, salt and pepper. Slowly whisk in oil. Set aside.

SALAD Cook quinoa according to package instructions; uncover. Meanwhile, in large skillet, heat oil over medium-high heat; sauté shiitake mushrooms, cremini mushrooms and shallot until mushrooms are beginning to turn golden, about 4 minutes. Add asparagus and sauté just until tender, about 3 minutes.

Remove from heat; stir in quinoa and two-thirds of the dressing. Scrape into large bowl; let cool slightly, about 5 minutes. Add kale, Parmesan and remaining dressing; toss to coat.

NUTRITIONAL INFORMATION, PER SERVING: about 479 cal, 13 g pro, 36 g total fat (5 g sat. fat), 32 g carb (7 g dietary fibre, 8 g sugar), 8 mg chol, 516 mg sodium, 947 mg potassium. % RDI: 24% calcium, 25% iron, 70% vit A, 132% vit C, 79% folate.

Tip from the Test Kitchen

If you can't find baby kale, use chopped stemmed kale instead. For a special garnish, top with a drizzle of truffle oil and extra Parmesan.

MARINATED WHITE BEAN & VEGETABLE SALAD

HANDS-ON TIME
10 minutes

TOTAL TIME
20 minutes

MAKES
2 servings

INGREDIENTS

2 cups	broccoli florets (about half large head)
4 tsp	extra-virgin olive oil
2 tsp	lemon juice
1 tsp	dried oregano
1	small clove garlic, finely grated or pressed
pinch	each salt and pepper
1 cup	rinsed drained canned white kidney beans
3	jarred roasted red peppers, drained and thinly sliced
⅓ cup	chopped fresh parsley
¼ cup	crumbled feta cheese

DIRECTIONS

In large saucepan of boiling salted water, cook broccoli until tender-crisp, about 1 minute. Using slotted spoon, transfer to bowl of ice water to chill; drain and pat dry. *(Make-ahead: Refrigerate in airtight container for up to 24 hours.)*

While broccoli is chilling, in large bowl, whisk together oil, lemon juice, oregano, garlic, salt and pepper. *(Make-ahead: Refrigerate in airtight container for up to 2 days.)* Add beans, red peppers, parsley and feta; toss to coat. Let stand for 10 minutes. *(Make-ahead: Refrigerate in airtight container for up to 6 hours.)* Stir in broccoli.

NUTRITIONAL INFORMATION, PER SERVING: about 275 cal, 13 g pro, 15 g total fat (5 g sat. fat), 26 g carb (9 g dietary fibre, 6 g sugar), 20 mg chol, 756 mg sodium, 584 mg potassium. % RDI: 20% calcium, 22% iron, 42% vit A, 190% vit C, 37% folate.

Tip from the Test Kitchen

Prep the components of this salad the night before, toss everything together in the morning, and you have a fresh, nutritious lunch to take to work or school.

HANDS-ON TIME
15 minutes
TOTAL TIME
15 minutes
MAKES
4 servings

VEGAN

GREEN BEAN & RADISH SALAD

INGREDIENTS

5 cups	green beans, trimmed
1 cup	shelled fresh or frozen peas
2 tbsp	sodium-reduced soy sauce
2 tsp	sesame oil
2 tsp	seasoned rice vinegar
1½ tsp	Dijon mustard
¾ tsp	grated fresh ginger
4	radishes, thinly sliced
1	avocado, pitted, peeled and sliced (optional)
2 tsp	sesame seeds, toasted

DIRECTIONS

In saucepan of boiling salted water, cook green beans until tender-crisp, about 4 minutes; add peas during last 2 minutes of cooking. Drain green beans and peas. Place in bowl of ice water; chill for 10 minutes. Drain again and pat dry.

In small bowl, whisk together soy sauce, sesame oil, vinegar, mustard and ginger.

In serving bowl, combine green beans, peas, radishes and avocado (if using). Drizzle with dressing, tossing to coat. Sprinkle with sesame seeds.

NUTRITIONAL INFORMATION, PER SERVING: about 150 cal, 5 g pro, 9 g total fat (1 g sat. fat), 18 g carb (7 g dietary fibre, 4 g sugar), 0 mg chol, 717 mg sodium, 438 mg potassium. % RDI: 6% calcium, 12% iron, 14% vit A, 33% vit C, 40% folate.

PANZANELLA
WITH ASPARAGUS & EGGS

HANDS-ON TIME
15 minutes
TOTAL TIME
15 minutes
MAKES
4 servings

INGREDIENTS

DIJON DRESSING

2 tbsp	extra-virgin olive oil
1 tbsp	red wine vinegar
1 tsp	Dijon mustard
¼ tsp	each salt and pepper

PANZANELLA

4	eggs (shell-on)
pinch	each salt and pepper
2	slices (½ inch thick) sourdough bread
1 tsp	extra-virgin olive oil
1	bunch asparagus (about 450 g), trimmed
1	clove garlic, halved lengthwise
1	avocado, pitted, peeled and sliced
1 cup	halved cherry tomatoes
½ cup	thinly sliced red onion
⅓ cup	torn fresh basil

DIRECTIONS

DIJON DRESSING In small bowl, whisk together oil, vinegar, mustard, salt and pepper. Set aside.

PANZANELLA In saucepan, add eggs and enough water to cover by at least 1 inch; bring to boil. Reduce heat; boil gently for 4 minutes. Remove from heat and let stand for 4 minutes. Drain and run eggs under cold water for 2 minutes; drain. *(Make-ahead: Refrigerate for up to 2 days.)* Peel eggs and halve lengthwise; sprinkle with salt and pepper. Set aside.

Brush both sides of bread with oil. Place bread and asparagus on greased grill over medium-high heat; close lid and grill, turning once, until asparagus is tender and slightly grill-marked and bread is grill-marked, about 7 minutes. Rub both sides of bread with cut sides of garlic; discard garlic. Let cool slightly; cube bread and halve asparagus crosswise.

In large bowl, gently toss together bread, asparagus, avocado, tomatoes, red onion and basil.

Toss bread mixture with dressing to coat. Top with eggs.

NUTRITIONAL INFORMATION, PER SERVING: about 330 cal, 13 g pro, 20 g total fat (4 g sat. fat), 27 g carb (6 g dietary fibre, 4 g sugar), 216 mg chol, 443 mg sodium, 556 mg potassium. % RDI: 7% calcium, 21% iron, 20% vit A, 25% vit C, 88% folate.

HANDS-ON TIME
15 minutes

TOTAL TIME
15 minutes

MAKES
4 servings

VEGAN

SUGAR SNAP PEAS & AVOCADO SALAD
WITH SESAME DRESSING

INGREDIENTS

6 cups	sugar snap peas, trimmed
1 tbsp	seasoned rice wine vinegar
2 tsp	sodium-reduced soy sauce
2 tsp	vegetable oil
1 tsp	Dijon mustard
½ tsp	sesame oil
1	small clove garlic, grated or pressed
1 tbsp	sesame seeds, toasted
4	green onions, sliced
half	avocado, diced

DIRECTIONS

In saucepan of boiling salted water, cook snap peas until tender-crisp, about 2 minutes. Drain and transfer to bowl of ice water. Chill; drain well and set aside.

Meanwhile, in large bowl, whisk together vinegar, soy sauce, vegetable oil, mustard, sesame oil and garlic until combined; stir in sesame seeds and green onions.

Stir in snap peas and avocado; toss to combine.

NUTRITIONAL INFORMATION, PER SERVING: about 131 cal, 4 g pro, 8 g total fat (1 g sat. fat), 12 g carb (5 g dietary fibre, 6 g sugar), 0 mg chol, 448 mg sodium, 386 mg potassium. % RDI: 5% calcium, 16% iron, 11% vit A, 77% vit C, 25% folate.

Tip from the Test Kitchen

To trim the snap peas, use a paring knife to snip and pull off the tough strings that run along the length of the pod.

CHARRED CORN & TOMATO SALAD
WITH CHIPOTLE VINAIGRETTE

HANDS-ON TIME
30 minutes
TOTAL TIME
30 minutes
MAKES
8 servings

INGREDIENTS

CHIPOTLE VINAIGRETTE

¼ cup	olive oil
3 tbsp	red wine vinegar
1	chipotle chili in adobo sauce, minced
2 tsp	liquid honey
1 tsp	adobo sauce
¼ tsp	each salt and pepper

SALAD

2	corn cobs, husked
1.25 kg	heirloom tomatoes, seeded and cut in 1½-inch chunks
½ cup	fresh parsley, torn
½ cup	fresh basil, torn
¼ cup	chopped fresh chives

DIRECTIONS

CHIPOTLE VINAIGRETTE In bowl, whisk together oil, vinegar, chipotle chili, honey, adobo sauce, salt and pepper. Set aside. *(Make-ahead: Refrigerate in airtight container for up to 24 hours.)*

SALAD Brush corn cobs with 2 tsp of the vinaigrette. Place on lightly greased grill over medium heat; close lid and grill, turning occasionally, until charred and tender, 15 to 20 minutes.

Cut kernels from corn cobs. In large bowl, toss together corn kernels, tomatoes, parsley, basil, chives and remaining vinaigrette. Serve warm.

NUTRITIONAL INFORMATION, PER SERVING: about 130 cal, 2 g pro, 8 g total fat (1 g sat. fat), 16 g carb (2 g dietary fibre, 5 g sugar), 0 mg chol, 102 mg sodium, 341 mg potassium. % RDI: 2% calcium, 7% iron, 16% vit A, 33% vit C, 19% folate.

Tip from the Test Kitchen

Seeding the tomatoes also removes much of their liquid, which would otherwise dilute the vinaigrette's flavour.

HANDS-ON TIME
15 minutes
TOTAL TIME
15 minutes
MAKES
4 to 6 servings

SHAVED BEET & CELERY ROOT SALAD
WITH MISO DRESSING

INGREDIENTS

MISO DRESSING

2 tsp	white miso paste
2 tsp	hot water
2 tbsp	vegetable oil
2 tbsp	lime juice
1 tsp	finely grated fresh ginger
1 tsp	sesame oil
1 tsp	liquid honey

BEET & CELERY ROOT SALAD

350 g	mixed golden and candy cane beets, peeled
200 g	celery root (about half root), peeled
2 tbsp	chopped fresh chives

DIRECTIONS

MISO DRESSING In large bowl, whisk miso paste with hot water until smooth; gradually whisk in vegetable oil, lime juice, ginger, sesame oil and honey.

BEET & CELERY ROOT SALAD Using mandoline, shave beets and celery root into paper-thin slices. (If they are too large for mandoline, cut in half.) Add beets, celery root and chives to dressing; toss to coat.

NUTRITIONAL INFORMATION, PER EACH OF 6 SERVINGS: about 90 cal, 2 g pro, 6 g total fat (trace sat. fat), 10 g carb (2 g dietary fibre, 5 g sugar), 0 mg chol, 143 mg sodium, 269 mg potassium. % RDI: 2% calcium, 5% iron, 1% vit A, 10% vit C, 25% folate.

Tip from the Test Kitchen

The easiest way to prep celery root is to trim both ends, then stand it on its base. Using a sharp knife, cut downward, following the contours of the root, to remove the skin.

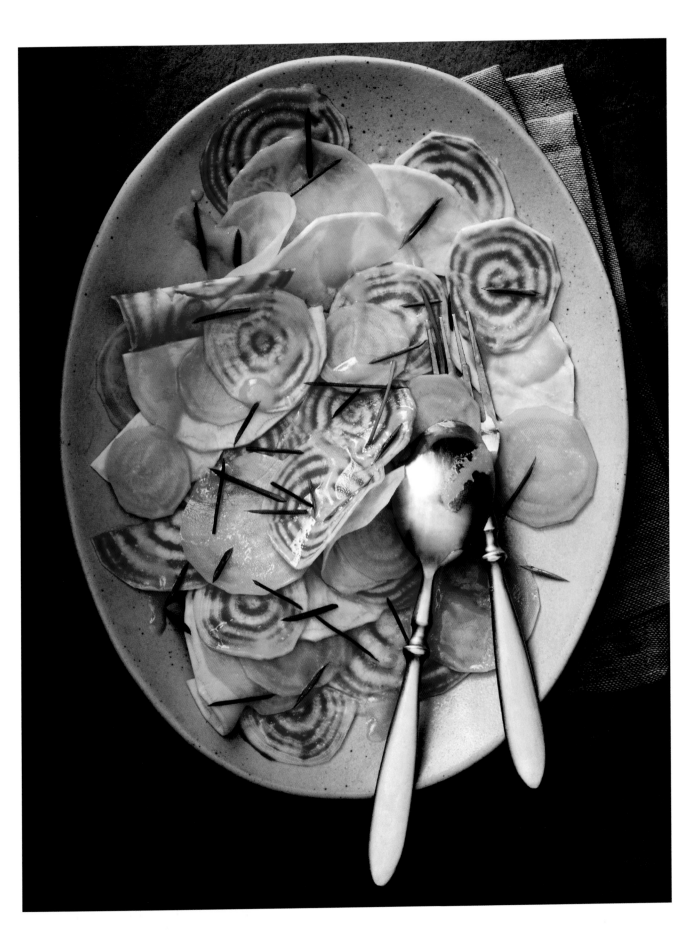

LAZY SKILLET LASAGNA
P 181

Complete Mains | 8

Vegetarian main dishes can range from hearty, everyday comfort food like lasagna, chili or meatless shepherd's pie to elegant dinner-party dishes such as risotto or homemade fresh pasta. From kid-friendly pizzas and burgers to home versions of restaurant favourites, these recipes will leave everyone satisfied.

HANDS-ON TIME
35 minutes
TOTAL TIME
40 minutes
MAKES
4 servings

SMOKY GRILLED CHEESE
WITH ALE-BRAISED ONIONS

INGREDIENTS

¼ cup	unsalted butter, softened
2	sweet onions, thinly sliced
1 cup	brown ale or porter beer
2 tsp	granulated sugar
pinch	pepper
4 tsp	Dijon mustard
8	thick (½ inch) slices sourdough bread (cut from 8-inch round loaf)
170 g	applewood-smoked Cheddar cheese, sliced, or Gruyère cheese, sliced

DIRECTIONS

In cast-iron or heavy skillet, melt 2 tbsp of the butter over medium-high heat; cook onions, stirring occasionally, until softened, about 5 minutes.

Add ale, sugar and pepper; cook, stirring occasionally, until no liquid remains and onions are golden brown, 20 to 25 minutes.

Meanwhile, spread mustard over 1 side of 4 of the bread slices; arrange Cheddar over top.

Divide onions over cheese. Sandwich with remaining bread. Spread remaining butter over outside of sandwiches. Cook in large skillet over medium heat, turning once, until golden brown, about 6 minutes.

NUTRITIONAL INFORMATION, PER SERVING: about 747 cal, 25 g pro, 30 g total fat (17 g sat. fat), 92 g carb (6 g dietary fibre, 11 g sugar), 75 mg chol, 1,222 mg sodium, 427 mg potassium. % RDI: 42% calcium, 32% iron, 22% vit A, 12% vit C, 68% folate.

Tip from the Test Kitchen
Use tortillas instead of bread for a delicious take on quesadillas.

TAHINI FALAFEL LETTUCE BURGERS
WITH CUCUMBER SALSA

HANDS-ON TIME
20 minutes
TOTAL TIME
20 minutes
MAKES
4 servings

INGREDIENTS

FALAFEL BURGERS

2	green onions, chopped
3	cloves garlic, chopped
1	can (540 mL) chickpeas, drained and rinsed
¼ cup	chopped fresh cilantro
1	egg
1 tsp	each ground cumin and chili powder
¼ tsp	each salt and pepper
¼ cup	chickpea flour or all-purpose flour
4 tsp	vegetable oil
4	large green or red lettuce leaves, separated
4 tsp	tahini

CUCUMBER SALSA

2	plum tomatoes, seeded and diced
1 cup	diced seeded English cucumber (about half cucumber)
1 tbsp	chopped fresh mint
2 tsp	white wine vinegar
pinch	each salt and pepper

DIRECTIONS

FALAFEL BURGERS In food processor, pulse green onions with garlic until finely chopped. Add chickpeas, cilantro, egg, cumin, chili powder, salt and pepper; pulse into fine paste. Add chickpea flour; pulse until combined. Shape into 4 balls; flatten each to ¾-inch thickness.

In large nonstick skillet, heat oil over medium heat; cook falafel, turning once, until golden, 6 to 8 minutes. Arrange 1 falafel in each lettuce leaf; drizzle with tahini.

CUCUMBER SALSA While falafel are cooking, in bowl, stir together tomatoes, cucumber, mint, vinegar, salt and pepper. Serve over falafel.

NUTRITIONAL INFORMATION, PER SERVING: about 242 cal, 10 g pro, 11 g total fat (1 g sat. fat), 27 g carb (7 g dietary fibre, 6 g sugar), 48 mg chol, 348 mg sodium, 374 mg potassium. % RDI: 9% calcium, 20% iron, 17% vit A, 12% vit C, 35% folate.

Tip from the Test Kitchen

If you only use chickpea flour occasionally, buy a small quantity at a bulk food store. For the longest shelf life, keep it in an airtight container and freeze.

HANDS-ON TIME
15 minutes

TOTAL TIME
40 minutes

MAKES
6 servings

VEGAN

CURRIED CAULIFLOWER & SPINACH WRAPS

INGREDIENTS

3	cloves garlic, smashed
1	small onion, quartered
1 tsp	grated fresh ginger
2 tbsp	vegetable oil
1 tbsp	packed brown sugar or liquid honey
2 tsp	Madras curry powder
½ tsp	cinnamon
¼ tsp	cayenne pepper
half	head cauliflower, cut in bite-size florets (about 3 cups)
1	can (398 mL) diced tomatoes, drained
1	can (540 mL) chickpeas, drained and rinsed
1	can (400 mL) light coconut milk
½ tsp	sea salt
5 cups	packed baby spinach
6	whole wheat soft flour tortillas (9 inches), warmed

DIRECTIONS

In food processor, pulse together garlic, onion and ginger, scraping down side occasionally, until finely chopped and onion is beginning to look mushy.

In nonstick skillet, heat oil over medium heat; cook onion mixture, stirring often, until softened, about 7 minutes. Add brown sugar, curry powder, cinnamon and cayenne pepper; cook, stirring often, for 2 minutes.

Stir in cauliflower, tomatoes, chickpeas, coconut milk and salt. Bring to boil over high heat; reduce heat and simmer, stirring often, until cauliflower is softened and most of the liquid is absorbed, about 25 minutes. Finely chop 2 cups of the spinach; stir in.

Arrange tortillas on flat surface; sprinkle with remaining spinach. Dollop cauliflower mixture over top; roll up tightly and serve.

NUTRITIONAL INFORMATION, PER SERVING: about 405 cal, 25 g pro, 13 g total fat (4 g sat. fat), 64 g carb (23 g dietary fibre, 9 g sugar), 0 mg chol, 835 mg sodium, 357 mg potassium. % RDI: 8% calcium, 36% iron, 25% vit A, 65% vit C, 41% folate.

Tip from the Test Kitchen

Madras curry powder, a mix of spices including fenugreek, coriander, cumin and turmeric, is often hotter than other curry powders. If you don't have any on hand, substitute with another curry powder.

P 6

MEDITERRANEAN VEGETABLE PANINI
WITH GRAPE TOMATOES & FETA PESTO

HANDS-ON TIME
15 minutes

TOTAL TIME
50 minutes

MAKES
4 servings

INGREDIENTS

ROASTED GRAPE TOMATOES

2¼ cups	grape tomatoes or cherry tomatoes, halved
1 tbsp	olive oil
1½ tsp	balsamic vinegar
¼ tsp	salt

FETA PESTO

2 cups	packed fresh basil leaves
⅓ cup	extra-virgin olive oil
¼ cup	toasted slivered almonds
1	small clove garlic, minced
1 tsp	lemon juice
¼ tsp	each salt and pepper
1 cup	crumbled feta cheese

VEGETABLE PANINI

2	zucchini (about 350 g total), sliced lengthwise ¼ inch thick
1	loaf focaccia (about 450 g)
4	bottled grilled artichokes, thinly sliced (about 1 cup)
20	Kalamata olives, halved and pitted

DIRECTIONS

ROASTED GRAPE TOMATOES In 8-inch square baking dish or ovenproof skillet, toss together tomatoes, oil, vinegar and salt. Roast in 400°F oven until shrivelled, 30 to 35 minutes.

FETA PESTO In food processor, purée basil, oil, almonds, garlic, lemon juice, salt and pepper. Pulse in feta.

VEGETABLE PANINI In greased panini press (or greased grill pan or skillet pressed with another heavy pan), grill zucchini on medium heat until tender, about 3 minutes.

Cut focaccia into 4 pieces; halve each to open. Spread ¾ cup of the pesto over cut sides. Layer bottoms with zucchini, artichokes, olives and tomatoes. Sandwich with tops.

Cook in greased panini press on medium heat until bread is crisp and golden, about 4 minutes.

NUTRITIONAL INFORMATION, PER SERVING: about 634 cal, 19 g pro, 30 g total fat (9 g sat. fat), 76 g carb (11 g dietary fibre), 34 mg chol, 1,931 mg sodium, 730 mg potassium. % RDI: 25% calcium, 51% iron, 31% vit A, 35% vit C, 80% folate.

Tip from the Test Kitchen
Whole grilled artichokes from the jar have a lovely earthy flavour and firm texture. If unavailable, use jarred marinated artichokes, rinsed and drained.

BLACK BEAN TOSTADAS
WITH MANGO AVOCADO SALAD

HANDS-ON TIME
15 minutes
TOTAL TIME
15 minutes
MAKES
4 servings

INGREDIENTS

TOSTADAS

1	can (540 mL) black beans, drained and rinsed
3 tbsp	light sour cream
1½ tsp	chili powder
4	soft flour tortillas (6 inches)
1 cup	shredded Monterey Jack cheese

MANGO AVOCADO SALAD

3 tbsp	olive oil
1 tbsp	lime juice
1 tsp	liquid honey
¼ tsp	chili powder
pinch	each salt and pepper
1	mango, peeled, pitted and cut in 1-inch chunks
1	avocado, peeled, pitted and cut in 1-inch chunks
3½ cups	packed watercress (about 1 bunch)
⅓ cup	thinly sliced red onion

DIRECTIONS

TOSTADAS In bowl using potato masher, roughly mash beans. Stir in sour cream and chili powder.

Spread one-quarter of the bean mixture onto each tortilla, leaving ½-inch border. Sprinkle with Monterey Jack. Place on greased grill over medium-low heat; close lid and grill until cheese is melted and tortillas are crisp, 6 to 7 minutes.

MANGO AVOCADO SALAD While tostadas are grilling, in large bowl, whisk together oil, lime juice, honey, chili powder, salt and pepper. Add mango, avocado, watercress and red onion; toss to coat. Serve over tostadas.

NUTRITIONAL INFORMATION, PER SERVING: about 523 cal, 18 g pro, 30 g total fat (9 g sat. fat), 50 g carb (13 g dietary fibre, 11 g sugar), 29 mg chol, 742 mg sodium, 841 mg potassium. % RDI: 28% calcium, 24% iron, 24% vit A, 60% vit C, 67% folate.

Tip from the Test Kitchen

To choose a ripe mango, squeeze it gently; it should yield slightly. Many mango varieties produce a fruity aroma at the stem end when ripe.

cover

HANDS-ON TIME
25 minutes
TOTAL TIME
30 minutes
MAKES
6 servings

VEGAN

CHILI-LIME SWEET POTATO TACOS

INGREDIENTS

QUICK-PICKLED RADISHES

5	radishes, trimmed and thinly sliced
1 tbsp	lime juice
pinch	each salt and pepper
1 tbsp	chopped fresh cilantro

SWEET POTATO TACOS

½ cup	dried green lentils, rinsed
1 tbsp	olive oil
350 g	sweet potato, peeled and cut in ½-inch chunks
1	onion, chopped
2 tsp	chili powder
½ tsp	salt
1 tbsp	lime juice
12	soft flour tortillas (6 inches), warmed
1	avocado, peeled, pitted and sliced

DIRECTIONS

QUICK-PICKLED RADISHES In bowl, stir together radishes, lime juice, salt and pepper. Let stand for 20 minutes. Stir in cilantro.

SWEET POTATO TACOS Meanwhile, in saucepan of boiling water, cook lentils until tender, 12 to 15 minutes; drain. *(Make-ahead: Rinse under cold water; drain again. Store in airtight container for up to 24 hours.)*

While lentils are cooking, in large nonstick skillet, heat oil over medium-high heat; cook sweet potato, onion and chili powder, stirring, until fragrant, about 2 minutes. Stir in 1 cup water; bring to boil. Reduce heat to medium; cook, stirring, until potatoes are softened, about 12 minutes.

Stir lentils and salt into sweet potato mixture; cook, stirring and adding water, 1 tbsp at a time, to reach desired consistency, about 1 minute. Stir in lime juice.

Spoon about ¼ cup of the sweet potato mixture onto each tortilla. Top with radishes and avocado.

NUTRITIONAL INFORMATION, PER SERVING: about 377 cal, 11 g pro, 11 g total fat (2 g sat. fat), 60 g carb (8 g dietary fibre, 7 g sugar), 0 mg chol, 530 mg sodium, 584 mg potassium. % RDI: 6% calcium, 31% iron, 88% vit A, 23% vit C, 88% folate.

Tip from the Test Kitchen

Check the label on the tortillas you buy. Many tortillas are vegan, but read the label to ensure you buy ones that are free of meat and milk products and have been processed at a dairy-free facility.

HANDS-ON TIME
15 minutes
TOTAL TIME
35 minutes
MAKES
8 servings

VEGAN

SWEET POTATO VEGGIE BURGERS

INGREDIENTS

2 cups	mashed cooked sweet potatoes (about 2 potatoes)
1	can (540 mL) chickpeas, drained and rinsed
2 cups	chopped fresh cilantro (with stems)
⅓ cup	quinoa flakes
2 tbsp	each tahini and Asian chili sauce (such as sriracha)
2 tbsp	lemon juice
3	cloves garlic, minced
1 tbsp	ground cumin
1 tsp	salt
¼ cup	vegetable oil
8	vegan buns, split and toasted

DIRECTIONS

In food processor, pulse together sweet potatoes, three-quarters of the chickpeas, the cilantro, quinoa flakes, tahini, chili sauce, lemon juice, garlic, cumin and salt, scraping down side occasionally, until well mixed. Add remaining chickpeas; pulse a few times to blend. Mixture should be chunky. Form by scant ¼ cup into 16 balls.

In large nonstick skillet, heat oil over medium-high heat. Working in batches, add balls, gently pressing to flatten slightly; cook until lightly browned, 2 to 3 minutes per side. Reduce heat if needed to prevent burning. Transfer to parchment paper–lined rimmed baking sheet. Bake in 375°F oven until warmed through, 8 to 10 minutes.

Place 2 patties on bottom halves of buns. Garnish with toppings such as sliced avocado, pickled red onion, microgreens or cucumber ribbons (optional). Sandwich with top halves of buns.

NUTRITIONAL INFORMATION, PER SERVING: about 390 cal, 11 g pro, 10 g total fat (1 g sat. fat), 65 g carb (6 g dietary fibre, 9 g sugar), 0 mg chol, 905 mg sodium, 333 mg potassium. % RDI: 6% calcium, 31% iron, 105% vit A, 22% vit C, 20% folate.

Tip from the Test Kitchen

To make mashed sweet potatoes in a flash, using a fork, prick 2 sweet potatoes; microwave on high until tender, 8 to 10 minutes. When cool enough to handle, slice in half; scrape out flesh and mash.

SLOW COOKER GARAM MASALA EGGPLANT

HANDS-ON TIME
15 minutes

TOTAL TIME
8¼ hours

MAKES
8 servings

INGREDIENTS

1	can (796 mL) diced tomatoes
1	sweet onion, diced
½ cup	whipping cream (35%)
3 tbsp	tomato paste
2 tbsp	minced fresh ginger
4	cloves garlic, minced
1 tbsp	garam masala
1 tbsp	mustard seeds
2 tsp	cumin seeds
2 tsp	granulated sugar
½ tsp	hot pepper flakes
½ tsp	salt
2	large Italian eggplants (about 1 kg total), trimmed and halved lengthwise
½ cup	chopped fresh cilantro (optional)

DIRECTIONS

In slow cooker, combine tomatoes, onion, cream, tomato paste, ginger, garlic, garam masala, mustard seeds, cumin seeds, sugar, hot pepper flakes and salt.

Arrange eggplant, cut sides up, over top of mixture. Cover and cook on low until eggplant is tender, about 8 hours.

Using 2 slotted spoons, remove eggplant to cutting board. Scoop flesh into fine-mesh sieve; with back of spoon, gently press on solids to remove excess liquid. Discard skin. Stir flesh into slow cooker; sprinkle with cilantro (if using).

NUTRITIONAL INFORMATION, PER SERVING: about 143 cal, 3 g pro, 6 g total fat (3 g sat. fat), 22 g carb (5 g dietary fibre, 10 g sugar), 19 mg chol, 290 mg sodium, 498 mg potassium. % RDI: 7% calcium, 16% iron, 8% vit A, 32% vit C, 15% folate.

HANDS-ON TIME
20 minutes
TOTAL TIME
50 minutes
MAKES
4 servings

CURRIED LENTIL CASHEW BURGER

INGREDIENTS

½ **cup**	unsalted cashews or walnuts
2 tbsp	vegetable oil
4 cups	sliced mushrooms
1	onion, chopped
1	clove garlic, minced
¼ **tsp**	each salt and pepper
1	can (540 mL) lentils, drained and rinsed
1 tbsp	curry paste
¼ **cup**	dried bread crumbs
¼ **cup**	chopped fresh coriander
4	slices Gouda cheese
4	leaves lettuce
4	slices red onion
4	hamburger buns, split

DIRECTIONS

In dry skillet, toast cashews over medium-low heat until fragrant, about 5 minutes; transfer to food processor.

In same pan, heat 1 tbsp of the oil over medium-high heat; cook mushrooms, chopped onion, garlic, salt and pepper, stirring occasionally, until liquid is evaporated, about 5 minutes. Add to food processor.

Add lentils and curry paste to food processor; pulse to combine. Mix in bread crumbs and coriander. Shape into four 1-inch thick patties.

In skillet, heat remaining oil over medium heat; cook patties until crusty, about 8 minutes per side. Top each with Gouda slice; cover and cook until Gouda is melted.

Sandwich patty, lettuce and red onion in buns.

NUTRITIONAL INFORMATION, PER SERVING: about 610 cal, 25 g pro, 27 g total fat (6 g sat. fat), 71 g carb (10 g dietary fibre), 24 mg chol, 878 mg sodium. % RDI: 27% calcium, 54% iron, 7% vit A, 15% vit C, 131% folate.

HANDS-ON TIME
20 minutes
TOTAL TIME
50 minutes
MAKES
4 servings

VEGAN

THAI-STYLE TOFU CURRY

INGREDIENTS

1	pkg (425 g) regular tofu
225 g	Japanese eggplant
1 tbsp	vegetable oil
⅓ cup	Thai Green Curry Paste (see recipe, page 62)
¾ tsp	salt
2	cans (each 400 mL) coconut milk
½ cup	vegetable broth
1 cup	green beans, halved
1 cup	frozen whole okra, thawed and halved lengthwise
¼ cup	chopped fresh cilantro
1 tbsp	lime juice

DIRECTIONS

Place tofu on paper towel–lined plate; place another paper towel and a flat, heavy plate over top. Set aside for 30 minutes; drain tofu and cut into ¾-inch cubes. Cut eggplant into same-size cubes. Set aside.

In Dutch oven or large heavy-bottomed saucepan, heat oil over medium heat; cook curry paste and ¼ tsp of the salt, stirring, for 2 minutes. Stir in coconut milk and vegetable broth; bring to boil.

Add tofu, eggplant, green beans and remaining salt. Reduce heat, cover and simmer, stirring occasionally, until eggplant is tender, about 8 minutes.

Add okra and cilantro; simmer for 1 minute. Stir in lime juice.

NUTRITIONAL INFORMATION, PER SERVING: about 571 cal, 13 g pro, 53 g total fat (41 g sat. fat), 21 g carb (6 g dietary fibre), 0 mg chol, 594 mg sodium. % RDI: 19% calcium, 67% iron, 7% vit A, 22% vit C, 60% folate.

HANDS-ON TIME
15 minutes
TOTAL TIME
30 minutes
MAKES
4 servings

VEGAN

CHANA MASALA

INGREDIENTS

3 tbsp	olive oil
2	onions, chopped
6	cloves garlic, minced
2 tbsp	grated fresh ginger
2 tsp	each chili powder, ground coriander, ground cumin and garam masala
2	cans (each 540 mL) chickpeas, drained and rinsed
½ cup	tomato paste
2 tsp	packed brown sugar
¼ tsp	salt
2 tbsp	lemon juice

DIRECTIONS

In saucepan, heat oil over medium-high heat; cook onions, stirring occasionally, until softened, about 5 minutes.

Add garlic and ginger; cook for 1 minute. Stir in chili powder, coriander, cumin and garam masala; cook until fragrant, about 1 minute.

Stir in 1 cup water, scraping up any browned bits. Stir in chickpeas, tomato paste, brown sugar and salt. Reduce heat, cover and simmer until thickened slightly, about 15 minutes. Stir in lemon juice.

NUTRITIONAL INFORMATION, PER SERVING: about 439 cal, 14 g pro, 14 g total fat (2 g sat. fat), 69 g carb (14 g dietary fibre, 17 g sugar), 0 mg chol, 778 mg sodium, 870 mg potassium. % RDI: 11% calcium, 38% iron, 9% vit A, 35% vit C, 65% folate.

LEEK & HAZELNUT RAVIOLI

HANDS-ON TIME
10 minutes
TOTAL TIME
15 minutes
MAKES
4 servings

INGREDIENTS

3	large leeks (white and light green parts only)
1 tbsp	butter
2 tsp	olive oil
3	cloves garlic, minced
pinch	each salt and pepper
450 g	cheese-filled ravioli
½ cup	crumbled soft goat cheese (chèvre)
⅓ cup	toasted hazelnuts, chopped
1 tbsp	chopped fresh chives

DIRECTIONS

Cut leeks in half lengthwise; thinly slice crosswise to make about 4 cups.

In saucepan, heat butter with oil over medium-high heat; cook leeks, garlic, salt and pepper, stirring occasionally, until leeks are tender and beginning to brown, about 10 minutes.

Meanwhile, in saucepan of boiling salted water, cook ravioli according to package directions; reserving ½ cup of the cooking liquid, drain.

Gently stir ravioli into leek mixture, adding enough of the reserved cooking liquid to coat. Top with goat cheese, hazelnuts and chives.

NUTRITIONAL INFORMATION, PER SERVING: about 559 cal, 20 g pro, 28 g total fat (9 g sat. fat), 60 g carb (6 g dietary fibre, 5 g sugar), 62 mg chol, 795 mg sodium, 318 mg potassium. % RDI: 25% calcium, 36% iron, 21% vit A, 17% vit C, 51% folate.

Tip from the Test Kitchen

There are two easy ways to toast nuts: In a dry skillet over medium heat, cook nuts, stirring frequently, until fragrant and lightly browned, about 6 minutes. Or spread nuts on a baking sheet and bake in 350°F oven, stirring halfway through, until fragrant and lightly browned, 8 to 12 minutes. Nuts burn quickly, so watch them carefully and remove them from the hot pan or baking sheet as soon as they're done.

HANDS-ON TIME
15 minutes
TOTAL TIME
15 minutes
MAKES
4 servings

CREAMY KALE & SUN-DRIED TOMATO CARBONARA

INGREDIENTS

375 g	spaghetti
1	large bunch kale, stemmed and sliced
3	eggs, lightly beaten
¼ cup	grated Parmesan cheese
60 g	soft goat cheese (chèvre), crumbled
4 tsp	chopped drained oil-packed sun-dried tomatoes
¼ tsp	pepper

DIRECTIONS

In large saucepan of boiling salted water, cook pasta according to package instructions, adding kale during last 2 minutes of cooking. Reserving ½ cup of the cooking liquid, drain. Return pasta mixture to pan. Set aside.

Whisk together eggs, Parmesan, goat cheese, sun-dried tomatoes and pepper; stir into pasta mixture until coated. Stir in reserved cooking liquid; cook over low heat, stirring, until sauce is thickened, about 1 minute.

NUTRITIONAL INFORMATION, PER SERVING: about 523 cal, 25 g pro, 12 g total fat (5 g sat. fat), 78 g carb (4 g dietary fibre, 4 g sugar), 157 mg chol, 719 mg sodium, 495 mg potassium. % RDI: 19% calcium, 35% iron, 93% vit A, 107% vit C, 114% folate.

Tip from the Test Kitchen

To avoid curdling the eggs, remove saucepan with pasta mixture from the heat before stirring in the egg mixture. Once everything is combined, return pan to the heat to thicken the sauce.

CACIO E PEPE

HANDS-ON TIME
15 minutes
TOTAL TIME
25 minutes
MAKES
4 servings

INGREDIENTS

1	batch Fresh Pasta Dough (see recipe, page 52)
½ cup	all-purpose flour (approx)
2 tbsp	olive oil
¾ tsp	pepper
1⅓ cups	finely shredded Pecorino-Romano or Parmesan cheese

DIRECTIONS

With pasta machine roller on widest setting and working with 1 sheet at a time, feed dough through lightly floured rollers. Fold dough in half, bringing short ends together; lightly dust dough with some of the flour. Feed dough through rollers 3 more times or until edges are smooth, cutting in half if too long to handle; continue feeding through rollers until third-widest setting (about ⅛ inch) is reached.

Lightly dust dough with some of the remaining flour. Working with 1 sheet at a time, fold dough in half, bringing short ends together; repeat twice to create 8-layer stack. Using sharp knife, cut crosswise into ⅛-inch thick strips. Using hands, separate pasta; dust generously with remaining flour. On lightly floured baking sheet, shape pasta into nests. Let stand until leathery but not dry, about 10 minutes. *(Make-ahead: Freeze until firm; transfer to resealable freezer bag and freeze for up to 3 weeks.)*

Gently separate pasta, removing excess flour. In large saucepan of boiling salted water, cook pasta until al dente, about 4 minutes. Reserving ¾ cup of the cooking liquid, drain.

In same pan, heat oil with pepper over medium heat; stir in pasta, 1 cup of the Pecorino-Romano and enough of the reserved cooking liquid to coat. Sprinkle with remaining Pecorino-Romano.

NUTRITIONAL INFORMATION, PER SERVING: about 469 cal, 23 g pro, 21 g total fat (8 g sat. fat), 45 g carb (2 g dietary fibre, 1 g sugar), 179 mg chol, 952 mg sodium, 139 mg potassium. % RDI: 35% calcium, 28% iron, 12% vit A, 51% folate.

VARIATION
AGLIO E OLIO

Omit pepper and Pecorino-Romano. Add 4 cloves garlic, sliced, and pinch hot pepper flakes to olive oil; cook as directed. Sprinkle with 2 tbsp chopped fresh parsley, if desired.

ZUCCHINI RIBBON & CAPER PASTA

HANDS-ON TIME
20 minutes
TOTAL TIME
20 minutes
MAKES
4 servings

INGREDIENTS

340 g	spaghetti
4	zucchini
1 tbsp	olive oil
half	red onion, thinly sliced
1 tbsp	capers, drained and rinsed
1	clove garlic, crushed
2 tsp	grated lemon zest
pinch	hot pepper flakes
¼ cup	grated Parmesan cheese
1 tbsp	lemon juice
pinch	each salt and pepper

DIRECTIONS

In large saucepan of boiling salted water, cook pasta according to package directions. Reserving ⅓ cup of the cooking liquid, drain.

Meanwhile, using vegetable peeler, slice zucchini lengthwise into long ribbons. In large skillet, heat oil over medium heat; cook zucchini, red onion and capers, stirring occasionally, until onion is softened, about 5 minutes. Add garlic, lemon zest and hot pepper flakes; cook, stirring, for 1 minute.

Stir in pasta, Parmesan, lemon juice and enough of the reserved pasta cooking liquid to coat; sprinkle with salt and pepper.

NUTRITIONAL INFORMATION, PER SERVING: about 417 cal, 15 g pro, 7 g total fat (2 g sat. fat), 75 g carb (7 g dietary fibre, 6 g sugar), 5 mg chol, 421 mg sodium, 557 mg potassium. % RDI: 11% calcium, 28% iron, 19% vit A, 18% vit C, 94% folate.

HANDS-ON TIME
15 minutes
TOTAL TIME
15 minutes
MAKES
4 servings

SEARED CHERRY TOMATO PASTA

INGREDIENTS

340 g	spaghettini
2 tbsp	olive oil
2 cups	cherry tomatoes, halved
2 tbsp	dried bread crumbs
½ tsp	salt
3	cloves garlic, sliced
pinch	crushed hot pepper flakes
⅓ cup	grated Parmesan cheese
¼ cup	chopped fresh basil

DIRECTIONS

In large saucepan of boiling lightly salted water, cook pasta according to package directions. Reserving ½ cup of the pasta water, drain.

Meanwhile, in large skillet, heat 1 tbsp of the oil over medium-high heat; sauté tomatoes until lightly seared, about 1 minute. Sprinkle with bread crumbs and salt; toss to coat. Remove from pan and set aside.

Add remaining oil to pan; cook garlic and hot pepper flakes over medium heat until fragrant and softened, about 2 minutes. Add tomato mixture, pasta and reserved pasta water, stirring to combine. Toss with Parmesan and basil.

NUTRITIONAL INFORMATION, PER SERVING: about 442 cal, 15 g pro, 11 g total fat (3 g sat. fat), 70 g carb (5 g dietary fibre, 4 g sugar), 7 mg chol, 714 mg sodium, 284 mg potassium. % RDI: 12% calcium, 26% iron, 8% vit A, 17% vit C, 85% folate.

BROCCOLI & BROWN BUTTER FUSILLI
WITH TOASTED ALMONDS

HANDS-ON TIME
20 minutes
TOTAL TIME
20 minutes
MAKES
4 servings

INGREDIENTS

375 g	fusilli
4 cups	bite-size broccoli florets
½ cup	butter
6	cloves garlic, thinly sliced
½ tsp	hot pepper flakes
½ tsp	pepper
¼ tsp	salt
¼ cup	shaved Parmesan cheese
¼ cup	sliced natural (skin-on) almonds, toasted

DIRECTIONS

In large saucepan of boiling salted water, cook pasta according to package instructions, adding broccoli during final minute of cooking. Reserving ½ cup of the cooking liquid, drain.

Meanwhile, in large skillet, melt butter over medium heat; continue to cook, swirling pan occasionally, until foamy, about 4 minutes. Add garlic and hot pepper flakes; cook, stirring, until butter is fragrant and nutty brown and garlic is golden, about 2 minutes.

Add pasta, broccoli, pepper and salt, tossing to coat. Stir in half of the Parmesan and enough of the reserved cooking liquid to make thin sauce. Top with remaining Parmesan and the almonds.

NUTRITIONAL INFORMATION, PER SERVING: about 640 cal, 19 g pro, 30 g total fat (16 g sat. fat), 76 g carb (5 g dietary fibre, 2 g sugar), 65 mg chol, 754 mg sodium, 369 mg potassium. % RDI: 13% calcium, 28% iron, 38% vit A, 57% vit C, 110% folate.

Tip from the Test Kitchen

Add the pasta to the skillet when the butter turns nutty brown. Watch the butter closely, as it can quickly go from browned to burned.

P 292

HANDS-ON TIME
15 minutes
TOTAL TIME
25 minutes
MAKES
4 servings

VEGAN

SPINACH & AVOCADO GREEN GODDESS PASTA

INGREDIENTS

4 cups	packed baby spinach
2	avocados, pitted and peeled
3	cloves garlic, smashed
⅓ cup	nutritional yeast
¼ cup	chopped fresh dill
¼ cup	each olive oil and cold water
2 tsp	grated lemon zest
3 tbsp	lemon juice
1 tsp	salt
¼ tsp	pepper
500 g	rigatoni or farfalle
1	bunch (about 450 g) asparagus, trimmed and cut in 2-inch lengths

DIRECTIONS

In food processor, pulse together spinach, avocados, garlic, nutritional yeast, dill, oil, water, lemon zest, lemon juice, salt and pepper until smooth. Mixture will resemble pesto. Set aside.

In large saucepan of boiling salted water, cook pasta according to package instructions. Add asparagus during last 4 minutes of cooking. Reserving ¼ cup of the cooking liquid, drain pasta and asparagus. Return to pan; gently stir in pesto until combined. If sauce is too thick, gradually stir in enough of the reserved cooking liquid to thin. Garnish with sprigs of fresh dill and sprinkle with more nutritional yeast, if you wish.

NUTRITIONAL INFORMATION, PER SERVING: about 757 cal, 24 g pro, 27 g total fat (4 g sat. fat), 107 g carb (12 g dietary fibre, 4 g sugar), 0 mg chol, 1,196 mg sodium, 890 mg potassium. % RDI: 8% calcium, 45% iron, 38% vit A, 47% vit C, 279% folate.

Tip from the Test Kitchen

Nutritional yeast is the secret ingredient in this dish. It's a good vegan source of protein and vitamin B, with a rich cheese-like flavour reminiscent of Parmesan.

RICOTTA GNOCCHI
WITH SAUTÉED BEETS

HANDS-ON TIME
30 minutes
TOTAL TIME
30 minutes
MAKES
4 servings

INGREDIENTS

RICOTTA GNOCCHI

1	tub (475 g) extra-smooth ricotta cheese
1¾ cups	all-purpose flour
2	eggs, beaten
½ cup	finely shredded Parmesan cheese
¼ tsp	salt

SAUTÉED BEETS

2 tbsp	olive oil
2	cloves garlic, thinly sliced
6	baby golden beets (about 2 inches diameter), peeled, halved and thinly sliced
2 cups	lightly packed chopped beet greens
⅔ cup	chopped walnuts, toasted
pinch	salt

DIRECTIONS

RICOTTA GNOCCHI In bowl, stir together ricotta, flour, eggs, Parmesan and salt to make ragged dough. Turn out onto lightly floured surface; divide into quarters. Working with one quarter at a time, with floured hands, roll dough into ¾-inch thick rope; cut crosswise into ¾-inch long pieces. Set aside on floured waxed paper–lined baking sheet.

In large pot of boiling salted water, cook gnocchi in batches, until floating and no longer doughy in centre, about 3 minutes. Using slotted spoon, transfer to plate. Set aside; keep warm.

SAUTÉED BEETS In large skillet, heat oil over medium heat; cook garlic, stirring, until fragrant and light golden, about 1 minute. Stir in beets; cook, stirring occasionally, until tender-crisp, about 8 minutes. Stir in beet greens, gnocchi, walnuts and salt; cook, stirring occasionally, until greens are wilted and gnocchi are warmed through, about 2 minutes.

NUTRITIONAL INFORMATION, PER SERVING: about 687 cal, 30 g pro, 40 g total fat (15 g sat. fat), 54 g carb (5 g dietary fibre, 11 g sugar), 132 mg chol, 1,035 mg sodium, 628 mg potassium. % RDI: 34% calcium, 36% iron, 42% vit A, 12% vit C, 80% folate.

Tip from the Test Kitchen

If your beets don't have the greens attached, substitute an equal amount of chopped Swiss chard leaves. And if you can't find baby golden beets, substitute a larger golden beet (about 3½ inches in diameter), cut into wedges and sliced thinly.

LEMONY RAVIOLI
WITH SUN-DRIED TOMATOES

HANDS-ON TIME
15 minutes

TOTAL TIME
20 minutes

MAKES
2 to 3 servings

INGREDIENTS

250 g	fresh vegetable- or cheese-filled ravioli
1 tbsp	butter
1 tbsp	olive oil
¼ cup	thinly sliced drained oil-packed sun-dried tomatoes
2	cloves garlic, minced
¼ cup	grated Parmesan cheese
¼ cup	chopped fresh parsley
1 tbsp	thinly sliced lemon zest
3 tbsp	lemon juice
1 tbsp	capers, drained and rinsed

DIRECTIONS

In saucepan of boiling salted water, cook pasta according to package instructions. Reserving ⅓ cup of the cooking liquid, drain.

In large nonstick skillet, heat butter and oil over medium heat until butter is melted; cook sun-dried tomatoes and garlic, stirring often, until fragrant, 2 to 3 minutes. Add pasta, Parmesan, parsley, lemon zest, lemon juice and capers; cook, stirring gently, for 2 minutes. Stir in enough of the reserved cooking liquid to coat.

NUTRITIONAL INFORMATION, PER EACH OF 3 SERVINGS: about 322 cal, 10 g pro, 18 g total fat (6 g sat. fat), 32 g carb (3 g dietary fibre, 3 g sugar), 39 mg chol, 779 mg sodium, 211 mg potassium. % RDI: 14% calcium, 18% iron, 9% vit A, 35% vit C, 5% folate.

SUN-DRIED TOMATO AGNOLOTTI
WITH WALNUTS & SWISS CHARD

HANDS-ON TIME
25 minutes

TOTAL TIME
25 minutes

MAKES
4 servings

INGREDIENTS

1 cup	ricotta cheese
⅓ cup	grated Pecorino-Romano cheese
⅓ cup	drained oil-packed sun-dried tomatoes, finely chopped
1	egg yolk
½ tsp	dried Italian herb seasoning
¼ tsp	pepper
1	egg
36	wonton wrappers (3 inches square)
2 tbsp	butter
2	shallots, thinly sliced
3	cloves garlic, sliced
¼ cup	chopped walnuts
½ cup	dry white wine
pinch	each salt and pepper
2 cups	chopped stemmed Swiss chard

DIRECTIONS

Stir together ricotta, Pecorino-Romano, sun-dried tomatoes, egg yolk, Italian seasoning and pepper.

Whisk egg with 1 tsp water to make egg wash. One at a time, lightly brush egg wash over wonton wrappers; spoon rounded 1 tsp ricotta mixture onto centre of each. Fold wrapper diagonally over filling to form triangle; press edges to seal.

In skillet over medium heat, melt butter; cook shallots and garlic, stirring occasionally, until softened, about 3 minutes. Stir in walnuts; cook until fragrant, about 2 minutes. Stir in wine, salt and pepper; simmer for 2 minutes.

Meanwhile, in large saucepan of boiling salted water, cook agnolotti until pale and floating, 2 minutes. Drain and return to pot. Add walnut mixture and Swiss chard; toss until chard is wilted, about 2 minutes.

NUTRITIONAL INFORMATION, PER SERVING: about 515 cal, 20 g pro, 25 g total fat (12 g sat. fat), 50 g carb (3 g dietary fibre, 3 g sugar), 132 mg chol, 776 mg sodium, 460 mg potassium. % RDI: 26% calcium, 29% iron, 30% vit A, 22% vit C, 42% folate.

Tip from the Test Kitchen

Packaged wonton wrappers are a clever shortcut for making homemade filled pasta, such as agnolotti. Use full-fat ricotta in the filling; it adds rich flavour.

HANDS-ON TIME
30 minutes
TOTAL TIME
35 minutes
MAKES
6 servings

CREAMY SKILLET MUSHROOM LASAGNA

INGREDIENTS

6	lasagna noodles (about 2 inches wide)
1 tbsp	olive oil
2	pkg (each 227 g) cremini mushrooms, sliced
1	pkg (142 g) baby spinach (about 5 cups)
¼ tsp	each salt and pepper
2 cups	milk
3 tbsp	all-purpose flour
1 cup	shredded mozzarella cheese
⅔ cup	extra-smooth ricotta cheese
4 tsp	Dijon mustard
pinch	cayenne pepper

DIRECTIONS

In large saucepan of boiling salted water, cook noodles for 2 minutes less than package instructions for al dente; drain. Arrange noodles, keeping edges from touching, in single layer on damp tea towels.

While noodles are cooking, in nonstick skillet, heat oil over medium-high heat; cook mushrooms, stirring occasionally, until softened and almost no liquid remains, about 7 minutes. Add spinach; cook, stirring, until spinach begins to wilt, about 2 minutes. Drain in colander; scrape into bowl. Stir in salt and pepper.

In small saucepan, whisk ¼ cup of the milk with the flour until smooth. Gradually whisk in remaining milk; cook over medium heat, whisking constantly, until thickened, about 8 minutes. Add ¾ cup of the mozzarella, the ricotta, mustard and cayenne pepper; cook, stirring, until mozzarella is melted. Remove from heat.

Spoon ½ cup of the sauce into bottom of lightly greased 10-inch cast-iron or ovenproof skillet. Arrange 3 of the noodles over top, trimming ends to fit; top with half of the mushroom mixture. Spoon half of the remaining sauce over top. Arrange remaining noodles, perpendicular to bottom noodles, over top; top with remaining mushroom mixture and sauce. Sprinkle with remaining mozzarella.

Bake in 425°F oven until mozzarella is melted, about 4 minutes; broil until top is golden, about 2 minutes.

NUTRITIONAL INFORMATION, PER SERVING: about 298 cal, 16 g pro, 13 g total fat (6 g sat. fat), 31 g carb (3 g dietary fibre, 7 g sugar), 31 mg chol, 389 mg sodium, 630 mg potassium. % RDI: 27% calcium, 16% iron, 39% vit A, 3% vit C, 49% folate.

HANDS-ON TIME
15 minutes

TOTAL TIME
25 minutes

MAKES
4 servings

LAZY SKILLET LASAGNA

INGREDIENTS

6	lasagna noodles
¼ cup	fresh basil
½ cup	ricotta cheese
1 tbsp	olive oil
2	zucchini
1	carrot
2 cups	jarred pasta sauce
1 cup	shredded mozzarella cheese

DIRECTIONS

Break noodles into thirds. In large saucepan of boiling salted water, cook according to package instructions until al dente, 7 to 9 minutes; drain. Meanwhile, chop half of the basil; stir with ricotta. Set aside.

In cast-iron or ovenproof skillet, heat oil over medium heat. Using vegetable peeler, slice zucchini and carrot lengthwise into long ribbons; cook until tender, 3 to 5 minutes. Add noodles and pasta sauce; simmer, stirring occasionally, until warm, about 3 minutes.

Sprinkle with mozzarella; dollop with ricotta mixture. Bake in 475°F oven until mozzarella is melted, 7 to 10 minutes. Tear remaining basil into small pieces; sprinkle over top.

NUTRITIONAL INFORMATION, PER SERVING: about 440 cal, 17 g pro, 19 g total fat (8 g sat. fat), 51 g carb (6 g dietary fibre, 15 g sugar), 43 mg chol, 675 mg sodium, 709 mg potassium. % RDI: 26% calcium, 14% iron, 79% vit A, 18% vit C, 20% folate.

Tip from the Test Kitchen

Looking for a flavourful way to use more zucchini when it's in season? Double the quantity of zucchini and carrot while omitting the noodles in this recipe.

P 148

ROASTED SQUASH & SPINACH LASAGNA

HANDS-ON TIME
45 minutes

TOTAL TIME
3 hours

MAKES
8 servings

INGREDIENTS

ROASTED SQUASH

1	butternut squash, peeled and cut in ¼-inch slices
2 tbsp	olive oil
½ tsp	salt
¼ tsp	pepper

TOMATO SAUCE

½ tbsp	olive oil
1	onion, finely chopped
1	rib celery, finely chopped
2	cloves garlic, minced
¼ tsp	hot pepper flakes
1	can (796 mL) diced tomatoes
½ cup	dry red wine
¼ cup	tomato paste
1 tsp	each dried oregano and dried sage

BÉCHAMEL SAUCE

¼ cup	butter
½ cup	all-purpose flour
3 cups	milk
1 cup	grated Parmesan cheese
½ tsp	nutmeg
2	eggs, lightly beaten

LASAGNA

16	lasagna noodles
3	bags (each 300 g) fresh spinach
3 cups	shredded mozzarella cheese

DIRECTIONS

ROASTED SQUASH Brush squash with oil. Place on 2 foil-lined rimmed baking sheets. Sprinkle with salt and pepper. Roast in 450°F oven until tender and lightly browned, about 30 minutes. Let cool on pans.

TOMATO SAUCE Meanwhile, in large nonstick skillet, heat oil over medium heat; cook onion, celery, garlic and hot pepper flakes, stirring until softened, about 3 minutes. Add tomatoes, red wine, tomato paste, oregano and sage. Reduce heat to low; cook, stirring occasionally, until thickened, about 30 minutes. Set aside.

BÉCHAMEL SAUCE In saucepan, melt butter over medium heat; stir in flour and cook, stirring, for 4 minutes. Gradually whisk in milk; cook, whisking constantly, until bubbly. Boil for 5 minutes, whisking often. Remove from heat. Whisk in Parmesan, nutmeg and eggs. Set aside.

LASAGNA In large saucepan of boiling salted water, cook noodles until al dente, 6 to 8 minutes. Drain and chill in cold water; arrange in single layer, keeping edges from touching, on damp tea towels.

Rinse spinach. In large saucepan over medium-high heat, cook spinach until wilted, about 5 minutes; drain in colander, squeezing out liquid. Chop spinach. Set aside.

ASSEMBLY In 13- × 9-inch baking dish, layer half of the tomato sauce, one-third of noodles, half each of the squash and béchamel sauce, and one-third of the mozzarella. Repeat noodle layer; cover with all of the spinach, the remaining squash and béchamel sauce, and half of the remaining mozzarella. Top with remaining noodles, tomato sauce and mozzarella.

Cover loosely with foil. *(Make-ahead: Refrigerate for up to 8 hours.)* Bake on rimmed baking sheet in 375°F oven for 25 minutes. Uncover and bake until cheese is lightly browned, about 30 minutes. Let stand for 10 minutes before serving.

NUTRITIONAL INFORMATION, PER SERVING: about 596 cal, 36 g pro, 18 g total fat (8 g sat. fat), 73 g carb, 1,048 mg sodium. % RDI: 83% calcium, 37% iron, 91% folate.

HANDS-ON TIME
25 minutes

TOTAL TIME
25 minutes

MAKES
4 servings

VEGAN

JAPCHAE

INGREDIENTS

280 g	sweet potato vermicelli
2 tbsp	sodium-reduced soy sauce
5 tsp	sesame oil
1 tsp	granulated sugar
2	cloves garlic, minced
1	carrot, cut in thin strips
2 cups	sliced stemmed shiitake mushrooms
1	sweet red pepper, thinly sliced
5	green onions, cut in 1½-inch lengths
1	bunch spinach, stemmed and chopped (about 4 cups)
2 tsp	sesame seeds, toasted

DIRECTIONS

In large saucepan of boiling water, cook vermicelli according to package instructions; drain. Using kitchen shears, cut into shorter lengths; toss with 2 tsp each of the soy sauce and sesame oil.

Meanwhile, stir together remaining soy sauce, 2 tsp of the sesame oil and the sugar. Set aside.

In wok or large nonstick skillet, heat remaining sesame oil over medium-high heat; sauté garlic until fragrant, about 1 minute. Add carrot, mushrooms, red pepper and green onions; sauté until pepper is tender-crisp, about 2 minutes. Add spinach; sauté just until wilted, about 1 minute. Remove from heat.

In large bowl, toss together vermicelli, carrot mixture and soy sauce mixture. Sprinkle with sesame seeds.

NUTRITIONAL INFORMATION, PER SERVING: about 348 cal, 6 g pro, 7 g total fat (1 g sat. fat), 67 g carb (4 g dietary fibre, 16 g sugar), 0 mg chol, 356 mg sodium, 425 mg potassium. % RDI: 9% calcium, 21% iron, 72% vit A, 92% vit C, 30% folate.

Tip from the Test Kitchen

Customize this Korean dish with your favourite vegetables, such as bok choy, bean sprouts or zucchini. Look for sweet potato vermicelli in Asian markets or specialty stores. They're long noodles, so we cut them with kitchen shears to make them easier to eat.

HANDS-ON TIME
15 minutes
TOTAL TIME
15 minutes
MAKES
4 servings

QUICK EGG & VEGGIE FRIED RICE

INGREDIENTS

2 tbsp	vegetable oil
3	green onions, thinly sliced (light and dark green parts separated)
1½ cup	sliced stemmed mushrooms, such as shiitake or cremini
1	carrot, diced
3	cloves garlic, minced
1 tbsp	minced fresh ginger
5 cups	cold cooked rice
½ cup	frozen peas
4	eggs, lightly beaten
2 tbsp	sodium-reduced soy sauce
1 tbsp	hoisin sauce
2 tsp	sriracha or other Asian chili sauce
1 tsp	sesame oil

DIRECTIONS

In wok or large nonstick skillet, heat vegetable oil over medium-high heat. Add light green parts of green onions; cook, stirring, until softened, about 1 minute.

Add mushrooms, carrot, garlic and ginger; cook, stirring, until softened, about 3 minutes.

Stir in rice and peas; cook, stirring often, until rice is hot, about 5 minutes. Push rice mixture into ring around edge of pan, leaving space in centre; pour eggs into centre. Cook, stirring eggs occasionally, until softly scrambled, about 2 minutes.

Stir rice mixture into eggs. Add soy sauce, hoisin sauce, sriracha and sesame oil; cook, stirring, for 1 minute. Sprinkle with dark green parts of green onions.

NUTRITIONAL INFORMATION, PER SERVING: about 444 cal, 14 g pro, 14 g total fat (2 g sat. fat), 65 g carb (3 g dietary fibre, 3 g sugar), 183 mg chol, 542 mg sodium, 315 mg potassium. % RDI: 6% calcium, 14% iron, 46% vit A, 7% vit C, 25% folate.

Tip from the Test Kitchen

For best results when making fried rice, use rice that has been cooked the day before and refrigerated; warm, freshly made rice becomes sticky and mushy when fried.

HANDS-ON TIME
30 minutes
TOTAL TIME
50 minutes
MAKES
4 to 6 servings

VEGETARIAN SINGAPORE NOODLES

INGREDIENTS

1	pkg (350 g) extra-firm tofu, drained and cut in ½-inch cubes
2 tbsp	sodium-reduced soy sauce
1 tsp	sesame oil
½ tsp	salt
¼ tsp	pepper
280 g	dried rice vermicelli (about ⅟₃₂-inch wide)
	boiling water
1 tbsp	vegetable oil
2	eggs, lightly beaten
1	small onion, thinly sliced
half	sweet red pepper, thinly sliced
2	cloves garlic, minced
2	green onions, cut in 1½-inch lengths
2 tsp	curry powder
1 tsp	turmeric
1 tsp	granulated sugar
2 cups	bean sprouts

DIRECTIONS

In bowl, stir together tofu, 2 tsp of the soy sauce, the sesame oil, pinch of the salt and the pepper. Cover and refrigerate for 30 minutes. *(Make-ahead: Refrigerate for up to 24 hours.)*

Meanwhile, in large bowl, add vermicelli and enough boiling water to cover; soak according to package instructions. Drain and rinse under cold water; drain well.

In wok or large nonstick skillet, heat 1 tsp of the vegetable oil over medium-high heat; cook eggs, stirring, just until set, about 1 minute. Scrape onto plate. Wipe pan clean. Add 1 tsp of the vegetable oil to pan; cook tofu mixture over medium-high heat until lightly browned, about 3 minutes. Transfer to plate.

Add remaining vegetable oil to pan; sauté onion, red pepper and garlic over medium-high heat until pepper is tender-crisp, about 2 minutes. Add vermicelli, eggs, tofu, green onions, curry powder, turmeric, sugar and remaining soy sauce and salt. Cook, stirring and tossing, until well combined and heated through, about 3 minutes. Add bean sprouts; cook, stirring, until softened, about 1 minute.

NUTRITIONAL INFORMATION, PER EACH OF 6 SERVINGS: about 264 cal, 9 g pro, 9 g total fat (3 g sat. fat), 40 g carb (3 g dietary fibre, 4 g sugar), 61 mg chol, 431 mg sodium, 184 mg potassium. % RDI: 41% calcium, 14% iron, 20% vit A, 42% vit C, 8% folate.

Tip from the Test Kitchen

This recipe makes a generous quantity; if you don't have a wok or skillet that's large enough to fit the noodles and other ingredients, you can use a Dutch oven or large saucepan.

HANDS-ON TIME
10 minutes

TOTAL TIME
35 minutes

MAKES
6 servings

VEGAN

ONE-POT QUINOA CHILI

INGREDIENTS

2 tsp	olive oil
1	onion, chopped
3	cloves garlic, minced
1	can (156 mL) tomato paste
2 tbsp	ground cumin
1 tbsp	each chili powder and smoked paprika
4 cups	vegetable broth
1	can (796 mL) diced tomatoes
¾ cup	quinoa, rinsed
1	can (540 mL) black beans, drained and rinsed
1	can (540 mL) kidney beans, drained and rinsed
1 cup	frozen corn
3 tbsp	fresh cilantro, chopped
1 tsp	pepper
½ tsp	salt (optional)

DIRECTIONS

In Dutch oven or large heavy-bottomed saucepan, heat oil over medium heat; cook onion, stirring often, until softened, about 5 minutes. Add garlic; cook, stirring occasionally, until fragrant, about 1 minute.

Stir in tomato paste, cumin, chili powder and paprika; cook for 2 minutes. Add broth and tomatoes; bring to boil over high heat, stirring often.

Stir in quinoa; reduce heat to low, cover and simmer for 15 minutes. Add black beans, kidney beans, corn, cilantro, pepper and salt (if using); simmer, uncovered, until quinoa is fluffy, 8 to 10 minutes.

Ladle into serving bowls; garnish with toppings such as sliced avocado, slivered red onion, thinly sliced radish, pickled jalapeño peppers or coconut crema (optional).

NUTRITIONAL INFORMATION, PER SERVING: about 334 cal, 17 g pro, 5 g total fat (1 g sat. fat), 62 g carb (16 g dietary fibre, 13 g sugar), 3 mg chol, 1,084 mg sodium, 1,204 mg potassium. % RDI: 14% calcium, 53% iron, 19% vit A, 50% vit C, 47% folate.

Tip from the Test Kitchen

To make coconut crema, skim the solid cream from the top of canned coconut milk. Thin with enough lemon juice to make a drizzle.

P 5

VEGAN

VEGETABLE SAFFRON PAELLA

HANDS-ON TIME
30 minutes

TOTAL TIME
1½ hours

MAKES
6 servings

INGREDIENTS

2	zucchini (about 375 g total)
2 cups	cubed eggplant
2 tbsp	olive oil
2	cloves garlic, minced
2 tsp	grated lemon zest
½ cup	chopped red onion
1	sweet red pepper, chopped
½ tsp	each salt and pepper
1½ cups	arborio rice
2	bay leaves
5 cups	vegetable broth
¼ tsp	saffron threads or turmeric
1 cup	frozen peas
1	can (400 mL) artichoke hearts, sliced
½ cup	oil-cured black olives, pitted and sliced
2 tbsp	chopped fresh parsley

DIRECTIONS

Cut zucchini in half lengthwise; cut crosswise into ½-inch thick slices. In bowl, toss together zucchini, eggplant, 1 tbsp of the oil, the garlic and lemon zest; let stand for 30 minutes. *(Make-ahead: Let stand for up to 2 hours.)*

In Dutch oven or large heavy-bottomed saucepan, heat remaining oil over medium-high heat; cook onion, red pepper, salt and pepper, stirring, until softened, about 3 minutes.

Add rice and bay leaves; stir for 1 minute to coat. Add zucchini mixture, broth and saffron; bring to boil. Reduce heat to medium-low; cover and cook, stirring occasionally, until rice is creamy and tender, about 25 minutes.

Stir in peas, artichokes and olives; heat through, about 3 minutes. Discard bay leaves. Sprinkle with parsley.

NUTRITIONAL INFORMATION, PER SERVING: about 338 cal, 8 g pro, 10 g total fat (1 g sat. fat), 57 g carb (6 g dietary fibre), 0 mg chol, 1,252 mg sodium. % RDI: 5% calcium, 14% iron, 11% vit A, 75% vit C, 25% folate.

VEGAN

PINE NUT, QUINOA & MUSHROOM STRUDEL

HANDS-ON TIME
30 minutes

TOTAL TIME
1 hour

MAKES
6 servings

INGREDIENTS

⅓ **cup**	red quinoa, rinsed
½ **cup**	pine nuts, toasted and chopped
1 tbsp	chopped fresh sage
½ tsp	each salt and pepper
6 tbsp	coconut oil
2	pkg (each 227 g) cremini mushrooms, sliced
1	small onion, chopped
3	cloves garlic, minced
1 tbsp	Dijon mustard
2 tsp	balsamic vinegar
8	sheets frozen phyllo pastry, thawed
1 cup	jarred roasted red peppers, drained and coarsely chopped
½ cup	bottled strained tomatoes (passata)
1½ cups	lightly packed baby arugula

DIRECTIONS

In saucepan of boiling water, cook quinoa according to package instructions. Stir in pine nuts, sage and half each of the salt and pepper.

Meanwhile, in nonstick skillet, heat 1 tbsp of the coconut oil over medium-high heat; cook mushrooms, onion, garlic and remaining salt and pepper, stirring occasionally, until softened and no liquid remains, about 12 minutes. Add mustard and vinegar; cook, stirring, for 1 minute.

In small microwaveable bowl, microwave remaining coconut oil until melted.

Place 1 sheet of phyllo on work surface with long end facing you; keep remainder covered with damp towel (to prevent drying out). Lightly brush phyllo with some of the remaining coconut oil. Top with second sheet of phyllo; lightly brush with some of the remaining coconut oil. Repeat layers with remaining phyllo and some of the remaining coconut oil.

Spoon quinoa mixture into 5-inch wide strip over top of phyllo, leaving 2-inch border at each short end and 2-inch border at long end farthest from you. Top with mushroom mixture, red peppers, strained tomatoes and arugula. Fold in short ends over borders. Starting from long end closest to you, roll up tightly.

Place strudel, seam side down, on parchment paper–lined rimmed baking sheet. Brush phyllo with remaining coconut oil. Bake in 400°F oven until golden, 25 to 30 minutes. Let cool on pan for 5 minutes. Slice crosswise into 6 pieces.

NUTRITIONAL INFORMATION, PER SERVING: about 381 cal, 8 g pro, 24 g total fat (13 g sat. fat), 35 g carb (5 g dietary fibre, 5 g sugar), 0 mg chol, 546 mg sodium, 602 mg potassium. % RDI: 5% calcium, 21% iron, 10% vit A, 92% vit C, 30% folate.

HANDS-ON TIME
40 minutes

TOTAL TIME
2¼ hours

MAKES
4 to 6 servings

BEET RISOTTO

INGREDIENTS

2	red beets
2½ cups	sodium-reduced vegetable broth
2 tbsp	butter
3	shallots, chopped
2 tsp	chopped fresh thyme
1⅓ cups	arborio rice
½ cup	dry white wine
¾ cup	grated Parmesan cheese
½ tsp	each salt and pepper
4 tsp	lemon juice
2 tsp	olive oil
2 cups	chopped beet greens (about 1 bunch)

DIRECTIONS

Wrap each beet in foil; roast in 400°F oven until tender, about 1 hour. Let cool enough to handle. Peel and dice to make 1½ cups. *(Make-ahead: Refrigerate in airtight container for up to 48 hours.)*

While beets are cooling, in small saucepan, bring broth and 1½ cups water to boil. Reduce heat to low and keep warm.

Meanwhile, in large skillet, melt butter over medium heat; cook shallots, stirring occasionally, until softened, about 5 minutes. Add thyme; cook, stirring, until fragrant, about 30 seconds. Add rice; cook, stirring to coat, until lightly toasted, about 1 minute. Pour in wine and cook, stirring, until most of the liquid is absorbed, about 1 minute.

Add broth mixture, ½ cup at a time, stirring after each addition until most of the liquid is absorbed before adding more, about 18 minutes total. Stir in beets, ½ cup of the Parmesan and all but pinch each of the salt and pepper. Remove from heat. Stir in lemon juice.

While risotto is cooking, in nonstick skillet, heat oil over medium heat; cook beet greens, stirring occasionally, until wilted, about 2 minutes. Sprinkle with remaining salt and pepper. Top risotto with beet greens and remaining Parmesan.

NUTRITIONAL INFORMATION, PER EACH OF 6 SERVINGS: about 303 cal, 9 g pro, 9 g total fat (5 g sat. fat), 44 g carb (2 g dietary fibre, 4 g sugar), 21 mg chol, 698 mg sodium, 357 mg potassium. % RDI: 16% calcium, 9% iron, 16% vit A, 10% vit C, 19% folate.

HANDS-ON TIME
40 minutes
TOTAL TIME
40 minutes
MAKES
4 to 6 servings

BUTTERNUT SQUASH RISOTTO

INGREDIENTS

3 cups	sodium-reduced chicken broth or vegetable broth
1	butternut squash (about 500 g)
2 tbsp	olive oil
1	onion, chopped
1	clove garlic, minced
1 tbsp	chopped fresh sage (or 1 tsp dried)
¼ tsp	each salt and pepper
1½ cups	arborio rice
½ cup	white wine
½ cup	grated Parmesan cheese
1 tbsp	butter

DIRECTIONS

In saucepan, cover and bring broth and 2 cups water to simmer over medium heat; reduce heat to low and keep warm. Meanwhile, peel and cube squash to make 4 cups.

In large saucepan, heat oil over medium heat; cook squash, onion, garlic, sage, salt and pepper, stirring occasionally, until onion is softened, about 5 minutes.

Add rice; stir to coat. Add wine; cook, stirring constantly, until no liquid remains.

Add 1 cup of the warm broth; simmer until absorbed. Continue adding broth, 1 cup at a time and stirring constantly, until all liquid is absorbed and rice is creamy and tender, about 18 minutes total.

Stir in Parmesan and butter; cook, stirring, until creamy, about 2 minutes.

NUTRITIONAL INFORMATION, PER EACH OF 6 SERVINGS: about 318 cal, 9 g pro, 9 g total fat (3 g sat. fat), 49 g carb (2 g dietary fibre), 12 mg chol, 538 mg sodium, 270 mg potassium. % RDI: 12% calcium, 6% iron, 72% vit A, 17% vit C, 8% folate.

Tip from the Test Kitchen

Risotto should be loose and creamy, with each grain of rice still slightly firm in the centre. It's best when served immediately, as it quickly loses its silky texture.

CRISPY POLENTA
WITH VEGETABLE RAGOUT

HANDS-ON TIME
30 minutes

TOTAL TIME
30 minutes

MAKES
8 servings

INGREDIENTS

CRISPY POLENTA

1	pkg (454 g) prepared polenta
2	eggs, lightly beaten
2 cups	grated Parmesan cheese

VEGETABLE RAGOUT

2 tbsp	olive oil
1	red onion, chopped
6	cloves garlic, minced
5	large portobello mushrooms, stemmed and chopped
2	sweet yellow peppers, chopped
⅔ cup	dry red wine
1	bottle (680 mL) strained tomatoes (passata)
3 tbsp	prepared pesto
½ tsp	each salt and pepper

DIRECTIONS

CRISPY POLENTA Slice polenta crosswise into 16 generous ½-inch thick rounds. Dip each round in egg, letting excess drip off; dredge in Parmesan. Arrange in single layer on 2 generously greased rimmed baking sheets. Bake in top and bottom thirds of 450°F oven, turning once and switching and rotating pans halfway through, until golden all over, about 20 minutes.

VEGETABLE RAGOUT While polenta is baking, in Dutch oven or large heavy-bottomed saucepan, heat oil over medium-high heat; cook red onion and garlic, stirring, until onion is softened, about 5 minutes. Add mushrooms and yellow peppers; cook, stirring, until softened, about 4 minutes.

Pour in wine; cook, stirring, until evaporated. Stir in strained tomatoes, pesto, salt and pepper; bring to boil. Reduce heat and simmer, stirring occasionally, until sauce is slightly thickened, about 5 minutes.

ASSEMBLY Divide polenta slices among 8 serving plates; spoon ragout over top.

NUTRITIONAL INFORMATION, PER SERVING: about 249 cal, 12 g pro, 12 g total fat (4 g sat. fat), 22 g carb (2 g dietary fibre, 7 g sugar), 51 mg chol, 780 mg sodium, 446 mg potassium. % RDI: 27% calcium, 9% iron, 7% vit A, 113% vit C, 11% folate.

Tip from the Test Kitchen

This recipe feeds a larger group, so it's ideal for easy entertaining, but it can easily be halved for an everyday dinner. Top the ragout with some extra shaved Parmesan, if you like.

HANDS-ON TIME
30 minutes
TOTAL TIME
30 minutes
MAKES
4 servings

GRILLED ASPARAGUS PIZZA

INGREDIENTS

2 tbsp	olive oil
2	cloves garlic, finely grated or pressed
2 tsp	dried oregano
½ tsp	grated lemon zest
¼ tsp	hot pepper flakes
pinch	each salt and pepper
1	bunch asparagus (about 450 g), trimmed
350 g	prepared pizza dough
1⅓ cups	shredded mozzarella cheese
½ cup	halved cherry tomatoes

DIRECTIONS

Whisk together half of the oil, the garlic, oregano, lemon zest, hot pepper flakes, salt and pepper; set aside.

Toss asparagus with 1 tsp of the remaining oil. Place on greased grill over medium-high heat; close lid and grill, turning often, until grill-marked and tender-crisp, 6 to 8 minutes. Set aside.

On lightly floured work surface, roll or press out dough to form 16- × 8½-inch oval. Brush 1 side with 1 tsp of the remaining oil. Place, oiled side down, on greased grill over medium heat; leave lid open and grill until bubbles form on top and bottom is grill-marked, about 3 minutes. Brush with remaining oil.

Reduce heat to medium-low; flip crust and brush with garlic mixture. Top with mozzarella, asparagus and tomatoes. Close lid and grill until mozzarella is melted and bottom of crust is browned, 5 to 8 minutes.

NUTRITIONAL INFORMATION, PER SERVING: about 436 cal, 17 g pro, 22 g total fat (8 g sat. fat), 45 g carb (4 g dietary fibre, 6 g sugar), 34 mg chol, 572 mg sodium, 364 mg potassium. % RDI: 31% calcium, 26% iron, 17% vit A, 15% vit C, 86% folate.

Tip from the Test Kitchen

The pizza dough will be easier to handle if you take it out of the fridge about 15 minutes before using it. Because barbecue temperatures vary, check the bottom of the crust often while grilling to avoid burning it.

VEGETABLE TIKKA MASALA NAAN PIZZA

HANDS-ON TIME
10 minutes

TOTAL TIME
25 minutes

MAKES
4 servings

INGREDIENTS

4	garlic or plain naan
2 cups	cubed seeded peeled butternut squash
4 cups	packed baby spinach
1 cup	jarred tikka masala sauce
1 cup	rinsed drained canned chickpeas
½ cup	crumbled feta cheese

DIRECTIONS

Arrange naan on 2 parchment paper–lined baking sheets. Place squash in microwaveable bowl; cover and microwave on high until tender, 2 to 3 minutes.

Meanwhile, coarsely chop 3 cups of the spinach. In small bowl, stir tikka masala sauce with chopped spinach; spread evenly over naan.

Top with squash, chickpeas and feta. Bake in 425°F oven until edge is crisp, 10 to 15 minutes. Top with remaining spinach.

NUTRITIONAL INFORMATION, PER SERVING: about 568 cal, 20 g pro, 16 g total fat (7 g sat. fat), 87 g carb (8 g dietary fibre, 11 g sugar), 17 mg chol, 1,083 mg sodium, 546 mg potassium. % RDI: 25% calcium, 42% iron, 115% vit A, 23% vit C, 137% folate.

Tip from the Test Kitchen
Legumes such as chickpeas are a good source of plant-based protein. You can also substitute lentils, if you wish.

HANDS-ON TIME
15 minutes
TOTAL TIME
25 minutes
MAKES
4 servings

DOUBLE MOZZARELLA & SPINACH PITA PIZZAS

INGREDIENTS

2 tsp	olive oil
4 cups	packed baby spinach
pinch	salt
½ cup	bottled strained tomatoes (passata)
2	cloves garlic, pressed or finely grated
1 tsp	Italian herb seasoning
pinch	pepper
4	whole wheat pita pockets (6 inches)
1 cup	shredded part-skim mozzarella cheese
125 g	fresh buffalo mozzarella cheese, torn in bite-size pieces and patted dry

DIRECTIONS

In nonstick skillet, heat oil over medium heat; cook spinach with salt, stirring, until wilted, 2 to 3 minutes. Set aside until cool enough to handle. Squeeze excess liquid from spinach; coarsely chop and set aside.

In bowl, combine strained tomatoes, garlic, Italian seasoning and pepper.

Arrange pitas on 2 baking sheets. Spread tomato mixture over top of pitas, leaving ½-inch border uncovered. Top with spinach, shredded mozzarella and buffalo mozzarella. Bake in 425°F oven until cheese is bubbly, about 10 minutes.

NUTRITIONAL INFORMATION, PER SERVING: about 356 cal, 18 g pro, 16 g total fat (8 g sat. fat), 38 g carb (5 g dietary fibre, 2 g sugar), 38 mg chol, 639 mg sodium, 325 mg potassium. % RDI: 22% calcium, 42% iron, 38% vit A, 10% vit C, 28% folate.

Tip from the Test Kitchen Store-bought whole wheat pitas make quick and easy pizza crusts, perfect for time-pressed weeknight meals. If you don't like spinach, top the pizzas with diced sweet red pepper or other favourite veggies.

SWEET ONION & GORGONZOLA PIZZA

HANDS-ON TIME
35 minutes

TOTAL TIME
50 minutes

MAKES
8 servings

INGREDIENTS

2 tbsp	extra-virgin olive oil (approx)
2	large sweet onions, such as Vidalia, thinly sliced
¼ cup	granulated sugar
¼ cup	balsamic vinegar
¼ tsp	salt
1	prepared pizza crust (12 inches)
2 tbsp	pine nuts
4 tsp	chopped fresh sage
225 g	gorgonzola cheese, crumbled

DIRECTIONS

In large skillet, heat half of the oil over medium-high heat; cook onions, stirring occasionally, until starting to turn golden, 10 to 12 minutes.

Reduce heat to medium. Add sugar and vinegar; cook, stirring occasionally, until almost no liquid remains, about 20 minutes. Stir in salt.

Place pizza crust on baking sheet; brush with remaining oil. Spread onions over top; sprinkle with pine nuts, sage and cheese. Bake in 400°F oven until cheese is bubbly, 7 to 10 minutes. Let stand 5 minutes before serving.

NUTRITIONAL INFORMATION, PER SERVING: about 313 cal, 10 g pro, 16 g total fat (7 g sat. fat), 34 g carb, 29 mg chol, 723 mg sodium. % RDI: 19% calcium, 10% iron, 9% vit A, 8% vit C.

Tip from the Test Kitchen

Let the onions cook slowly and gently; if they start to burn, reduce the heat to medium-low.

HANDS-ON TIME
25 minutes
TOTAL TIME
25 minutes
MAKES
4 servings

ARUGULA MUSHROOM PIZZA

INGREDIENTS

1	pkg (200 g) multigrain thin pizza crust
¾ cup	shredded Gruyère cheese
1 tbsp	butter
2 tsp	olive oil
2	shallots, chopped
2	cloves garlic, chopped
2 tsp	minced fresh thyme
225 g	cremini mushrooms, quartered
pinch	each salt and pepper
1 cup	frozen peas, thawed
55 g	light cream cheese, cubed
2 cups	arugula
1 tsp	lemon juice

DIRECTIONS

Place crust on parchment paper–lined baking sheet or pizza pan. Sprinkle with Gruyère, leaving ½-inch border uncovered. Bake in 400°F oven until Gruyère is melted and crust is golden and no longer doughy, 6 to 8 minutes.

Meanwhile, in large skillet, heat butter and half of the oil over medium heat; cook shallots, garlic and thyme, stirring occasionally, until shallots are softened, about 2 minutes.

Add mushrooms, salt and pepper; cook for 4 minutes. Add peas and cream cheese; cook until peas are warm and cheese is melted. Spread on baked crust.

Toss together arugula, lemon juice and remaining oil; scatter over pizza.

NUTRITIONAL INFORMATION, PER SERVING: about 362 cal, 15 g pro, 18 g total fat (8 g sat. fat), 36 g carb (5 g dietary fibre, 4 g sugar), 40 mg chol, 384 mg sodium, 548 mg potassium. % RDI: 30% calcium, 25% iron, 26% vit A, 13% vit C, 41% folate.

Tip from the Test Kitchen

Arugula, also known as rocket, is an iron-rich leafy green with a sharp, peppery flavour. The more mature it is, the stronger the flavour. If you love spicy, bitter greens, look for fully grown arugula.

CORN & FETA TART
WITH FRESH TARRAGON

HANDS-ON TIME
30 minutes

TOTAL TIME
3¼ hours

MAKES
8 servings

INGREDIENTS

CORNMEAL PASTRY

1¼ cups	all-purpose flour
¼ cup	cornmeal
½ tsp	salt
½ cup	cold unsalted butter, cubed
3 tbsp	sour cream
2 tbsp	ice water (approx)

FILLING

1	corn cob, husked
1 tbsp	olive oil
¾ cup	chopped leek (white and light green parts only)
4	eggs
⅓ cup	milk
2 tbsp	10% cream
¼ tsp	each salt and pepper
½ cup	crumbled feta cheese
2 tsp	chopped fresh tarragon

DIRECTIONS

CORNMEAL PASTRY In large bowl, whisk together flour, cornmeal and salt. Using pastry blender or 2 knives, cut in butter until mixture resembles large crumbs. Whisk sour cream with ice water; drizzle over flour mixture, tossing with fork and adding up to 1 tbsp more ice water if needed, until dough comes together. Shape into disc; wrap in plastic wrap and refrigerate until chilled, about 1 hour.

On lightly floured work surface, roll out dough to ¼-inch thickness; fit into fluted 9-inch tart pan with removable bottom, trimming excess. Prick crust all over with fork and refrigerate until firm, about 30 minutes.

Line crust with foil and fill with pie weights or dried beans. Bake on rimmed baking sheet on bottom rack of 400°F oven until edge is golden, about 20 minutes. Remove pie weights and foil; bake until crust is golden, about 10 minutes. Let cool slightly on rack.

FILLING While crust is baking, cut kernels from corn cob. In skillet, heat oil over medium heat; cook corn kernels and leek, stirring occasionally, until corn is deep yellow and tender and leek is softened, about 5 minutes. Set aside.

In large bowl, whisk together eggs, milk, cream, salt and pepper. Stir in corn mixture, feta and tarragon. Pour over crust.

TO FINISH Bake on rimmed baking sheet in 375°F oven until knife inserted in centre comes out clean, about 40 minutes. Let cool on rack for 15 minutes.

NUTRITIONAL INFORMATION, PER SERVING: about 265 cal, 8 g pro, 17 g total fat (9 g sat. fat), 21 g carb (1 g dietary fibre, 2 g sugar), 132 mg chol, 340 mg sodium, 149 mg potassium. % RDI: 8% calcium, 11% iron, 17% vit A, 3% vit C, 25% folate.

HANDS-ON TIME
25 minutes

TOTAL TIME
25 minutes

MAKES
4 servings

MEATLESS SHEPHERD'S PIE

INGREDIENTS

¾ cup	no-salt-added vegetable broth
1 tbsp	sodium-reduced soy sauce
1 tbsp	cornstarch
½ tsp	salt
¼ tsp	pepper
2	large russet potatoes (about 700 g total)
2 tsp	olive oil
1	pkg (227 g) button mushrooms, finely chopped
1	onion, finely chopped
1	carrot, finely chopped
1½ tsp	chopped fresh thyme
1	can (540 mL) lentils, drained and rinsed
¼ cup	chopped fresh parsley
¼ cup	milk
2 tbsp	butter
½ tsp	grainy mustard

DIRECTIONS

In small bowl, whisk together broth, soy sauce, cornstarch and half each of the salt and pepper until smooth. Set aside.

Using fork, prick potatoes all over. Microwave on high, turning once, until fork-tender, 8 to 10 minutes. Set aside until just cool enough to handle.

Meanwhile, in large skillet, heat oil over medium-high heat; cook mushrooms, onion, carrot and thyme, stirring occasionally, until softened and no liquid remains, 6 to 8 minutes. Stir in lentils; cook for 1 minute.

Stir in broth mixture; cook, whisking, until slightly thickened, about 2 minutes. Stir in 3 tbsp of the parsley. Scrape into 6-cup casserole dish.

Peel potatoes. Using potato masher, mash together potatoes, milk, half of the butter and the remaining salt and pepper. Stir in remaining parsley and the mustard. Spoon over mushroom mixture, spreading to edge; dot with remaining butter. Broil on centre rack until top is golden, 3 to 5 minutes.

NUTRITIONAL INFORMATION, PER SERVING: about 358 cal, 18 g pro, 9 g total fat (4 g sat. fat), 57 g carb (8 g dietary fibre, 8 g sugar), 16 mg chol, 764 mg sodium, 1,286 mg potassium. % RDI: 7% calcium, 39% iron, 38% vit A, 53% vit C, 100% folate.

Tip from the Test Kitchen

For faster prep, pulse together the mushrooms, onion, carrot and thyme in a food processor until they're finely chopped.

VEGAN

CRISPY TOFU & BROCCOLI
WITH UDON NOODLES

HANDS-ON TIME
30 minutes

TOTAL TIME
30 minutes

MAKES
4 servings

INGREDIENTS

1	pkg (420 g) firm tofu, drained and cut in ¾-inch cubes
1 tbsp	cornstarch
2 tbsp	vegetable oil
1	pkg (227 g) cremini mushrooms, thinly sliced
4	cloves garlic, minced
1 tbsp	grated peeled fresh ginger
3 cups	bite-size broccoli florets
3 tbsp	hoisin sauce
1 tsp	Asian chili sauce (such as sriracha)
3	pkg (each 200 g) fresh udon noodles
2	green onions, thinly sliced
1 tsp	sesame oil

DIRECTIONS

Using paper towel, pat tofu dry; toss gently with cornstarch to coat. In wok or large nonstick skillet, heat all but 2 tsp of the vegetable oil over medium-high heat; cook tofu, turning occasionally, until crisp and golden, 8 to 10 minutes. Remove to paper towel–lined plate to drain. Set aside.

In same wok, heat remaining vegetable oil over medium-high heat; stir-fry mushrooms, garlic and ginger until mushrooms are beginning to soften, about 2 minutes. Add broccoli; stir-fry until tender-crisp, about 3 minutes. Stir in hoisin sauce, chili sauce and ¾ cup water; bring to boil.

Reduce heat to low; add noodles, tossing gently to coat. Simmer, stirring gently, until sauce is slightly thickened, about 2 minutes. Add tofu, green onions and sesame oil; cook, tossing to coat, for 1 minute.

NUTRITIONAL INFORMATION, PER SERVING: about 515 cal, 28 g pro, 17 g total fat (2 g sat. fat), 68 g carb (5 g dietary fibre, 6 g sugar), 0 mg chol, 261 mg sodium, 717 mg potassium. % RDI: 20% calcium, 41% iron, 16% vit A, 53% vit C, 26% folate.

HANDS-ON TIME
20 minutes
TOTAL TIME
20 minutes
MAKES
4 servings

VEGAN

TOFU & CHOW MEIN NOODLES

INGREDIENTS

1	pkg (425 g) firm tofu, cut in ½-inch cubes
2 tbsp	sodium-reduced soy sauce
3 tsp	sesame oil
2 tsp	vegetable oil
1 cup	frozen peas
¾ cup	finely chopped green onions
2 tbsp	grated fresh ginger
2	cloves garlic, minced
1 cup	vegetable broth
280 g	Cantonese-style steamed chow mein noodles
⅓ cup	chopped roasted cashews

DIRECTIONS

Using paper towel, pat tofu dry. In bowl, whisk together half each of the soy sauce and sesame oil; add tofu and toss to coat.

In wok or large nonstick skillet, heat vegetable oil over medium-high heat; stir-fry tofu until light golden and crisp, about 5 minutes. Transfer to plate.

Add peas, green onions, ginger, garlic and remaining soy sauce to wok; stir-fry for 2 minutes. Stir in broth and bring to boil; boil for 2 minutes.

Meanwhile, cook noodles according to package directions. Drain and add to wok along with tofu; stir-fry to coat and warm through, about 2 minutes. Stir in remaining sesame oil; sprinkle with cashews.

NUTRITIONAL INFORMATION, PER SERVING: about 482 cal, 27 g pro, 20 g total fat (3 g sat. fat), 52 g carb (3 g dietary fibre, 4 g sugar), 5 mg chol, 635 mg sodium, 407 mg potassium. % RDI: 18% calcium, 38% iron, 9% vit A, 10% vit C, 24% folate.

Tip from the Test Kitchen

In the grocery store, look for fresh ginger with smooth, shiny skin and a spicy aroma. Wrinkles and cracks indicate it's dry and past its prime. When it's young, ginger doesn't need peeling, but older roots have a tough skin that should be scraped off with a vegetable peeler or knife.

HANDS-ON TIME
25 minutes
TOTAL TIME
25 minutes
MAKES
4 servings

VEGAN

SPICY GREEN BEAN & TOFU STIR-FRY

INGREDIENTS

1	pkg (350 g) extra-firm tofu, cut in 1-inch cubes
1 tbsp	cornstarch
3 tbsp	vegetable oil
3	cloves garlic, minced
2	green onions, thinly sliced (light and dark green parts separated)
1 tbsp	minced fresh ginger
¼ tsp	hot pepper flakes
2 tbsp	tomato paste
450 g	green beans, trimmed (about 6 cups)
1 cup	vegetable broth
1 tbsp	hoisin sauce
2 tsp	sodium-reduced soy sauce

DIRECTIONS

Using paper towel, pat tofu dry; toss gently with cornstarch to coat. In wok, heat oil over medium-high heat; cook tofu, turning occasionally, until crisp and golden, about 10 minutes. Drain on paper towel–lined plate.

Drain all but 2 tsp oil from wok. Add garlic, light green parts of green onions, ginger and hot pepper flakes; stir-fry for 1 minute. Add tomato paste; stir-fry for 30 seconds. Add green beans, broth, ¼ cup water, the hoisin sauce and soy sauce; stir-fry until green beans are tender-crisp, 5 to 6 minutes.

Add tofu and dark green parts of green onions; stir-fry until coated and heated through, about 1 minute.

NUTRITIONAL INFORMATION, PER SERVING: about 239 cal, 16 g pro, 14 g total fat (1 g sat. fat), 17 g carb (3 g dietary fibre, 5 g sugar), 1 mg chol, 370 mg sodium, 399 mg potassium. % RDI: 17% calcium, 18% iron, 10% vit A, 20% vit C, 24% folate.

VEGAN

OVEN-BAKED TERIYAKI TOFU

HANDS-ON TIME 10 minutes
TOTAL TIME 35 minutes
MAKES 4 to 6 servings

INGREDIENTS

2	pkg (each 350 g) extra-firm tofu, drained and cut in 1-inch chunks
½ tsp	salt
pinch	pepper
¼ cup	cornstarch
2 tbsp	vegetable oil
½ cup	Molasses Teriyaki Sauce (see recipe, right)
1	green onion, thinly sliced
1	red finger chili pepper, thinly sliced
¼ tsp	sesame seeds, toasted

DIRECTIONS

Using paper towel, pat tofu dry. In bowl, toss together tofu, salt and pepper. Sprinkle with cornstarch; toss until well coated. Drizzle with oil; toss to coat. Arrange in single layer on greased rimmed baking sheet. Bake in 400°F oven, turning occasionally, until golden all over, about 25 minutes.

Arrange tofu on serving dish; drizzle with Molasses Teriyaki Sauce. Sprinkle with green onion, chili pepper and sesame seeds.

NUTRITIONAL INFORMATION, PER EACH OF 6 SERVINGS: about 250 cal, 17 g pro, 13 g total fat (1 g sat. fat), 17 g carb (trace dietary fibre, 7 g sugar), 0 mg chol, 667 mg sodium, 315 mg potassium. % RDI: 18% calcium, 18% iron, 1% vit A, 3% vit C, 11% folate.

VEGAN

MOLASSES TERIYAKI SAUCE

HANDS-ON TIME 10 minutes
TOTAL TIME 10 minutes
MAKES about 1 cup

INGREDIENTS

½ cup	sodium-reduced soy sauce
¼ cup	fancy molasses
2 tbsp	packed brown sugar
1	piece (1 inch) fresh ginger
2 tbsp	cornstarch

DIRECTIONS

In small saucepan, stir together soy sauce, molasses, brown sugar, ginger and ¾ cup water; bring to boil. Reduce heat to medium and simmer, stirring occasionally, until slightly thickened, about 5 minutes. Discard ginger. Whisk cornstarch with 2 tbsp water; whisk into soy sauce mixture and cook, stirring, until thickened, about 1 minute. *(Make-ahead: Refrigerate in airtight container for up to 1 week.)*

NUTRITIONAL INFORMATION, PER 1 TBSP: about 31 cal, trace pro, 0 g total fat (0 g sat. fat), 7 g carb (trace dietary fibre, 5 g sugar), 0 mg chol, 269 mg sodium, 99 mg potassium. % RDI: 1% calcium, 3% iron.

HANDS-ON TIME
20 minutes
TOTAL TIME
25 minutes
MAKES
4 servings

VEGAN

VEGETARIAN MA PO TOFU

INGREDIENTS

1 cup	20-minute whole grain brown rice
1 tbsp	vegetable oil or sesame oil
1	carrot, quartered lengthwise and cut crosswise in scant ½-inch thick pieces
4	green onions, sliced
1 tbsp	minced peeled fresh ginger
120 g	green beans, trimmed and cut in 1-inch lengths
100 g	shiitake mushrooms, stemmed and sliced
2 tbsp	black bean garlic sauce
2 tsp	Korean hot pepper paste (gochujang)
1 tbsp	cornstarch
1	pkg (454 g) medium-firm tofu, cut in ¾-inch cubes

DIRECTIONS

In saucepan, cook rice according to package instructions.

Meanwhile, in large nonstick skillet or wok, heat oil over medium-high heat; stir-fry carrot, three-quarters of the green onions and the ginger until carrot is beginning to soften, about 4 minutes. Add green beans and mushrooms; stir-fry until green beans are beginning to soften, about 3 minutes. Stir in black bean garlic sauce and hot pepper paste; cook, stirring, until fragrant, about 1 minute.

Whisk cornstarch with 1 cup water; stir into vegetable mixture. Bring to boil; boil, stirring, until thickened, about 1 minute. Reduce heat to medium. Add tofu; cook, stirring gently, until tofu is coated and warmed through, about 3 minutes. If necessary, add water, 1 tbsp at a time, to reach desired consistency.

Divide rice among serving bowls; top with ma po tofu. Sprinkle with remaining green onions.

NUTRITIONAL INFORMATION, PER SERVING: about 370 cal, 26 g pro, 15 g total fat (1 g sat. fat), 52 g carb (4 g dietary fibre, 6 g sugar), 0 mg chol, 226 mg sodium, 470 mg potassium. % RDI: 18% calcium, 25% iron, 114% vit A, 8% vit C, 27% folate.

Tip from the Test Kitchen

Korean hot pepper paste isn't traditionally found in ma po tofu, but it adds a nice kick. Look for it in the Asian section of your grocery store, or substitute with 1 tsp of sriracha.

HANDS-ON TIME
15 minutes
TOTAL TIME
25 minutes
MAKES
4 servings

VEGAN

BROCCOLI & BROILED TOFU
WITH NO-COOK PEANUT SAUCE

INGREDIENTS

NO-COOK PEANUT SAUCE

¼ cup	reduced-fat peanut butter
1 tbsp	grated fresh ginger
2 tsp	each sodium-reduced soy sauce and rice vinegar
1 tsp	sesame oil
½ tsp	Asian chili paste (such as sambal oelek)
2	green onions, thinly sliced

BROCCOLI AND TOFU

1	pkg (454 g) firm tofu, cut in 8 slices
2 tbsp	olive oil
1	large stalk broccoli, stems removed and separated in florets
1 tbsp	toasted sesame seeds

DIRECTIONS

NO-COOK PEANUT SAUCE In small bowl, whisk together peanut butter, ginger, soy sauce, vinegar, sesame oil and chili paste; slowly whisk in ¼ cup hot water. Stir in green onions.

BROCCOLI AND TOFU Using paper towels, pat tofu dry. Brush baking sheet with 1 tsp of the oil. Arrange tofu on pan; brush remaining oil over top. Broil, about 8 inches from heat, until crisp and dry looking, about 15 minutes.

Meanwhile, in steamer, cover and steam broccoli until tender-crisp, about 3 minutes.

Serve tofu over broccoli. Drizzle with peanut sauce; sprinkle with sesame seeds.

NUTRITIONAL INFORMATION, PER SERVING: about 347 cal, 22 g pro, 24 g total fat (3 g sat. fat), 15 g carb (4 g dietary fibre, 4 g sugar), 0 mg chol, 241 mg sodium, 461 mg potassium. % RDI: 21% calcium, 23% iron, 22% vit A, 73% vit C, 38% folate.

Tip from the Test Kitchen

Try this versatile peanut sauce tossed with cold pasta or as a dip for raw vegetables or Vietnamese-style fresh rolls.

HANDS-ON TIME
15 minutes

TOTAL TIME
1 hour 50 minutes

MAKES
6 servings

VEGAN

TEMPEH & RICE–STUFFED PEPPERS

INGREDIENTS

6	sweet peppers
1 cup	long-grain rice
1¼ tsp	salt
2	pkg (each 240 g) tempeh
¼ cup	olive oil
1	onion, finely diced
1	rib celery, finely diced
3	cloves garlic, minced
¼ cup	dry white wine or tomato juice
3 tbsp	sodium-reduced soy sauce
2 tsp	dried oregano
½ tsp	pepper
¼ cup	chopped fresh parsley
¼ cup	nutritional yeast flakes (optional)
1	can (796 mL) crushed tomatoes
2 tbsp	chopped fresh basil

DIRECTIONS

About 1 inch down from stem end, slice tops off peppers. Reserve tops; scrape out ribs and seeds from peppers.

In saucepan, bring 1½ cups water, the rice and ¼ tsp salt to boil. Reduce heat; simmer, covered, until no liquid remains, about 20 minutes. Remove from heat; let stand, covered, for 10 minutes. Scrape into large bowl; let cool.

Using coarse side of box grater, grate tempeh.

In large skillet, heat half of the oil over medium heat; cook onion, celery and garlic, stirring often, until softened, about 5 minutes. Add tempeh, wine, soy sauce, oregano, pepper and remaining salt. Cook until no liquid remains, about 1 minute.

Add tempeh mixture, parsley and yeast (if using) to rice; toss to combine. Divide stuffing among peppers, mounding tops. Snugly arrange peppers in single layer in 10- × 10- × 4-inch baking dish; cover peppers with reserved tops.

Mix tomatoes with basil and 1 cup water; spoon around peppers. Drizzle peppers with remaining oil.

Cover with lid or foil; bake in 350°F oven until peppers are almost tender, 1 hour. Uncover; bake until tender, 20 minutes.

NUTRITIONAL INFORMATION, PER SERVING: about 434 cal, 20 g pro, 18 g total fat (4 g sat. fat), 53 g carb, 10 mg chol, 981 mg sodium, 1039 mg potassium. % RDI: 15% calcium, 35% iron, 28% vit A, 280% vit C, 28% folate.

Tip from the Test Kitchen

Tempeh is made from fermented soybeans and grains; it has a nutty, mushroomy flavour and a denser texture than tofu. To make it easier to grate, freeze it first for about 10 minutes.

HANDS-ON TIME
20 minutes
TOTAL TIME
40 minutes
MAKES
4 servings

VEGAN

SWEET POTATO & CAULIFLOWER TAGINE

INGREDIENTS

1	bag (284 g) white pearl onions (about 2 cups)
1 tbsp	vegetable oil
3	cloves garlic, minced
1½ tsp	ground cumin
1 tsp	paprika
½ tsp	ground ginger
½ tsp	salt
¼ tsp	pepper
¼ tsp	cayenne pepper
3 cups	cubed peeled sweet potato (about 1 large potato)
1	can (540 mL) chickpeas, drained and rinsed
1½ cups	vegetable broth
2 cups	cauliflower florets
1 cup	frozen peas
2 tbsp	minced fresh cilantro

DIRECTIONS

Place pearl onions in heatproof bowl; cover with boiling water. Let stand for 5 minutes; drain and peel.

In large deep skillet, heat oil over medium heat; cook pearl onions, stirring occasionally, until golden, 5 minutes. Add garlic, cumin, paprika, ginger, salt, pepper and cayenne pepper; cook, stirring, for 1 minute.

Add sweet potato, chickpeas and broth; bring to boil. Reduce heat, cover and simmer for 5 minutes. Stir in cauliflower; simmer, covered, until almost tender, 20 minutes. Add peas; simmer, covered, until hot. Sprinkle with coriander.

NUTRITIONAL INFORMATION, PER SERVING: about 337 cal, 11 g pro, 6 g total fat (1 g sat. fat), 63 g carb (10 g dietary fibre), 0 mg chol, 852 mg sodium. % RDI: 8% calcium, 24% iron, 177% vit A, 82% vit C, 55% folate.

Tip from the Test Kitchen

You can replace the pearl onions with 2 white or yellow onions, cut in wedges.

HANDS-ON TIME
5 minutes

TOTAL TIME
30 minutes

MAKES
4 servings

VEGAN

MEDITERRANEAN STEWED CHICKPEAS

INGREDIENTS

2 tbsp	olive oil
1	onion, chopped
1	sweet green pepper, chopped
2	cloves garlic, minced
½ tsp	crushed fennel seeds
¼ tsp	each pepper and hot pepper flakes
1	can (796 mL) diced no-salt-added tomatoes
1	can (540 mL) chickpeas, drained and rinsed
½ cup	sliced large stuffed green olives
½ cup	chopped fresh parsley
¼ tsp	dried mint
1 cup	whole wheat couscous

DIRECTIONS

In Dutch oven or large heavy-bottomed saucepan, heat oil over medium heat; cook onion, green pepper, garlic, fennel seeds, pepper and hot pepper flakes, stirring occasionally, until onion is tender, about 5 minutes.

Stir in tomatoes, chickpeas, olives, half of the parsley and the mint; bring to boil. Reduce heat and simmer, stirring often, until slightly thickened, about 15 minutes. Stir in remaining parsley; cook for 5 minutes.

Meanwhile, in bowl, stir couscous with 1½ cups boiling water; cover with plastic wrap and let stand for 5 minutes. Fluff with fork. Serve with stew.

NUTRITIONAL INFORMATION, PER SERVING: about 462 cal, 15 g pro, 12 g total fat (2 g sat. fat), 78 g carb (14 g dietary fibre), 0 mg chol, 617 mg sodium, 317 mg potassium. % RDI: 18% calcium, 52% iron, 18% vit A, 83% vit C, 38% folate.

HANDS-ON TIME
15 minutes
TOTAL TIME
35 minutes
MAKES
4 servings

CREAMY LEEK & CORN BAKED EGGS

INGREDIENTS

1 tbsp	butter
⅔ cup	diced leeks (white and light green parts only)
¼ tsp	each salt and pepper
1½ cups	frozen corn kernels
2 tbsp	chopped fresh parsley
4	eggs
6 tbsp	whipping cream (35%
¼ cup	crumbled goat cheese (chèvre)
pinch	nutmeg

DIRECTIONS

In skillet, melt butter over medium heat; cook leeks, salt and pepper, stirring occasionally, until softened, about 4 minutes. Stir in corn; cook, stirring occasionally, until tender, about 3 minutes. Stir in parsley. Divide among 4 greased 6-oz ramekins.

Crack 1 egg into each ramekin; drizzle with whipping cream. Sprinkle with goat cheese and nutmeg.

Place ramekins in 8-inch square baking dish; pour enough hot water into baking dish to come halfway up sides of ramekins. Bake in 375°F oven until egg whites are set but still jiggle slightly and yolks are still runny, 25 to 28 minutes. Let ramekins stand in water in pan for 10 minutes before serving.

NUTRITIONAL INFORMATION, PER SERVING: about 254 cal, 10 g pro, 18 g total fat (10 g sat. fat), 15 g carb (2 g dietary fibre, 3 g sugar), 224 mg chol, 274 mg sodium. % RDI: 6% calcium, 11% iron, 27% vit A, 10% vit C, 27% folate.

HANDS-ON TIME
10 minutes
TOTAL TIME
25 minutes
MAKES
4 servings

BAKED PHYLLO EGG NESTS

INGREDIENTS

½ cup	shredded Gruyère cheese
2 tbsp	chopped drained oil-packed sun-dried tomatoes
1 tbsp	chopped fresh chives and parsley
4	sheets phyllo pastry, thawed
2 tbsp	butter, melted
4	eggs
¼ tsp	pepper
pinch	salt

DIRECTIONS

Stir together Gruyère, sun-dried tomatoes, chives and parsley; set aside.

Place 1 sheet of phyllo on work surface with long edge facing you; cover remainder with damp towel (to prevent drying out). Lightly brush phyllo with some of the butter. Push edges in to form 4-inch wide nest, keeping centre flat; transfer nest to parchment paper–lined rimmed baking sheet. Repeat with remaining phyllo and butter to make 3 more nests.

Crack 1 egg into centre of each nest; sprinkle pepper and salt over eggs. Leaving yolk uncovered, sprinkle white of each egg with one-quarter of the cheese mixture.

Bake in 425°F oven until whites are set but yolks are still runny and phyllo is golden and crisp, 8 to 10 minutes. Let stand 3 minutes before serving.

NUTRITIONAL INFORMATION, PER SERVING: about 261 cal, 12 g pro, 17 g total fat (8 g sat. fat), 14 g carb (1 g dietary fibre, 1 g sugar), 213 mg chol, 277 mg sodium, 151 mg potassium. % RDI: 15% calcium, 12% iron, 20% vit A, 8% vit C, 24% folate.

Tip from the Test Kitchen

Be sure to thaw frozen phyllo pastry for 24 hours in the refrigerator or 3 hours at room temperature before working with it. Rewrap unused phyllo and refrigerate for up to 2 days.

HANDS-ON TIME
20 minutes
TOTAL TIME
30 minutes
MAKES
4 servings

TURKISH EGG TARTINES

INGREDIENTS

YOGURT SAUCE

½ cup	grated English cucumber
½ tsp	salt
1 cup	2% plain Greek yogurt
2	cloves garlic, minced
2 tbsp	chopped fresh dill

PAPRIKA BUTTER

2 tbsp	unsalted butter
1½ tsp	smoked paprika
½ tsp	chili powder
¼ tsp	ground cumin

HERB SALAD

1 tbsp	olive oil
1 tbsp	lemon juice
½ cup	lightly packed arugula
½ cup	fresh cilantro or parsley
¼ cup	fresh mint
1 tbsp	fresh dill (optional)
pinch	each salt and pepper
4	thick slices pumpernickel bread, toasted
8	soft-poached eggs

DIRECTIONS

YOGURT SAUCE Mix cucumber with salt; let stand for 10 minutes. Squeeze out and discard excess liquid. In small bowl, stir together cucumber, yogurt, garlic and dill. *(Make-ahead: Cover with plastic wrap; refrigerate for up to 2 days.)*

PAPRIKA BUTTER In small microwaveable bowl, combine butter, paprika, chili powder and cumin. Microwave on medium until melted, about 45 seconds.

HERB SALAD In bowl, whisk oil with lemon juice. Add arugula, cilantro, mint and dill (if using); toss to coat. Sprinkle with salt and pepper.

ASSEMBLY Spread each slice of toast with Yogurt Sauce. Top each with 2 poached eggs; drizzle with warm Paprika Butter. Top with Herb Salad.

NUTRITIONAL INFORMATION, PER SERVING: about 534 cal, 28 g pro, 24 g total fat (9 g sat. fat), 53 g carb (8 g dietary fibre, 4 g sugar), 404 mg chol, 973 mg sodium, 542 mg potassium. % RDI: 28% calcium, 39% iron, 36% vit A, 8% vit C, 60% folate.

Tip from the Test Kitchen

To keep poached eggs heated, place them in a bowl of warm water. Transfer to a paper towel–lined plate to dry briefly before serving. Substitute prepared tzatziki for Yogurt Sauce if you're pressed for time.

ROASTED PEPPERS
WITH EGGS

HANDS-ON TIME
10 minutes
TOTAL TIME
30 minutes
MAKES
4 servings

INGREDIENTS

2	large red peppers
⅓ cup	shredded Havarti cheese
2	green onions, thinly sliced (white and green parts separated)
4	eggs
pinch	each salt and pepper

DIRECTIONS

Leaving stems intact, halve and core red peppers. Arrange, cut sides down, on foil-lined rimmed baking sheet. Bake in 425°F oven just until beginning to soften, about 10 minutes.

Turn red peppers cut sides up; sprinkle with one-quarter of the Havarti and the white parts of green onions. Crack 1 egg into each red pepper half; sprinkle with salt and pepper.

Bake in 425°F oven until egg whites are just set but yolks are still runny, 8 to 10 minutes. Sprinkle with remaining Havarti and green parts of green onions. Broil until cheese is melted, about 1 minute.

NUTRITIONAL INFORMATION, PER SERVING: about 136 cal, 9 g pro, 9 g total fat (4 g sat. fat), 6 g carb (1 g dietary fibre, 4 g sugar), 194 mg chol, 136 mg sodium, 208 mg potassium. % RDI: 9% calcium, 9% iron, 35% vit A, 225% vit C, 20% folate.

Tip from the Test Kitchen

Be sure to leave the stems on the peppers when halving and coring them—they help hold the pepper together as it cooks and softens.

HANDS-ON TIME
15 minutes
TOTAL TIME
35 minutes
MAKES
8 servings

SPINACH & FETA OMELETTE SOUFFLÉ

INGREDIENTS

2 tbsp	butter
4 cups	packed baby spinach, chopped
4	green onions, finely chopped
10	eggs, separated
½ cup	crumbled feta cheese
½ tsp	pepper
¼ tsp	salt

DIRECTIONS

In ovenproof nonstick skillet, melt 2 tsp of the butter over medium heat; cook spinach and green onions, stirring occasionally, until spinach is wilted, about 3 minutes. Scrape into bowl; let cool slightly. Stir in egg yolks, feta, pepper and salt.

In bowl, beat egg whites until stiff peaks form; fold into egg yolk mixture.

Add remaining butter to pan; melt over medium-low heat. Scrape in egg mixture, smoothing top; cook for 5 minutes. Transfer to 425°F oven; bake until top is dry and springs back when touched, 12 to 15 minutes.

NUTRITIONAL INFORMATION, PER SERVING: about 147 cal, 9 g pro, 11 g total fat (5 g sat. fat), 2 g carb (1 g dietary fibre, 1 g sugar), 245 mg chol, 287 mg sodium. % RDI: 9% calcium, 11% iron, 31% vit A, 3% vit C, 28% folate.

Tip from the Test Kitchen

Beating the whites separately might seem fussy, but it's well worth the effort. The extra volume gives the dish a light, airy texture you won't get from beating whole eggs.

CRUSTLESS ZUCCHINI QUICHE
WITH GRILLED CORN SALAD

HANDS-ON TIME
25 minutes

TOTAL TIME
45 minutes

MAKES
6 to 8 servings

INGREDIENTS

QUICHE

1 tsp	vegetable oil
2	cloves garlic, minced
3 cups	baby spinach
1	zucchini, grated
5	eggs
1 cup	whipping cream (35%)
½ cup	milk
pinch	each nutmeg, salt and pepper
½ cup	crumbled soft goat cheese (chèvre)
⅓ cup	grated Parmesan cheese

GRILLED CORN SALAD

1 tbsp	butter, melted
¼ tsp	each salt and pepper
pinch	dried Italian herb seasoning
2	corn cobs, husked
2 tbsp	olive oil
1 tbsp	lemon juice
2 tsp	Dijon mustard
2 tsp	liquid honey
4 cups	packed baby spinach
1 cup	cherry tomatoes, halved

DIRECTIONS

QUICHE In skillet, heat oil over medium heat; cook garlic until fragrant, 1 minute. Add spinach; cook, stirring often, until wilted, 2 minutes. Let cool.

Wrap spinach and zucchini in clean tea towel; twist and squeeze to release excess liquid; discard liquid. Set spinach and zucchini aside.

In large bowl, whisk eggs just until blended. Whisk in cream, milk, nutmeg, salt and pepper just until combined. Stir in goat cheese, Parmesan, zucchini and spinach. Pour into greased 9-inch pie plate. Bake in 425°F oven until golden brown and centre is set, 35 to 40 minutes.

GRILLED CORN SALAD Combine butter, half each of the salt and pepper and the Italian seasoning.

Place corn cobs on greased grill over medium-high heat; close lid and grill, turning often and brushing with half of the butter mixture, until tender and grill-marked, 10 to 15 minutes. Brush with remaining butter mixture; cut kernels from corn cobs.

In large bowl, whisk together oil, lemon juice, mustard, honey and remaining salt and pepper. Add spinach, tomatoes and corn; toss to coat. Serve with quiche.

NUTRITIONAL INFORMATION, PER EACH OF 8 SERVINGS: about 294 cal, 10 g pro, 23 g total fat (11 g sat. fat), 14 g carb (2 g dietary fibre, 5 g sugar), 166 mg chol, 280 mg sodium, 403 mg potassium. % RDI: 14% calcium, 13% iron, 51% vit A, 18% vit C, 39% folate.

Tip from the Test Kitchen
Wring out as much liquid as possible from the zucchini and spinach, so the quiche doesn't become soggy.

P 303

HANDS-ON TIME
15 minutes
TOTAL TIME
1½ hours
MAKES
4 servings

ASPARAGUS & GRUYÈRE CUPS

INGREDIENTS

ASPARAGUS & GRUYÈRE CUPS

2½ cups	cubed day-old crusty French bread or Italian bread
half	bunch (about 450 g bunch) asparagus, trimmed and cut in bite-size pieces
⅔ cup	shredded Gruyère cheese
1 tbsp	chopped fresh chives
5	eggs
1 cup	milk
1 tbsp	Dijon mustard
pinch	each salt and pepper

WATERCRESS SALAD

3 tbsp	extra-virgin olive oil
1 tbsp	white or red wine vinegar
1 tsp	Dijon mustard
½ tsp	liquid honey
pinch	each salt and pepper
1	bunch watercress, stemmed
1 cup	grape tomatoes, halved
1	shallot, thinly sliced

DIRECTIONS

ASPARAGUS & GRUYÈRE CUPS In bowl, toss together bread, asparagus, all but ¼ cup of the Gruyère and the chives. Divide among 4 greased 1-cup ramekins.

In separate bowl, whisk together eggs, milk, mustard, salt and pepper; pour generous ½ cup into each ramekin. Sprinkle with remaining Gruyère. Cover and refrigerate for 1 hour. *(Make-ahead: Refrigerate for up to 24 hours.)* Bake on rimmed baking sheet in 425°F oven until puffed and slightly jiggly, about 20 minutes.

WATERCRESS SALAD Meanwhile, in large bowl, whisk together oil, vinegar, mustard, honey, salt and pepper. Add watercress, tomatoes and shallot; toss to coat. Serve with Asparagus & Gruyère Cups.

NUTRITIONAL INFORMATION, PER SERVING: about 405 cal, 20 g pro, 25 g total fat (8 g sat. fat), 24 g carb (2 g dietary fibre, 6 g sugar), 266 mg chol, 452 mg sodium, 506 mg potassium. % RDI: 34% calcium, 19% iron, 41% vit A, 42% vit C, 63% folate.

Tip from the Test Kitchen

Wash and dry watercress thoroughly—the leaves can easily trap dirt.

LOADED CHEDDAR BROCCOLI POTATOES
WITH TOSSED SALAD

HANDS-ON TIME
20 minutes
TOTAL TIME
1¾ hours
MAKES
4 servings

INGREDIENTS

POTATOES

4	large yellow-fleshed potatoes (about 900 g total)
1	clove garlic, minced
¼ tsp	each salt and pepper
1½ cups	chopped broccoli florets (about 120 g)
1	carrot, peeled and grated
half	sweet red pepper, finely diced
1½ cups	shredded Cheddar cheese
½ cup	light sour cream
1	green onion, thinly sliced

TOSSED SALAD

4 tsp	olive oil
2 tsp	balsamic vinegar
pinch	each salt and pepper
5 cups	lightly packed baby salad greens
½ cup	grape tomatoes or cherry tomatoes, halved

DIRECTIONS

POTATOES Using fork, prick potatoes several times. Bake in 400°F oven until fork-tender, about 1 hour. (Or microwave on high until fork-tender, about 7 minutes.) Set aside until cool enough to handle.

Cut potatoes in half lengthwise; scoop flesh into bowl, leaving ¼-inch thick shells. Using potato masher, mash flesh with garlic, salt and pepper until smooth. Stir in broccoli, carrot, red pepper and ⅔ cup of the Cheddar. Spoon into potato shells, packing gently. Bake on parchment paper–lined baking sheet in 400°F oven for 15 minutes. Sprinkle with remaining Cheddar; bake until melted, about 10 minutes. Top with sour cream and green onion.

TOSSED SALAD Meanwhile, in large bowl, whisk together oil, vinegar, salt and pepper; toss with salad greens and tomatoes. Serve with potatoes.

NUTRITIONAL INFORMATION, PER SERVING: about 459 cal, 20 g pro, 21 g total fat (11 g sat. fat), 51 g carb (7 g dietary fibre, 8 g sugar), 49 mg chol, 502 mg sodium, 1,565 mg potassium. % RDI: 43% calcium, 27% iron, 119% vit A, 127% vit C, 81% folate.

HANDS-ON TIME
20 minutes
TOTAL TIME
30 minutes
MAKES
4 servings

EGGS POACHED IN TOMATO & FENNEL SAUCE

INGREDIENTS

2 tsp	olive oil
1	small bulb fennel, trimmed, cored and thinly sliced
2	green onions, sliced (white and light green parts separated)
2 cups	Fresh Tomato Sauce (page 49) or good-quality plain tomato sauce
1 tsp	sherry vinegar or red wine vinegar
½ tsp	granulated sugar
4	eggs
pinch	each salt and pepper

DIRECTIONS

In large skillet, heat oil over medium heat; cook fennel and ½ cup water, stirring occasionally, until fennel is softened and water has evaporated, about 15 minutes. Add white parts of green onions; cook, stirring, until fragrant, about 1 minute.

Stir in tomato sauce, vinegar and sugar. Bring to boil; reduce heat to simmer.

Using back of spoon, make 4 wells in sauce; gently break 1 egg into each. Sprinkle with salt and pepper. Simmer, partially covered, until egg whites are set but yolks are still slightly runny, about 9 minutes. Sprinkle with green parts of green onions.

NUTRITIONAL INFORMATION, PER SERVING: about 201 cal, 9 g pro, 13 g total fat (3 g sat. fat), 14 g carb (4 g dietary fibre, 9 g sugar), 193 mg chol, 247 mg sodium, 775 mg potassium. % RDI: 7% calcium, 14% iron, 24% vit A, 45% vit C, 28% folate.

Tip from the Test Kitchen

To avoid getting any bits of shell in the tomato-fennel sauce, crack each egg into a small bowl before tipping it into a well.

COUSCOUS & CHEESE-STUFFED ZUCCHINI
P 241

Complete Sides | 9

Side dishes may be members of the supporting cast, rounding out a meal and balancing flavours while letting the main course shine—but often it's the sides, not the mains, that become the must-have dishes at holiday dinners. Looking for some new family favourites? You'll find them in our Tested-Till-Perfect sides.

ROASTED LEEK & ENDIVE
WITH CITRUS DRESSING

HANDS-ON TIME
10 minutes

TOTAL TIME
40 minutes

MAKES
6 to 8 servings

INGREDIENTS

CITRUS DRESSING

1 tbsp	chopped fresh parsley
1 tbsp	olive oil
1 tsp	grated orange zest
1½ tsp	orange juice
1½ tsp	lemon juice
1 tsp	liquid honey
half	clove garlic, grated
pinch	each salt and pepper

LEEK & ENDIVE

4	leeks (white and light green parts only), trimmed and halved lengthwise
3	heads Belgian endive, halved lengthwise
1 tbsp	olive oil
pinch	each salt and pepper

DIRECTIONS

CITRUS DRESSING Whisk together parsley, oil, orange zest, orange juice, lemon juice, honey, garlic, salt and pepper. *(Make-ahead: Refrigerate in airtight container for up to 24 hours.)*

LEEK AND ENDIVE In large bowl, toss together leeks, endives, oil, salt and pepper. Spread on foil-lined rimmed baking sheet. Roast in 425°F oven, turning once, until tender and lightly golden, about 25 minutes. Let cool for 5 minutes.

In large bowl, toss citrus dressing with leek mixture.

NUTRITIONAL INFORMATION, PER EACH OF 8 SERVINGS: about 55 cal, 1 g pro, 4 g total fat (1 g sat. fat), 6 g carb (1 g dietary fibre, 2 g sugar), 0 mg chol, 43 mg sodium, 94 mg potassium. % RDI: 2% calcium, 6% iron, 1% vit A, 8% vit C, 9% folate.

Tip from the Test Kitchen

To get some prep done in advance, halve and wash the leeks ahead of time. Be sure to spread out the leeks and endives on the baking sheet, so everything has room to roast.

SLOW COOKER DAL

HANDS-ON TIME
20 minutes
TOTAL TIME
8¼ hours
MAKES
6 to 8 servings

INGREDIENTS

2	onions
2 cups	dried green lentils, rinsed
2	tomatoes, seeded and chopped
1	jalapeño pepper, seeded and sliced
4	cloves garlic, minced
4 tsp	minced fresh ginger
1 tbsp	each cumin seeds and ground coriander
¼ cup	butter
1 tbsp	lemon juice
1½ tsp	salt
½ tsp	pepper
½ cup	plain Balkan-style yogurt
¼ cup	chopped fresh cilantro

DIRECTIONS

Slice 1 of the onions; set aside. Finely chop remaining onion.

In slow cooker, combine chopped onion, lentils, half of the tomatoes, the jalapeño pepper, garlic, ginger and half each of the cumin seeds and coriander. Stir in 6 cups water. Cover and cook on low until lentils are tender, 8 to 10 hours.

Using immersion blender, purée mixture to desired consistency and thickness, leaving some lentils whole. *(Make-ahead: Refrigerate in airtight container for up to 24 hours or freeze for up to 3 weeks; reheat before continuing with recipe.)*

Meanwhile, in skillet, melt butter over medium heat; cook sliced onion, stirring, until dark golden, about 7 minutes. Add remaining cumin seeds and coriander; cook, stirring, until fragrant, about 1 minute. Stir in lemon juice, salt and pepper.

Stir onion mixture into slow cooker. Serve dal with yogurt, cilantro and remaining tomatoes.

NUTRITIONAL INFORMATION, PER EACH OF 8 SERVINGS: about 251 cal, 14 g pro, 7 g total fat (4 g sat. fat), 35 g carb (7 g dietary fibre, 5 g sugar), 18 mg chol, 486 mg sodium, 720 mg potassium. % RDI: 6% calcium, 37% iron, 10% vit A, 18% vit C, 119% folate.

Tip from the Test Kitchen

Green lentils hold their shape even after hours of cooking, so they're ideal for slow cooker recipes.

SWISS CHARD
WITH FRIZZLED ONIONS

HANDS-ON TIME
35 minutes
TOTAL TIME
35 minutes
MAKES
8 to 10 servings

INGREDIENTS

3	bunches Swiss chard, stems and leaves separated
3 cups	thinly sliced onion (about 1 large)
¼ cup	cornstarch
½ tsp	salt
	vegetable oil for frying
2 tbsp	olive oil
6	cloves garlic, thinly sliced
pinch	hot pepper flakes
¼ tsp	pepper
1 tbsp	lemon juice
½ tsp	grainy mustard
½ tsp	liquid honey

DIRECTIONS

Cut Swiss chard stems into ½-inch lengths; coarsely chop Swiss chard leaves. Set aside.

In large bowl, sprinkle onion with cornstarch and pinch of the salt; toss to coat. Shake off any excess.

In cast-iron or heavy-bottomed skillet, add enough vegetable oil to come ¼ inch up side; heat over medium heat. Working in batches, cook onions, stirring occasionally, until crisp and golden, 2 to 3 minutes. Using slotted spoon, remove to paper towel–lined plate to drain. *(Make-ahead: Store at room temperature for up to 2 hours.)*

In large nonstick skillet, heat together olive oil, garlic and hot pepper flakes over medium heat; cook, stirring often, until fragrant and edges of garlic are golden, about 2 minutes. Add Swiss chard stems, remaining salt and the pepper; cook, stirring occasionally, until tender-crisp, 8 to 10 minutes. Add half of the Swiss chard leaves; cook, stirring, until beginning to wilt, about 1 minute. Add remaining Swiss chard leaves; cook, stirring, until wilted, about 4 minutes.

In small bowl, whisk together lemon juice, mustard and honey. Stir into Swiss chard mixture. Scrape into bowl; top with onions.

NUTRITIONAL INFORMATION, PER EACH OF 10 SERVINGS: about 129 cal, 2 g pro, 10 g total fat (1 g sat. fat), 10 g carb (2 g dietary fibre, 3 g sugar), 0 mg chol, 254 mg sodium, 470 mg potassium. % RDI: 5% calcium, 14% iron, 46% vit A, 27% vit C, 5% folate.

COUSCOUS & CHEESE–STUFFED ZUCCHINI

HANDS-ON TIME
10 minutes

TOTAL TIME
40 minutes

MAKES
6-8 servings

INGREDIENTS

1 tbsp	butter
2	shallots, diced
1	clove garlic, minced
1	tomato, seeded and chopped
¼ tsp	each salt and pepper
½ cup	vegetable broth
½ cup	whole wheat couscous
1 cup	shredded Gouda cheese
3 tbsp	fresh basil leaves, thinly sliced
1 tbsp	each chopped fresh parsley and fresh oregano
6–8	small zucchini (about 675 g total)

DIRECTIONS

In saucepan, melt butter over medium-high heat; cook shallots and garlic until softened, about 3 minutes. Add tomato and pinch each of the salt and pepper; cook for 1 minute.

Add broth and bring to boil; stir in couscous. Cover and remove from heat; let stand for 5 minutes. Fluff with fork. Stir in ⅔ cup of the Gouda, the basil, parsley and oregano.

Meanwhile, trim ends off zucchini; slice lengthwise in half. Using melon baller or spoon, scoop out pulp, leaving scant ½-inch thick walls. Sprinkle with remaining salt and pepper.

Divide couscous mixture among zucchini; sprinkle with remaining cheese. Place on baking sheet and cover with foil; bake in 400°F oven until fork-tender, 25 to 30 minutes.

NUTRITIONAL INFORMATION, PER EACH OF 8 SERVINGS: about 124 cal, 6 g pro, 6 g total fat (4 g sat. fat), 14 g carb (3 g dietary fibre, 2 g sugar), 21 mg chol, 248 mg sodium, 258 mg potassium. % RDI: 11% calcium, 6% iron, 14% vit A, 9% vit C, 9% folate.

Tip from the Test Kitchen

To serve this recipe as a main dish, simply divide the filling among 4 medium zucchini.

P 234

VEGAN

ROASTED CILANTRO LIME SQUASH

HANDS-ON TIME 10 minutes

TOTAL TIME 35 minutes

MAKES 4 to 6 servings

INGREDIENTS

2	acorn squash, halved, seeded and cut in 1-inch wedges
3 tbsp	Lemongrass Chili Oil (see recipe, right)
½ tsp	each salt and pepper
3 tbsp	chopped fresh cilantro
2 tbsp	lime juice

DIRECTIONS

Toss together squash, oil, salt and pepper; spread on foil-lined rimmed baking sheet. Roast in 425°F oven, turning once, until tender and golden, 25 to 30 minutes. Sprinkle with cilantro and lime juice. Garnish with additional cilantro to taste.

NUTRITIONAL INFORMATION, PER EACH OF 6 SERVINGS: about 123 cal, 2 g pro, 7 g total fat (1 g sat. fat), 17 g carb (2 g dietary fibre, 3 g sugar), 0 mg chol, 197 mg sodium, 468 mg potassium. % RDI: 5% calcium, 7% iron, 5% vit A, 20% vit C, 8% folate.

VEGAN

LEMONGRASS CHILI OIL

HANDS-ON TIME 20 minutes

TOTAL TIME 35 minutes

MAKES 5 tbsp

INGREDIENTS

1	stalk lemongrass
⅓ cup	vegetable oil
3	fresh red finger chili peppers, sliced
4	cloves garlic, smashed

DIRECTIONS

Cut lemongrass into 1½-inch pieces. Smash with chef's knife. In small saucepan, cook lemongrass, oil, chili peppers and garlic over medium heat, stirring occasionally, until fragrant, about 15 minutes. Let cool for 15 minutes. Strain. *(Make-ahead: Refrigerate in airtight container for up to 5 days.)*

NUTRITIONAL INFORMATION, PER 1 TSP: about 43 cal, 0 g pro, 5 g total fat (trace sat. fat), 0 g carb (0 g dietary fibre, 0 g sugar), 0 mg chol, 0 mg sodium, 1 mg potassium.

ROASTED CILANTRO LIME SQUASH

HANDS-ON TIME
15 minutes

TOTAL TIME
40 minutes

MAKES
4 servings

VEGAN

CRUNCHY CURRY RICE & SQUASH

INGREDIENTS

4 cups	cubed (½ inch) seeded peeled butternut, turban, acorn or kabocha squash
1 tbsp	olive oil
¼ tsp	each salt and pepper
¼ tsp	ground cumin
1	onion, chopped
2	cloves garlic, chopped
1 cup	basmati rice
1	cinnamon stick
2 tsp	curry powder
2 cups	sodium-reduced vegetable broth
⅓ cup	chopped fresh cilantro
¼ cup	roasted almonds, chopped
2 tsp	lemon juice
¼ cup	fresh pomegranate seeds

DIRECTIONS

On greased rimmed baking sheet, toss together squash, half each of the oil, salt and pepper, and the cumin. Roast in 425°F oven, turning once, until tender and golden, about 20 minutes.

Meanwhile, in saucepan, heat remaining oil over medium heat; cook onion, garlic and remaining salt and pepper, stirring often, until onion is softened, about 3 minutes.

Add rice, cinnamon stick and curry powder; stir to coat. Add broth and bring to boil. Reduce heat, cover and simmer until rice is tender and no liquid remains, about 12 minutes. Let stand, covered, for 5 minutes; fluff with fork. Discard cinnamon stick. Stir in squash, cilantro, almonds and lemon juice. Top with pomegranate seeds.

NUTRITIONAL INFORMATION, PER SERVING: about 353 cal, 9 g pro, 10 g total fat (1 g sat. fat), 61 g carb (5 g dietary fibre, 7 g sugar), 0 mg chol, 450 mg sodium, 659 mg potassium. % RDI: 12% calcium, 15% iron, 175% vit A, 45% vit C, 20% folate.

Tip from the Test Kitchen

If you can't find a fresh pomegranate, add the same amount of golden raisins, dried currants or chopped dried apricots instead.

HANDS-ON TIME
15 minutes
TOTAL TIME
1 hour
MAKES
16 servings

TWIN PEAS
WITH ROASTED GARLIC BUTTER

INGREDIENTS

ROASTED GARLIC BUTTER

1	head garlic
1 tsp	olive oil
¼ cup	butter, softened

PEAS

8 cups	whole sugar snap peas (about 750 g), trimmed
4 cups	frozen green peas
1 tsp	salt
¼ tsp	pepper
2 tbsp	chopped fresh tarragon (optional)

DIRECTIONS

ROASTED GARLIC BUTTER Slice off top third of garlic head to expose cloves; discard. Place garlic head on small square of foil; drizzle with oil and fold foil over to seal. Roast in 375°F oven until tender, about 45 minutes. Let cool slightly. Squeeze cloves into small bowl; stir in butter until well combined. *(Make-ahead: Cover with plastic wrap; refrigerate for up to 2 days. Soften at room temperature for 20 minutes before continuing with recipe.)*

PEAS In large saucepan of boiling salted water, cook snap peas for 1 minute; add frozen peas and cook until heated through, about 30 seconds. Drain well.

In large bowl, toss together peas, garlic butter, salt and pepper until butter is melted and well combined. Sprinkle with tarragon (if using).

NUTRITIONAL INFORMATION, PER SERVING: about 74 cal, 3 g pro, 3 g total fat (2 g sat. fat), 8 g carb (3 g dietary fibre, 3 g sugar), 8 mg chol, 361 mg sodium, 146 mg potassium. % RDI: 3% calcium, 10% iron, 13% vit A, 38% vit C, 14% folate.

Tip from the Test Kitchen

This recipe is easily halved or quartered for a smaller group.

MEDITERRANEAN BAKED PEPPERS

HANDS-ON TIME
10 minutes

TOTAL TIME
30 MINUTES

MAKES
4 servings

INGREDIENTS

2	sweet peppers (red, orange and/or yellow), halved and cored
2 tsp	olive oil
1	small clove garlic, thinly sliced
½ tsp	dried oregano
¼ tsp	grated lemon zest
pinch	each salt and pepper
⅓ cup	crumbled or chopped feta cheese
1 tbsp	chopped fresh parsley
1 tsp	lemon juice

DIRECTIONS

Cut each pepper half into thirds. In bowl, toss together peppers, oil, garlic, oregano, lemon zest, salt and pepper. Arrange in 12-cup baking dish; sprinkle with feta. Bake in 425°F oven until peppers are tender, about 20 minutes. Sprinkle with parsley and drizzle with lemon juice.

NUTRITIONAL INFORMATION, PER SERVING: about 71 cal, 3 g pro, 5 g total fat (2 g sat. fat), 5 g carb (1 g dietary fibre, 3 g sugar), 11 mg chol, 141 mg sodium, 116 mg potassium. % RDI: 7% calcium, 4% iron, 19% vit A, 167% vit C, 7% folate.

Tip from the Test Kitchen

To test if the peppers are fully cooked, insert the tip of a knife into the pepper flesh—it should slide through with minimal resistance.

HANDS-ON TIME
30 minutes
TOTAL TIME
1 hour
MAKES
8 servings

AFGHAN-STYLE BAKED EGGPLANT
WITH MINT-GARLIC YOGURT SAUCE

INGREDIENTS

MINT-GARLIC YOGURT SAUCE

2	cloves garlic
½ tsp	salt
1 cup	Balkan-style plain yogurt
2 tbsp	chopped fresh mint

BAKED EGGPLANT

3	eggplants (1.5 kg total)
⅓ cup	olive oil
1 tsp	each salt and pepper
1	onion, minced
3	cloves garlic, minced
1	can (796 mL) diced tomatoes, drained
2 tbsp	tomato paste
1 tsp	turmeric
¼ tsp	cayenne pepper
3 tbsp	chopped fresh cilantro

DIRECTIONS

MINT-GARLIC YOGURT SAUCE On cutting board and using side of knife, mash garlic with salt into smooth paste. Whisk together yogurt, garlic paste and all but 2 tsp of the mint.

BAKED EGGPLANT Cut eggplants into ½-inch thick rounds. Whisk ¼ cup of the oil with ½ tsp each of the salt and pepper; brush over eggplant slices. Arrange in single layer on foil-lined rimmed baking sheets; broil, 1 sheet at a time and turning once, until softened and browned and edges are wrinkled, about 10 minutes.

Meanwhile, in skillet, heat remaining oil over medium-high heat; cook onion and garlic until golden, about 5 minutes. Add tomatoes, tomato paste, turmeric, cayenne pepper and remaining salt and pepper; bring to boil. Reduce heat and simmer until sauce is thick, about 8 minutes.

Arrange half of the eggplant slices in greased 13- × 9-inch glass baking dish; top with 1 cup of the tomato sauce. Repeat with remaining eggplant and tomato sauce. Sprinkle with 2 tbsp of the cilantro.

Bake in 375°F oven until bubbly, about 25 minutes. Let cool for 15 minutes. Before serving, pour Mint-Garlic Yogurt Sauce over eggplant; sprinkle with remaining mint and cilantro.

NUTRITIONAL INFORMATION, PER SERVING: about 169 cal, 4 g pro, 10 g total fat (2 g sat. fat), 18 g carb (5 g dietary fibre), 3 mg chol, 556 mg sodium. % RDI: 8% calcium, 10% iron, 7% vit A, 27% vit C, 16% folate.

Tip from the Test Kitchen

Choose eggplants that feel plump and heavy for their size, with a dark purple, glossy skin. They should be free of scars or soft spots, with a fresh green cap. Eggplants should be used quickly but can be stored in the refrigerator, covered in plastic wrap, for up to 5 days.

ARUGULA & BULGUR–STUFFED TOMATOES

HANDS-ON TIME
15 minutes

TOTAL TIME
45 minutes

MAKES
4 servings

INGREDIENTS

¾ cup	whole grain bulgur
4 cups	baby arugula
⅓ cup	light cream cheese, softened
½ cup	chopped fresh dill
½ cup	chopped fresh mint
1 tbsp	lemon juice
1	clove garlic, minced
¾ tsp	salt
½ tsp	pepper
1 cup	shredded smoked Gouda cheese or white Cheddar cheese
4	large beefsteak tomatoes

DIRECTIONS

In saucepan, bring 1½ cups water to boil. Stir in bulgur; cover and simmer until tender and water is absorbed, about 15 minutes.

Add arugula and cream cheese; stir until arugula is wilted and cheese is melted. Add dill, mint, lemon juice, garlic, ½ tsp of the salt and pepper. Stir in ½ cup of the Gouda.

Meanwhile, cut thin slice from stem ends of tomatoes; using melon baller or small spoon, scoop out centres. Sprinkle cavities with remaining salt. Place, cut side down, on towel to drain, about 5 minutes.

Divide bulgur mixture evenly among tomato cavities, packing firmly. Sprinkle with remaining Gouda.

Bake on baking sheet in 375°F oven until tomato skin is wilted and cheese is golden brown, about 20 minutes.

NUTRITIONAL INFORMATION, PER SERVING: about 284 cal, 16 g pro, 13 g total fat (8 g sat. fat), 31 g carb (6 g dietary fibre, 6 g sugar), 44 mg chol, 751 mg sodium, 791 mg potassium. % RDI: 32% calcium, 22% iron, 37% vit A, 45% vit C, 33% folate.

HANDS-ON TIME
25 minutes
TOTAL TIME
30 minutes
MAKES
4 servings

VEGAN

GREEN BEANS
WITH MUSTARD SEED & ONIONS

INGREDIENTS

450 g	green beans, trimmed and halved diagonally
4 tsp	vegetable oil
2	onions, thinly sliced
2 tsp	black or yellow mustard seeds
1 tsp	ground coriander
¼ tsp	ground cumin
pinch	each salt and pepper
½ cup	sodium-reduced vegetable broth
1 tsp	white wine vinegar
¼ tsp	Asian chili sauce (such as sriracha)

DIRECTIONS

In saucepan of boiling salted water, cook beans until tender-crisp, about 4 minutes. Drain and set aside.

Meanwhile, in nonstick skillet, heat oil over medium heat; cook onions and mustard seeds, stirring occasionally, until onions are softened and golden, about 15 minutes. Stir in coriander, cumin, salt and pepper; cook, stirring, until fragrant, about 1 minute.

Stir in green beans and vegetable broth; cook, stirring occasionally, until almost no liquid remains, about 2 minutes. Stir in vinegar and chili sauce.

NUTRITIONAL INFORMATION, PER SERVING: about 107 cal, 3 g pro, 6 g total fat (1 g sat. fat), 13 g carb (4 g dietary fibre, 4 g sugar), 0 mg chol, 77 mg sodium, 242 mg potassium. % RDI: 6% calcium, 7% iron, 7% vit A, 23% vit C, 20% folate.

Tip from the Test Kitchen

To trim green beans quickly, grab a handful of beans with the stems pointing upward and use kitchen shears to snip off the stem ends.

HONEY-LIME CARROTS
WITH CIPOLLINI ONIONS

HANDS-ON TIME
1 hour
TOTAL TIME
1 hour
MAKES
8 servings

INGREDIENTS

2	bags (each 175 g) cipollini onions
2 tbsp	butter
750 g	carrots
1 tbsp	liquid honey
½ tsp	salt
pinch	pepper
½ tsp	grated lime zest
1 tbsp	lime juice

DIRECTIONS

In saucepan of boiling water, cook onions until skins begin to loosen, about 1 minute. Drain and rinse under cold water. Peel onions, trimming root ends if necessary. Cut onions through root end into quarters.

In large skillet, melt one-quarter of the butter over medium heat; cook onions, stirring occasionally, until softened and golden, about 40 minutes. If onions begin to stick to pan, add 1 to 2 tbsp water, as needed (about every 4 minutes). *(Make-ahead: Refrigerate in airtight container for up to 2 days.)*

While onions are cooking, peel carrots and cut crosswise on the diagonal into 2-inch lengths. Cut lengthwise into ½-inch thick pieces. In large saucepan of boiling salted water, cook carrots until tender-crisp, about 8 minutes. Drain and transfer to bowl of ice water to chill. Drain and pat dry with clean towel. *(Make-ahead: Refrigerate in airtight container for up to 24 hours.)*

In large skillet, melt remaining butter over medium-high heat; cook carrots, stirring often, until light golden, about 4 minutes. Stir in onions, honey, salt and pepper; cook, stirring often, just until carrots are tender, about 2 minutes. Remove from heat; stir in lime zest and lime juice.

NUTRITIONAL INFORMATION, PER SERVING: about 76 cal, 1 g pro, 3 g total fat (2 g sat. fat), 12 g carb (3 g dietary fibre, 6 g sugar), 8 mg chol, 361 mg sodium, 229 mg potassium. % RDI: 3% calcium, 3% iron, 116% vit A, 8% vit C, 7% folate.

Tip from the Test Kitchen
Cippolini onions become delicate after you peel off their skins, so stir and shake the pan very gently until they're softened and golden. If you can't find them, substitute with halved pearl onions.

HANDS-ON TIME
15 minutes
TOTAL TIME
15 minutes
MAKES
4 to 6 servings

CARDAMOM- & GINGER-GLAZED CARROTS

INGREDIENTS

2 tbsp	butter
2	cloves garlic, minced
1 tbsp	minced fresh ginger
5	green cardamom pods
2	bunches thin carrots (stem-on), trimmed and halved lengthwise
¼ tsp	each salt and pepper
pinch	nutmeg
4 tsp	liquid honey
1 tbsp	chopped fresh tarragon
2 tsp	lemon juice

DIRECTIONS

In large nonstick skillet, melt butter over medium heat; cook garlic, ginger and cardamom pods, stirring, until fragrant, about 1 minute. Add carrots, salt, pepper and nutmeg; cook, stirring occasionally, until slightly softened, about 4 minutes.

Add honey and ½ cup water; cook, stirring often, until carrots are tender-crisp and most of the liquid has evaporated, about 6 minutes. Remove from heat. Discard cardamom pods. Stir in tarragon and lemon juice.

NUTRITIONAL INFORMATION, PER EACH OF 6 SERVINGS: about 78 cal, 1 g pro, 4 g total fat (2 g sat. fat), 11 g carb (2 g dietary fibre, 7 g sugar), 10 mg chol, 168 mg sodium, 225 mg potassium. % RDI: 2% calcium, 2% iron, 94% vit A, 7% vit C, 4% folate.

Tip from the Test Kitchen

If you find the anise-like flavour of fresh tarragon overwhelming, substitute with parsley, which is milder in flavour. If you can't find whole cardamom pods, use a generous pinch of ground cardamom instead.

FROM TOP
CRUNCHY PARMESAN-TOPPED DOUBLE POTATO MASH P 258 AND **CREAMED BRUSSELS SPROUTS**

HANDS-ON TIME
25 minutes

TOTAL TIME
25 minutes

MAKES
6 to 8 servings

CREAMED BRUSSELS SPROUTS

INGREDIENTS

1½ tsp	butter
1	large clove garlic, minced
1	shallot, thinly sliced
450 g	brussels sprouts, trimmed and thinly sliced lengthwise
¼ cup	sodium-reduced vegetable broth
⅓ cup	whipping cream (35%)
¼ tsp	each salt and pepper

DIRECTIONS

In large saucepan or skillet, heat butter over medium heat; cook garlic and shallot, stirring often, until shallot is softened, about 2 minutes.

Add brussels sprouts and broth; cook, stirring often, until sprouts are softened, about 5 minutes.

Stir in cream, salt and pepper; cook, stirring, until reduced and brussels sprouts are tender, about 3 minutes.

NUTRITIONAL INFORMATION, PER EACH OF 8 SERVINGS: about 61 cal, 2 g pro, 5 g total fat (3 g sat. fat), 5 g carb (2 g dietary fibre, 1 g sugar), 14 mg chol, 110 mg sodium, 192 mg potassium. % RDI: 3% calcium, 5% iron, 8% vit A, 58% vit C, 16% folate.

VARIATION
CREAMED CABBAGE
Substitute green cabbage for brussels sprouts.

CRUNCHY PARMESAN-TOPPED DOUBLE POTATO MASH

HANDS-ON TIME
25 minutes

TOTAL TIME
25 minutes

MAKES
6 to 8 servings

INGREDIENTS

DOUBLE POTATO MASH

575 g	russet potatoes, peeled and cubed (about 5)
3	cloves garlic
575 g	sweet potatoes, peeled and cubed (about 4)
¼ cup	milk
2 tbsp	chopped fresh chives
2 tbsp	butter, softened
pinch	each salt and pepper

CRUNCHY PARMESAN TOPPING

½ cup	fresh bread crumbs
¼ cup	grated Parmesan cheese
1 tbsp	chopped fresh chives
1 tbsp	butter, melted

DIRECTIONS

DOUBLE POTATO MASH In large saucepan of boiling lightly salted water, cook russet potatoes and garlic just until beginning to soften, about 4 minutes.

Add sweet potatoes; cook until tender, about 5 minutes. Drain and return to pot. Mash with milk, chives, butter, salt and pepper.

Spread in lightly greased 8- × 8-inch baking dish. *(Make-ahead: Cover with foil; refrigerate for up to 24 hours. Let stand at room temperature for 1½ hours; bake, covered, in 425°F oven until warmed through, about 40 minutes.)*

CRUNCHY PARMESAN TOPPING Stir together bread crumbs, Parmesan, chives and butter; sprinkle over potato mixture. Broil until golden brown, about 1 minute.

NUTRITIONAL INFORMATION, PER EACH OF 8 SERVINGS: about 158 cal, 4 g pro, 6 g total fat (3 g sat. fat), 24 g carb (2 g dietary fibre, 5 g sugar), 15 mg chol, 438 mg sodium, 386 mg potassium. % RDI: 7% calcium, 8% iron, 103% vit A, 28% vit C, 7% folate.

VARIATION

CRUNCHY PARMESAN-TOPPED POTATO & CELERY ROOT MASH

Substitute celery root for sweet potatoes.

Tip from the Test Kitchen

If you're making this recipe ahead of time, choose a large shallow ovenproof dish, which will decrease the time needed to warm it in the oven while the turkey is resting.

P 256

SMOOTH & CREAMY MASHED POTATOES

HANDS-ON TIME
15 minutes

TOTAL TIME
30 minutes

MAKES
8 to 10 servings

INGREDIENTS

2.25 kg	russet potatoes, peeled and cut in chunks
1¼ cups	10% cream
¼ cup	butter
1 tsp	salt
¼ tsp	pepper

DIRECTIONS

In saucepan of boiling lightly salted water, cook potatoes until fork-tender, about 15 minutes; drain well. Press potatoes through potato ricer. *(Make-ahead: Spread onto parchment paper–lined rimmed baking sheet; let cool. Cover and refrigerate for up to 24 hours. Continue with recipe, adding 8 minutes to cook time.)*

In large saucepan, heat together cream, butter, salt and pepper over medium heat until butter is melted. Add potatoes; cook, stirring often, until smooth and hot, about 4 minutes.

NUTRITIONAL INFORMATION, PER EACH OF 10 SERVINGS: about 226 cal, 5 g pro, 8 g total fat (5 g sat. fat), 36 g carb (2 g dietary fibre, 1 g sugar), 22 mg chol, 730 mg sodium, 751 mg potassium. % RDI: 5% calcium, 11% iron, 6% vit A, 47% vit C, 11% folate.

Tip from the Test Kitchen

If you like super-fluffy, smooth mashed potatoes, a ricer is the tool you need; wavy, wire mashers are better for a rustic mash with more texture.

RAINBOW ROOT FRIES
WITH CHIVE MAYO

HANDS-ON TIME
20 minutes
TOTAL TIME
1 hour
MAKES
4 to 6 servings

INGREDIENTS

ROOT FRIES

1	sweet potato
1	small celery root
1	small rutabaga
1	red beet
2 tbsp	olive oil
1 tsp	each garlic powder and dried rosemary
½ tsp	pepper
¼ tsp	salt
1 tbsp	chopped fresh parsley

CHIVE MAYO

⅓ cup	mayonnaise
1 tbsp	chopped fresh chives
1	small clove garlic, finely grated or pressed
1 tsp	grainy mustard
1 tsp	lemon juice

DIRECTIONS

ROOT FRIES Peel and cut sweet potato, celery root and rutabaga lengthwise into scant ½-inch thick sticks; cut in half crosswise. Transfer to bowl. Set aside.

Peel and cut beet into scant ½-inch thick sticks. Transfer to separate bowl.

Drizzle sweet potato, celery root, rutabaga and beet with oil. Sprinkle with garlic powder, rosemary, salt and pepper; toss each to coat.

Arrange sweet potato, celery root, rutabaga and beet in single layer on parchment paper–lined rimmed baking sheets. Bake in top and bottom thirds of 425°F oven, turning fries once and switching and rotating pans halfway through, until tender and golden, 40 to 45 minutes. Sprinkle with parsley.

CHIVE MAYO While fries are baking, in small bowl, whisk together mayonnaise, chives, garlic, mustard and lemon juice. *(Make-ahead: Refrigerate in airtight container for up to 2 days.)* Serve with fries.

NUTRITIONAL INFORMATION, PER EACH OF 6 SERVINGS: about 245 cal, 4 g pro, 15 g total fat (2 g sat. fat), 27 g carb (5 g dietary fibre, 14 g sugar), 5 mg chol, 292 mg sodium, 776 mg potassium. % RDI: 8% calcium, 12% iron, 91% vit A, 50% vit C, 29% folate.

Tip from the Test Kitchen

Keep the beets separated until they're cooked; otherwise they'll stain the other vegetables.

ROASTED WINTER VEGETABLES
WITH MAPLE CANDIED NUTS

HANDS-ON TIME
15 minutes

TOTAL TIME
35 minutes

MAKES
10 to 12 servings

INGREDIENTS

VEGETABLES

600 g	brussels sprouts, trimmed
450 g	parsnips, peeled and cut lengthwise in ½-inch thick wedges
1	small rutabaga (about 450 g), peeled, halved crosswise and cut in ½-inch thick wedges
1	bunch (about 400 g) small carrots, halved diagonally
1	bag (250 g) shallots, halved
¼ cup	olive oil
1 tbsp	chopped fresh thyme
¾ tsp	salt
¼ tsp	pepper

MAPLE CANDIED NUTS

¼ cup	maple syrup
1 tbsp	butter
1 cup	mixed pecan halves and walnut halves, coarsely chopped
1 tsp	chopped fresh thyme
pinch	salt

DIRECTIONS

VEGETABLES In large bowl, toss together brussels spouts, parsnips, rutabaga, carrots, shallots, oil, thyme, salt and pepper. Spread in single layer on 2 lightly greased rimmed baking sheets. Roast in top and bottom thirds of 425°F oven, turning vegetables and switching and rotating pans halfway through, 25 to 30 minutes. Scrape onto serving platter.

MAPLE CANDIED NUTS Meanwhile, in small skillet, heat maple syrup and butter over medium heat, stirring, until butter is melted; bring to boil and cook, stirring occasionally, until thickened, about 5 minutes. Stir in nuts and thyme; cook, stirring, until sticky and liquid is mostly evaporated, about 3 minutes.

Spread in single layer on parchment paper–lined rimmed baking sheet. Let stand until firm, about 10 minutes. Break into bite-size pieces. *(Make-ahead: Store in airtight container for up to 3 days.)* Sprinkle over vegetables.

NUTRITIONAL INFORMATION, PER EACH OF 12 SERVINGS: about 176 cal, 3 g pro, 12 g total fat (2 g sat. fat), 18 g carb (4 g dietary fibre, 7 g sugar), 3 mg chol, 176 mg sodium, 381 mg potassium. % RDI: 5% calcium, 9% iron, 41% vit A, 45% vit C, 22% folate.

Tip from the Test Kitchen

Trim the brussels sprouts to a uniform size, halving any larger pieces so that they cook evenly.

GRILLED CORN
WITH SRIRACHA AIOLI

HANDS-ON TIME
25 minutes
TOTAL TIME
25 minutes
MAKES
8 servings

INGREDIENTS

SRIRACHA AIOLI

3	egg yolks
2 tsp	Dijon mustard
1	clove garlic, pressed or finely grated
¼ tsp	salt
pinch	pepper
½ cup	vegetable oil
¼ cup	extra-virgin olive oil
1 tsp	red wine vinegar
2 tsp	sriracha
1 tbsp	chopped fresh cilantro (optional)

GRILLED CORN

8	corn cobs, husked

DIRECTIONS

SRIRACHA AIOLI In bowl, whisk together egg yolks, mustard, garlic, salt and pepper. Gradually whisk in vegetable oil until mixture is pale yellow and thickened. Gradually whisk in olive oil. Stir in vinegar, sriracha and cilantro (if using). *(Make-ahead: Refrigerate in airtight container for up to 5 days.)*

GRILLED CORN Place corn cobs on lightly greased grill over medium heat; close lid and grill, turning occasionally and brushing each corn cob with 1 tbsp of the aioli during last 5 minutes of grilling, until kernels are deep yellow and tender, 15 to 20 minutes. Serve with remaining aioli.

NUTRITIONAL INFORMATION, PER SERVING: about 388 cal, 7 g pro, 25 g total fat (3 g sat. fat), 43 g carb (5 g dietary fibre, 6 g sugar), 72 mg chol, 134 mg sodium, 430 mg potassium. % RDI: 1% calcium, 10% iron, 8% vit A, 18% vit C, 40% folate.

VARIATION
SRIRACHA MAYONNAISE

Omit egg yolks, salt, vegetable oil, extra-virgin olive oil and red wine vinegar; substitute with 1 cup prepared mayonnaise.

GRILLED PARMESAN CORN

HANDS-ON TIME 25 minutes
TOTAL TIME 25 minutes
MAKES 6 servings

INGREDIENTS

1 tbsp	butter, melted
1 tbsp	olive oil
½ tsp	smoked or sweet paprika
pinch	salt
6	corn cobs, husked
½ cup	grated Parmesan cheese
1 tbsp	chopped fresh parsley

DIRECTIONS

Whisk together butter, oil, paprika and salt; set aside.

Place corn cobs on greased grill over medium-high heat; close lid and grill, turning occasionally, for 8 minutes. Brush corn cobs with some of the butter mixture; grill, turning and brushing with remaining butter mixture, until grill-marked and tender, 12 to 15 minutes. Sprinkle with Parmesan and parsley.

NUTRITIONAL INFORMATION, PER SERVING: about 127 cal, 5 g pro, 7 g total fat (3 g sat. fat), 13 g carb (1 g dietary fibre, 2 g sugar), 12 mg chol, 150 mg sodium, 142 mg potassium. % RDI: 9% calcium, 4% iron, 5% vit A, 7% vit C, 11% folate.

GRILLED GARAM MASALA CORN

HANDS-ON TIME 20 minutes
TOTAL TIME 20 minutes
MAKES 10 servings

INGREDIENTS

⅔ cup	butter, softened
2	green onions, minced
2	cloves garlic, minced
2 tsp	garam masala
½ tsp	pepper
pinch	each cinnamon and salt
10	corn cobs, husked

DIRECTIONS

In small bowl, stir together butter, green onions, garlic, garam masala, pepper, cinnamon and salt. *(Make-ahead: Cover and refrigerate for up to 5 days. Let soften at room temperature for 15 minutes.)*

Place corn cobs on greased grill over medium-high heat; close lid and grill, turning occasionally, for 8 minutes. Continue grilling, brushing occasionally with butter mixture, until grill-marked and tender, 12 to 15 minutes.

NUTRITIONAL INFORMATION, PER SERVING: about 242 cal, 4 g pro, 14 g total fat (8 g sat. fat), 31 g carb (4 g dietary fibre, 4 g sugar), 33 mg chol, 109 mg sodium, 320 mg potassium. % RDI: 1% calcium, 7% iron, 14% vit A, 13% vit C, 26% folate.

HANDS-ON TIME
25 minutes
TOTAL TIME
25 minutes
MAKES
10 servings

JALAPEÑO CORN FRITTERS
WITH CILANTRO SOUR CREAM

INGREDIENTS

CILANTRO SOUR CREAM

⅔ cup	sour cream
2 tbsp	chopped fresh cilantro
2 tsp	lime juice

FRITTERS

3	corn cobs, husked
2	green onions, thinly sliced
1	jalapeño pepper, seeded and minced
½ cup	all-purpose flour
1 tsp	baking powder
½ tsp	salt
¼ tsp	pepper
¼ cup	milk
1	egg, lightly beaten
	vegetable oil for frying

DIRECTIONS

CILANTRO SOUR CREAM In small bowl, stir together sour cream, cilantro and lime juice. Set aside. *(Make-ahead: Cover and refrigerate for up to 4 hours.)*

FRITTERS Cut kernels from corn cobs. In large bowl, stir together corn kernels, green onions, jalapeño pepper, flour, baking powder, salt and pepper. Stir in milk and egg until combined.

In large skillet, add enough oil to come ¼ inch up side; heat over medium heat. Working in batches, drop batter by heaping 1 tbsp into oil, using back of spoon to flatten into discs. Cook, gently turning once, until deep golden, about 5 minutes. Using slotted spoon, remove to paper towel–lined plate to drain; keep warm. Serve with Cilantro Sour Cream.

NUTRITIONAL INFORMATION, PER SERVING: about 183 cal, 4 g pro, 12 g total fat (2 g sat. fat), 17 g carb (1 g dietary fibre, 2 g sugar), 25 mg chol, 173 mg sodium, 170 mg potassium. % RDI: 4% calcium, 5% iron, 5% vit A, 7% vit C, 16% folate.

Tip from the Test Kitchen
Use a splatter screen when frying, as the corn can pop right out of the pan.

CHEESY POLENTA SQUARES

HANDS-ON TIME
20 minutes
TOTAL TIME
1½ hours
MAKES
10 to 12 servings

INGREDIENTS

2 tbsp	butter
2 tsp	dried thyme
2 tsp	dried sage
¼ tsp	garlic powder
¼ tsp	each salt and pepper
pinch	nutmeg
2 cups	sodium-reduced vegetable broth
1 cup	cornmeal
⅓ cup	grated Parmesan cheese
¼ cup	shredded Gruyère cheese
¼ cup	sour cream
1 tbsp	Dijon mustard
1 tbsp	lemon juice
2 tbsp	olive oil
2 tbsp	chopped fresh parsley or fresh chives

DIRECTIONS

In saucepan, melt butter over medium heat; cook thyme, sage, garlic powder, salt, pepper and nutmeg, stirring, until fragrant, about 1 minute. Stir in broth and ⅓ cup water; bring to boil. Reduce heat to medium and gradually whisk in cornmeal; cook, stirring often, until thick enough to mound on spoon, about 5 minutes. Stir in Parmesan and Gruyère until melted, about 30 seconds. Remove from heat; stir in sour cream, mustard and lemon juice.

Scrape polenta into parchment paper–lined 9-inch square cake pan, smoothing top. Let cool slightly, about 15 minutes. Refrigerate until firm, about 1 hour. *(Make-ahead: Refrigerate for up to 48 hours.)* Cut into generous 1-inch squares.

In large skillet, heat half of the oil over medium-high heat; cook half of the polenta, gently turning occasionally, until golden, about 5 minutes. Transfer to serving platter. Repeat with remaining oil and polenta. Sprinkle with parsley.

NUTRITIONAL INFORMATION, PER EACH OF 12 SERVINGS: about 121 cal, 4 g pro, 7 g total fat (3 g sat. fat), 12 g carb (1 g dietary fibre, trace sugar), 12 mg chol, 234 mg sodium, 45 mg potassium. % RDI: 6% calcium, 4% iron, 4% vit A, 2% vit C, 3% folate.

VEGAN

SAUTÉED KALE WITH RAISINS

HANDS-ON TIME 10 minutes
TOTAL TIME 10 minutes
MAKES 8 servings

INGREDIENTS

4 tsp	olive oil
2	large bunches kale, stemmed and chopped
½ cup	golden raisins
¼ tsp	each salt and pepper
2 tbsp	toasted sliced almonds

DIRECTIONS

In large skillet, heat oil over medium-high heat; cook kale, golden raisins, salt, pepper and ½ cup water, stirring, until kale is slightly softened and water has evaporated, about 6 minutes. Sprinkle with toasted sliced almonds.

NUTRITIONAL INFORMATION, PER SERVING: about 47 cal, 1 g pro, 1 g total fat (trace sat. fat), 10 g carb (1 g dietary fibre, 6 g sugar), 0 mg chol, 82 mg sodium, 173 mg potassium. % RDI: 3% calcium, 4% iron, 29% vit A, 37% vit C, 3% folate.

MUSHROOM & SPINACH SAUTÉ

HANDS-ON TIME 10 minutes
TOTAL TIME 10 minutes
MAKES 4 servings

INGREDIENTS

2 tbsp	butter
180 g	chanterelle and/or shiitake mushroom caps, sliced
¼ tsp	each salt and pepper
2	bunches spinach (about 500 g total), stemmed

DIRECTIONS

In large skillet, melt butter over medium-high heat; cook mushrooms and half each of the salt and pepper, stirring, until mushrooms are beginning to soften, about 5 minutes. Add spinach and remaining salt and pepper; cook, stirring, until spinach is wilted, about 2 minutes.

NUTRITIONAL INFORMATION, PER SERVING: about 78 cal, 3 g pro, 6 g total fat (4 g sat. fat), 5 g carb (2 g dietary fibre, 1 g sugar), 15 mg chol, 82 mg sodium, 387 mg potassium. % RDI: 7% calcium, 15% iron, 61% vit A, 8% vit C, 37% folate.

ROASTED CABBAGE WEDGES
WITH BUFFALO SAUCE

HANDS-ON TIME
5 minutes

TOTAL TIME
1½ hours

MAKES
4 servings

INGREDIENTS

half	head green cabbage, cut in 4 wedges
2 tbsp	olive oil
½ tsp	kosher salt
¼ cup	crumbled blue cheese
3 tbsp	2% plain Greek yogurt
2 tbsp	cayenne pepper sauce (such as Frank's RedHot Original)
2 tbsp	buttermilk
¼ tsp	granulated sugar

DIRECTIONS

Arrange cabbage on rimmed baking sheet; brush cabbage all over and between leaves with oil. Sprinkle with salt. Let stand for 1 hour.

Place cast-iron or ovenproof skillet in oven; heat to 450°F. Transfer cabbage to skillet; roast, gently turning once, until tender, about 30 minutes.

While cabbage is roasting, in blender, purée together 3 tbsp of the blue cheese, the yogurt, cayenne pepper sauce, buttermilk and sugar until smooth; drizzle over roasted cabbage. Sprinkle with remaining blue cheese.

NUTRITIONAL INFORMATION, PER SERVING: about 129 cal, 4 g pro, 10 g total fat (3 g sat. fat), 7 g carb (2 g dietary fibre, 5 g sugar), 7 mg chol, 644 mg sodium, 170 mg potassium. % RDI: 11% calcium, 2% iron, 5% vit A, 42% vit C, 13% folate.

Tip from the Test Kitchen
Salting the cabbage in advance draws out some of the liquid from the leaves.

HANDS-ON TIME
30 minutes
TOTAL TIME
30 minutes
MAKES
12 cakes

SOUTHWESTERN CAULIFLOWER CAKES

INGREDIENTS

4 cups	bite-size cauliflower florets (about half a head)
2	eggs
1 tbsp	grainy mustard
1 tsp	chili powder
1	clove garlic, pressed or grated
¼ tsp	each salt and pepper
¾ cup	dried bread crumbs
½ cup	frozen corn kernels
2 tbsp	chopped fresh chives
2 tbsp	olive oil
⅓ cup	light sour cream

DIRECTIONS

In covered steamer basket set over saucepan of boiling water, steam cauliflower until tender, about 5 minutes. Transfer to large bowl. Using potato masher, mash until cauliflower resembles coarse crumbs. Set aside.

In separate bowl, whisk together eggs, mustard, chili powder, garlic, salt and pepper. Add cauliflower, bread crumbs, corn and half of the chives; stir until well combined. Shape by 2 tbsp into twelve 1½-inch wide patties.

In large nonstick skillet, heat oil over medium heat. Working in batches, cook patties, flattening with spatula and turning once, until browned and heated through, about 6 minutes.

Top with sour cream and remaining chives.

NUTRITIONAL INFORMATION, PER CAKE: about 83 cal, 3 g pro, 5 g total fat (1 g sat. fat), 8 g carb (1 g dietary fibre, 1 g sugar), 133 mg chol, 136 mg sodium, 107 mg potassium. % RDI: 3% calcium, 5% iron, 3% vit A, 25% vit C, 14% folate.

SPICED CAULIFLOWER & LEEK PURÉE

HANDS-ON TIME
25 minutes
TOTAL TIME
50 minutes
MAKES
4 servings

INGREDIENTS

8 cups	cauliflower florets (about 1 head)
1 tbsp	olive oil
1 tsp	ground coriander
½ tsp	ground cumin
1 tbsp	butter
2 tsp	chopped fresh thyme
2	leeks (white and light green parts only), halved lengthwise and thinly sliced crosswise
2	cloves garlic, minced
¾ cup	warm milk
1 tbsp	lemon juice
1 tsp	Dijon mustard
¼ tsp	each salt and pepper
2 tsp	chopped fresh chives.

DIRECTIONS

Toss together cauliflower florets, oil, coriander and cumin. Arrange in single layer on lightly greased rimmed baking sheet. Bake in 425°F oven, turning once, until tender and light golden, about 25 minutes.

Meanwhile, in nonstick skillet, melt butter over medium heat; cook thyme, stirring, until fragrant, about 1 minute. Add leeks and garlic; cook, stirring occasionally, for 5 minutes. Add ¼ cup water; cook, stirring occasionally, until leeks are very soft, about 15 minutes. In food processor, purée together leek mixture, cauliflower, milk, lemon juice, mustard, salt and pepper until smooth. Scrape into serving bowl; sprinkle with chives.

NUTRITIONAL INFORMATION, PER SERVING: about 157 cal, 6 g pro, 8 g total fat (3 g sat. fat), 18 g carb (7 g dietary fibre, 7 g sugar), 11 mg chol, 242 mg sodium, 448 mg potassium. % RDI: 12% calcium, 14% iron, 13% vit A, 155% vit C, 50% folate.

Tip from the Test Kitchen

As leeks grow, sand can get trapped between their layers; after halving them, rinse well in a colander.

HANDS-ON TIME
7 minutes

TOTAL TIME
50 minutes

MAKES
4 servings

ROASTED CAULIFLOWER
WITH PARMESAN & CAPERS

INGREDIENTS

8 cups	cauliflower florets (about 1 head)
4 tsp	olive oil
2 tsp	chopped fresh thyme
3 tbsp	grated Parmesan cheese
2 tbsp	chopped fresh parsley
2 tsp	drained capers
2 tsp	lemon juice
¼ tsp	pepper
pinch	salt

DIRECTIONS

Toss together cauliflower florets, oil and thyme. Arrange in single layer on lightly greased rimmed baking sheet. Bake in 425°F oven, turning once, until tender and deep golden, about 40 minutes.

Transfer to bowl; gently stir in Parmesan, parsley, capers, lemon juice, pepper and salt.

NUTRITIONAL INFORMATION, PER SERVING: about 107 cal, 6 g pro, 7 g total fat (2 g sat. fat), 9 g carb (5 g dietary fibre, 3 g sugar), 4 mg chol, 145 mg sodium, 299 mg potassium. % RDI: 8% calcium, 7% iron, 3% vit A, 148% vit C, 40% folate.

Tip from the Test Kitchen

For best results, use a baking sheet that's large enough to fit the cauliflower florets in a single layer; otherwise they will steam rather than roast.

POMEGRANATE, PISTACHIO & APRICOT BARK
P 278

Complete Desserts | 10

The best desserts are as simple as they are tasty. Fresh and dried fruits, velvety chocolate and wonderful home-baked treats all make for satisfying sweet finishes to great meals. Since it can be hard to find dessert options without dairy products and eggs, we've showcased several of our best vegan dessert recipes here (and a few non-vegan ones), including refreshing summery granitas and a rich, dark chocolate cake.

HANDS-ON TIME
15 minutes

TOTAL TIME
1 hour

MAKES
about 18 pieces

VEGAN

POMEGRANATE, PISTACHIO & APRICOT BARK

INGREDIENTS

600 g	good-quality dairy-free dark chocolate (about 21 oz), chopped
½ cup	pomegranate seeds
¼ cup	dried apricots, finely chopped
2 tbsp	salted shelled pistachios, chopped

DIRECTIONS

In heatproof bowl set over saucepan of gently simmering (not boiling) water, melt chocolate, stirring, until smooth. Scrape into parchment paper–lined 13- × 9-inch cake pan, smoothing top. Sprinkle with pomegranate seeds, apricots and pistachios. Refrigerate until set, about 45 minutes. Cut into shards. *(Make-ahead: Refrigerate in airtight container for up to 2 days.)*

NUTRITIONAL INFORMATION, PER PIECE: about 206 cal, 2 g pro, 13 g total fat (7 g sat. fat), 20 g carb (3 g dietary fibre, 14 g sugar), 2 mg chol, 7 mg sodium, 231 mg potassium. % RDI: 2% calcium, 16% iron, 1% vit A, 2% vit C, 1% folate.

Tip from the Test Kitchen

Try substituting chopped candied oranges, almonds or crystallized ginger for the apricots and the pistachios.

P 276

HANDS-ON TIME
7 minutes
TOTAL TIME
8¼ hours
MAKES
4 servings

VEGAN

STRAWBERRY GRANITA

INGREDIENTS

½ **cup**	granulated sugar
1 tbsp	lemon juice
6 cups	hulled strawberries (about 750 g)

DIRECTIONS

In small saucepan, bring sugar and ¼ cup water to boil, stirring often; boil for 1 minute. Let cool completely. Stir in lemon juice.

Meanwhile, in food processor or blender, purée strawberries. Add syrup; whirl to combine. Pour into 8-inch square metal cake pan; freeze until firm, about 8 hours. *(Make-ahead: Cover and freeze for up to 1 week.)*

Scrape fork across surface of frozen purée to form crystals. Spoon into dishes.

NUTRITIONAL INFORMATION, PER SERVING: about 148 cal, 1 g pro, 1 g total fat (0 g sat. fat), 37 g carb (4 g dietary fibre), 0 mg chol, 3 mg sodium. % RDI: 2% calcium, 5% iron, 1% vit A, 162% vit C, 14% folate.

VARIATION

STRAWBERRY MINT GRANITA

Add ¾ cup chopped fresh mint to sugar and water before boiling. Let cool completely. Cover and refrigerate for 6 hours; strain. Stir in lemon juice and 1 tsp more chopped fresh mint; stir into puréed strawberries.

HANDS-ON TIME
20 minutes
TOTAL TIME
30 minutes
MAKES
8 to 10 servings

VEGAN

ROSÉ SNOW CONES

INGREDIENTS

1 cup	rosé wine
½ cup	granulated sugar
quarter	vanilla bean
1½ tsp	lemon juice
4 cups	ice cubes
⅓ cup	chopped pitted fresh cherries (optional)
⅓ cup	chopped hulled fresh strawberries (optional)

DIRECTIONS

In large skillet, whisk wine with sugar over medium-high heat. Using paring knife, halve vanilla bean lengthwise; scrape out seeds. Add seeds and pod to pan.

Bring to boil. Reduce heat to medium; simmer, stirring occasionally, until thickened and syrupy, 10 to 15 minutes. Strain into bowl; discard pod. Stir in lemon juice; let cool to room temperature.

In food processor or blender, crush ice. Scoop ½ cup of the crushed ice into each of 8 to 10 paper cones or glass cups. Drizzle each with 1 tbsp of the wine syrup. Top with cherries and strawberries (if using).

NUTRITIONAL INFORMATION, PER EACH OF 10 SERVINGS: about 50 cal, 0 g pro, 0 g total fat (0 g sat. fat), 11 g carb (0 g dietary fibre, 10 g sugar), 0 mg chol, 4 mg sodium, 29 mg potassium. % RDI: 1% iron.

Tip from the Test Kitchen
For a kid-friendly version, swap out the wine for grape juice.

PEACH BLACKBERRY CHEESECAKE TART

HANDS-ON TIME
30 minutes
TOTAL TIME
2 hours
MAKES
8 servings

INGREDIENTS

FRUIT TOPPING

3 to 4	peaches, pitted and cut in wedges
¼ cup	granulated sugar
2 tbsp	lemon juice

CRUST

2 cups	finely ground amaretti cookies
¼ cup	packed chopped dried apricots
⅓ cup	unsalted butter, melted

CHEESECAKE FILLING

½ cup	whipping cream (35%)
1	pkg (227 g) cream cheese, softened
½ cup	icing sugar, sifted
1 tsp	grated lemon zest
1 tsp	vanilla
½ cup	fresh blackberries, halved

DIRECTIONS

FRUIT TOPPING In bowl, toss together peaches, sugar and lemon juice. Let stand at room temperature, stirring occasionally, until peaches are softened and sugar is dissolved, about 30 minutes.

CRUST Meanwhile, in food processor, pulse together amaretti cookies and apricots until in fine crumbs. Drizzle in butter; pulse until mixture is moistened. Press into bottom and up side of 9-inch tart pan with removable bottom. Bake on rimmed baking sheet in 350°F oven until fragrant and crust is set, about 10 minutes. Let cool.

CHEESECAKE FILLING In large bowl, whip cream until stiff peaks form; scrape into small bowl. In same large bowl, beat together cream cheese, icing sugar, lemon zest and vanilla until smooth and fluffy. Fold whipped cream into cream cheese mixture until combined.

ASSEMBLY Spoon Cheesecake Filling over cooled crust, smoothing top. Refrigerate until set, about 1 hour. Drain Fruit Topping, reserving syrup for another use. Mound Fruit Topping over top of tart and top with blackberries.

NUTRITIONAL INFORMATION PER SERVING: about 438 cal, 4 g pro, 28 g total fat (18 g sat. fat), 47 g carb (3 g dietary fibre, 44 g sugar), 74 mg chol, 183 mg sodium, 298 mg potassium. % RDI: 5% calcium, 5% iron, 28% vit A, 10% vit C, 5% folate.

HANDS-ON TIME
25 minutes
TOTAL TIME
35 minutes
MAKES
25 pieces

VEGAN

FRUIT & NUT TRUFFLES

INGREDIENTS

⅓ cup	finely chopped dried apricots
2 tbsp	red wine or rum
250 g	dairy-free bittersweet chocolate (about 9 oz), chopped
1½ cups	slivered almonds, coarsely chopped
3 tbsp	finely chopped crystallized ginger

DIRECTIONS

Stir apricots with wine; let stand for 5 minutes. Drain; discard wine.

Meanwhile, in heatproof bowl over saucepan of hot (not boiling) water, melt 140 g (about 5 oz) of the chocolate, stirring until smooth. In separate bowl, stir almonds with ginger; stir in apricot mixture and melted chocolate.

Roll by 1 tbsp into balls; arrange on waxed paper–lined rimmed baking sheet. Refrigerate until set, about 5 minutes.

Meanwhile, in clean heatproof bowl over saucepan of hot (not boiling) water, melt remaining chocolate, stirring until smooth. Using fork, dip each ball into chocolate, tapping on edge and letting excess drip back into bowl. Return to baking sheet; let stand until coating is firm, about 15 minutes. *(Make-ahead: Store in airtight container for up to 5 days).*

NUTRITIONAL INFORMATION, PER PIECE: about 95 cal, 2 g pro, 7 g total fat (2 g sat. fat), 8 g carb (2 g dietary fibre, 6 g sugar), 0 mg chol, 4 mg sodium, 154 mg potassium. % RDI: 2% calcium, 8% iron, 1% vit A, 2% vit C, 1% folate.

Tip from the Test Kitchen
Cold, clean hands make shaping truffles easier. Work quickly, occasionally rinsing your hands in cold water and drying them.

VEGAN

DAIRY-FREE CHOCOLATE FONDUE

HANDS-ON TIME
10 minutes

TOTAL TIME
10 minutes

MAKES
1 cup

INGREDIENTS

2 tbsp	boiling water
1 tsp	instant espresso powder
140 g	dairy-free bittersweet chocolate (about 5 oz), chopped
⅓ cup	coconut milk
1 tsp	granulated sugar
pinch	salt
	Assorted fruit, such as sliced banana, pineapple or strawberries, or dried fruit

DIRECTIONS

Stir boiling water with espresso powder; set aside.

In heatproof bowl over saucepan of hot (not boiling) water, melt together chocolate, coconut milk, sugar and salt. Stir in espresso mixture until smooth.

Pour into fondue pot or espresso cups; keep warm. Serve with fruit for dipping.

NUTRITIONAL INFORMATION, PER 1 TBSP (WITHOUT FRUIT): about 61 cal, 1 g pro, 4 g total fat (3 g sat. fat), 5 g carb (1 g dietary fibre, 4 g sugar), 1 mg chol, 2 mg sodium, 64 mg potassium. % RDI: 1% calcium, 5% iron.

Tip from the Test Kitchen

Coconut milk sometimes separates in the can. Just give it a whisk to recombine and to make it easier to pour.

HANDS-ON TIME
35 minutes

TOTAL TIME
2¾ hours

MAKES
8 to 10 servings

STRAWBERRIES & CREAM LOAF

INGREDIENTS

LOAF

1½ cups	hulled fresh or frozen strawberries
1 cup	granulated sugar
1 tsp	cornstarch
1 tsp	grated lemon zest
⅔ cup	plain Balkan-style yogurt
3	eggs
⅓ cup	vegetable oil
1½ cups	all-purpose flour
1¾ tsp	baking powder
¾ tsp	baking soda
½ tsp	salt

CREAM CHEESE ICING

quarter	pkg (250 g pkg) cream cheese, softened
1 tbsp	butter, softened
1 cup	icing sugar
1 tbsp	10% cream or milk
	quartered strawberries (optional)

DIRECTIONS

LOAF In small saucepan, cook strawberries, 2 tbsp of the sugar and 1 tbsp water over medium-high heat, stirring often and breaking up strawberries with spoon, until strawberries are broken down and mixture resembles chunky jam.

Whisk cornstarch with 1 tsp water; stir into strawberry mixture. Cook, stirring, for 1 minute. Scrape into bowl. Refrigerate until chilled, about 20 minutes. *(Make-ahead: Cover and refrigerate for up to 24 hours.)*

Meanwhile, in large bowl, using fingers, rub remaining sugar with lemon zest. Whisk in yogurt and eggs; gradually whisk in oil. In separate bowl, whisk together flour, baking powder, baking soda and salt; stir into lemon zest mixture in 2 additions.

Stir half of the batter into strawberry mixture until combined. Alternately drop spoonfuls of white and strawberry batters into parchment paper–lined 8- × 4-inch loaf pan. Using butter knife, gently swirl batters to create marble effect.

Bake in 350°F oven until loaf springs back when lightly touched and cake tester inserted in centre comes out clean, 40 to 45 minutes. Let cool in pan for 10 minutes. Transfer to rack; peel off parchment paper. Let cool completely. *(Make-ahead: Wrap in plastic wrap; store at room temperature for up to 24 hours.)*

CREAM CHEESE ICING While loaf is cooling, in bowl, beat cream cheese with butter until light and fluffy; beat in icing sugar and cream until smooth. Spread over top of loaf. Refrigerate until set, about 15 minutes. Garnish with quartered strawberries if desired.

NUTRITIONAL INFORMATION, PER EACH OF 10 SERVINGS: about 335 cal, 5 g pro, 14 g total fat (4 g sat. fat), 49 g carb (1 g dietary fibre, 34 g sugar), 71 mg chol, 320 mg sodium, 108 mg potassium. % RDI: 6% calcium, 9% iron, 8% vit A, 15% vit C, 18% folate.

VEGAN

GLUTEN- & DAIRY-FREE MAPLE CARROT LOAF

HANDS-ON TIME
15 minutes

TOTAL TIME
1¼ hours

MAKES
8 servings

INGREDIENTS

3 tbsp	flaxseed meal
1½ cups	gluten-free all-purpose flour
¾ cup	maple sugar
2 tsp	each baking soda and cinnamon
¾ tsp	xanthan gum
½ tsp	salt
¼ tsp	nutmeg
pinch	ground cloves
⅓ cup	unsweetened applesauce
¼ cup	coconut milk
2 tbsp	lemon juice
2 tsp	vanilla
1 cup	finely shredded carrot (about 1 large)

DIRECTIONS

In small bowl, mix flaxseed meal with ⅓ cup water. Let stand for 5 minutes.

In large bowl, whisk together flour, maple sugar, baking soda, cinnamon, xanthan gum, salt, nutmeg and cloves. In separate bowl, whisk together applesauce, coconut milk, lemon juice, vanilla and flaxseed meal mixture; stir into flour mixture just until combined. Fold in carrot. Scrape into greased 8- × 4-inch loaf pan, smoothing top.

Bake in 350°F oven until golden and cake springs back when touched, 35 to 40 minutes. Let cool in pan for 20 minutes; transfer directly to rack to cool completely.

NUTRITIONAL INFORMATION, PER SERVING: about 175 cal, 3 g pro, 3 g total fat (1 g sat. fat), 36 g carb (4 g dietary fibre, 16 g sugar), 0 mg chol, 480 mg sodium, 146 mg potassium. % RDI: 6% calcium, 12% iron, 21% vit A, 3% vit C, 3% folate.

Tip from the Test Kitchen

Xanthan gum is a common ingredient in gluten-free baking; like gluten, it provides structure to baked goods. Look for it in health-food stores and some grocery stores.

HANDS-ON TIME
20 minutes

TOTAL TIME
1½ hours

MAKES
8 to 10 servings

VEGAN

DARK & DELICIOUS VEGAN CHOCOLATE CAKE

INGREDIENTS

CHOCOLATE CAKE

1¼ cups	all-purpose flour
1 cup	coconut sugar
½ cup	cocoa powder, sifted
1½ tsp	baking soda
¼ tsp	salt
¼ cup	light-tasting olive oil
¼ cup	unsweetened applesauce
1 tsp	vanilla
4 tsp	cider vinegar

CHOCOLATE GLAZE

140 g	dairy-free semisweet chocolate (about 5 oz), finely chopped
2 tbsp	coconut milk

DIRECTIONS

CHOCOLATE CAKE In large bowl, whisk together flour, coconut sugar, cocoa powder, baking soda and salt; whisk in oil, applesauce, vanilla and 1 cup water. Stir in vinegar. Scrape into greased parchment paper–lined 9-inch square cake pan.

Bake in 350°F oven until cake tester inserted in centre comes out clean, 25 to 30 minutes. Let cool in pan for 20 minutes. Invert onto rack; peel off parchment paper. Let cool completely. *(Make-ahead: Store in airtight container for up to 24 hours.)*

CHOCOLATE GLAZE While cake is baking, in heatproof bowl set over saucepan of hot (not boiling) water, heat chocolate with coconut milk, whisking, until melted, about 5 minutes. Let cool for 25 minutes. Pour over cake, spreading to edges. Refrigerate until set, about 20 minutes. Bring to room temperature before serving.

NUTRITIONAL INFORMATION, PER EACH OF 10 SERVINGS: about 274 cal, 3 g pro, 11 g total fat (4 g sat. fat), 45 g carb (3 g dietary fibre, 30 g sugar), 0 mg chol, 260 mg sodium, 415 mg potassium. % RDI: 1% calcium, 17% iron, 12% folate.

Tip from the Test Kitchen
When baking with coconut milk, use a brand that contains an emulsifier, such as guar gum, which will prevent the milk from separating.

BROCCOLI & BROWN BUTTER FUSILLI WITH TOASTED ALMONDS
P 173

About Our Nutrition Information

To meet nutrient needs each day, moderately active women aged 25 to 49 need about 1,900 calories, 51 g protein, 261 g carbohydrate, 25 to 35 g fibre and not more than 63 g total fat (21 g saturated fat). Men and teenagers usually need more. Canadian sodium intake of approximately 3,500 mg daily should be reduced, whereas the intake of potassium from food sources should be increased to 4,700 mg per day. The percentage of recommended daily intake (% RDI) is based on the values used for Canadian food labels for calcium, iron, vitamins A and C, and folate.

Figures are rounded off. They are based on the first ingredient listed when there is a choice and do not include optional ingredients or those with no specified amounts.

Abbreviations

cal = calories   **pro** = protein   **carb** = carbohydrate   **sat. fat** = saturated fat   **chol** = cholesterol

Complete Index

v vegan

A

Afghan-Style Baked Eggplant With
Mint-Garlic Yogurt Sauce, **248**
Aglio e Olio, **171**
Ale-Braised Onions, **150**
almonds. See nuts
appetizers, **70–93**
Apple & Blue Cheese Tartlets With
Icewine Glaze, **89**
apples
Apple & Blue Cheese Tartlets With
Icewine Glaze, **89**
Cozy Apple Pie Oatmeal, **24**
arugula
Arugula & Bulgur–Stuffed Tomatoes, **251**
Arugula Mushroom Pizza, **203**
Pine Nut, Quinoa & Mushroom
Strudel, **190** V
Turkish Egg Tartines, **224**
Arugula & Bulgur–Stuffed Tomatoes, **251**
Arugula Mushroom Pizza, **203**
asparagus
Asparagus & Gruyère Cups, **230**
Grilled Asparagus Pizza, **196**
Panzanella With Asparagus & Eggs, **143**
Poached Eggs & Asparagus With
Herbed Mustard, **19**
Spinach & Avocado Green Goddess
Pasta, **174** V
Warm Kale & Quinoa Salad, **138**
Asparagus & Gruyère Cups, **230**
avocado
Black Bean Tostadas With Mango
Avocado Salad, **156**
Chili-Lime Sweet Potato Tacos, **157** V
Edamame Guacamole, **82** V
Green Bean & Radish Salad, **140** V
Mexican Tortilla Soup, **107** V
Panzanella With Asparagus & Eggs, **143**
Spinach & Avocado Green Goddess
Pasta, **174** V

Sugar Snap Peas & Avocado Salad With
Sesame Dressing, **144** V
Vegetarian Watermelon Poke Bowl, **134**

B

baguette. See bread (as ingredient)
Baked Phyllo Egg Nests, **223**
Baked Spring Rolls With Chili Garlic
Dipping Sauce, **77**
bananas
Clementine Yogurt Smoothie, **14**
Gingery Fruit Salad, **32** V
Gluten-Free, Dairy-Free Banana
Pancakes, **27**
Peanut Butter & Banana French Toast
Sandwiches, **26**
Swiss Chard & Mango Smoothie, **14**
basics, **46–69**
beans
Black Bean Tostadas With Mango
Avocado Salad, **156**
Cauliflower & White Bean Dip, **81**
Chipotle Bean Cakes With Lime Mayo, **72**
Huevos Rancheros Casserole, **20**
Jalapeño Bean Cakes With Lime
Mayo, **72**
Marinated White Bean & Vegetable
Salad, **139**
One-Pot Quinoa Chili, **188** V
beans, green
Green Bean & Radish Salad, **140** V
Green Beans With Mustard Seed &
Onions, **252** V
Spicy Green Bean & Tofu Stir-Fry, **211** V
Thai-Style Tofu Curry, **163** V
Vegetarian Ma Po Tofu, **215** V
bean sprouts
Vegetarian Singapore Noodles, **187**
Béchamel Sauce, **182**
Beet Borscht, **110** V
Beet Risotto, **193**

beets
Beet Borscht, **110** V
Beet Risotto, **193**
Rainbow Root Fries With Chive
Mayo, **260**
Ricotta Gnocchi With Sautéed Beets, **177**
Shaved Beet & Celery Root Salad With
Miso Dressing, **146**
black beans. See beans
Black Bean Tostadas With Mango
Avocado Salad, **156**
Blood Orange & Fennel Salad, **117**
blue cheese. See cheese
bread (as ingredient). See also pita;
tortillas
Asparagus & Gruyère Cups, **230**
Broccoli Soup With Cheddar
Croutons, **105**
Curried Lentil Cashew Burger, **162**
Mediterranean Vegetable Panini With
Grape Tomatoes & Feta Pesto, **155**
Panzanella With Asparagus & Eggs, **143**
Peanut Butter & Banana French Toast
Sandwiches, **26**
Slow Cooker French Leek Soup, **106**
Smoked Tomato Bruschetta With
Gouda, **92**
Smoky Grilled Cheese With Ale-Braised
Onions, **150**
Sweet Potato Veggie Burgers, **158** V
Tomato & Vegetable Soup With
Halloumi, **99**
Turkish Egg Tartines, **224**
breads, **37–45**
breakfast, **12–35**
broccoli
Broccoli & Broiled Tofu With No-Cook
Peanut Sauce, **216** V
Broccoli & Brown Butter Fusilli, **173**
Broccoli Soup With Cheddar
Croutons, **105**

Crispy Tofu & Broccoli With Udon Noodles, **209** V

Loaded Cheddar Broccoli Potatoes With Tossed Salad, **231**

Marinated White Bean & Vegetable Salad, **139**

Miso Ginger Soba Salad, **128** V

Wheat Berry & Chickpea Salad With Garam Masala Dressing, **125**

Broccoli & Broiled Tofu With No-Cook Peanut Sauce, **216** V

Broccoli & Brown Butter Fusilli With Toasted Almonds, **173**

Broccoli Soup With Cheddar Croutons, **105**

Brown Rice & Baby Kale Salad With Curry Dressing, **126**

brussels sprouts

Creamed Brussels Sprouts, **257**

Roasted Winter Vegetables With Maple Candied Nuts, **263**

Buffalo Sauce, **271**

bulgur

Arugula & Bulgur–Stuffed Tomatoes, **251**

Heirloom Tomato Tabbouleh Salad, **124** V

buns. See bread (as ingredient)

burgers

Curried Lentil Cashew Burger, **162**

Sweet Potato Veggie Burgers, **158** V

Tahini Falafel Lettuce Burgers With Cucumber Salsa, **153**

butternut squash. See squash

Butternut Squash Risotto, **194**

C

cabbage

Baked Spring Rolls With Chili Garlic Dipping Sauce, **77**

Beet Borscht, **110** V

Creamed Cabbage, **257**

Roasted Cabbage Wedges With Buffalo Sauce, **271**

Cacio e Pepe, **169**

cake

Dark & Delicious Vegan Chocolate Cake, **290** V

cannellini beans. See beans

Caraway & Thyme Irish Soda Bread, **43**

Cardamom- & Ginger-Glazed Carrots, **254**

carrots

Cardamom- & Ginger-Glazed Carrots, **254**

Gluten- & Dairy-Free Maple Carrot Loaf, **289** V

Honey-Lime Carrots With Cipollini Onions, **253**

Rice Salad With Quick-Pickled Carrot & Daikon, **127** V

Roasted Winter Vegetables With Maple Candied Nuts, **263**

cashews. See nuts

cauliflower

Cauliflower & White Bean Dip, **81**

Cauliflower Corn Chowder, **109**

Curried Cauliflower & Spinach Wraps, **154** V

Roasted Cauliflower With Parmesan & Capers, **274**

Southwestern Cauliflower Cakes, **272**

Spiced Cauliflower & Leek Purée, **273**

Sweet Potato & Cauliflower Tagine, **218** V

Warm Roasted Cauliflower Salad With Garlicky Tahini Dressing, **133**

Cauliflower & White Bean Dip, **81**

Cauliflower Corn Chowder, **109**

celery root

Crunchy Parmesan-Topped Potato & Celery Root Mash, **258**

Rainbow Root Fries With Chive Mayo, **260**

Shaved Beet & Celery Root Salad With Miso Dressing, **146**

Chana Masala, **164** V

Charred Corn & Tomato Salad With Chipotle Vinaigrette, **145**

Cheddar cheese. See cheese

Cheddar Croutons, **105**

cheese

Apple & Blue Cheese Tartlets With Icewine Glaze, **89**

Arugula & Bulgur–Stuffed Tomatoes, **251**

Arugula Mushroom Pizza, **203**

Asparagus & Gruyère Cups, **230**

Baked Phyllo Egg Nests, **223**

Black Bean Tostadas With Mango Avocado Salad, **156**

Broccoli Soup With Cheddar Croutons, **105**

Cacio e Pepe, **169**

Cheesy Polenta Squares, **269**

Couscous & Cheese–Stuffed Zucchini, **241**

Curried Lentil Cashew Burger, **162**

Huevos Rancheros Casserole, **20**

Loaded Cheddar Broccoli Potatoes With Tossed Salad, **231**

Roasted Peppers With Eggs, **227**

Slow Cooker French Leek Soup, **106**

Smoked Cheddar Pancakes With Pickled Beets, **75**

Smoked Tomato Bruschetta With Gouda, **92**

Smoky Grilled Cheese With Ale-Braised Onions, **150**

Sweet Onion & Gorgonzola Pizza, **201**

Sweet Potato & Two-Cheese Tarte Tatin, **91**

cheesecake

Peach Blackberry Cheesecake Tart, **283**

cheese, feta. See also cheese

Corn & Feta Tart, **205**

Feta & Dill Scrambled Eggs, **18**

Mediterranean Baked Peppers, **247**

Spinach & Feta Omelette Soufflé, **228**

Swiss Chard, Strawberry & Feta Salad, **114**

Vegetable Tikka Masala Naan Pizza, **199**

cheese, goat. See also cheese

Creamy Kale & Sun-Dried Tomato Carbonara, **166**

Creamy Leek & Corn Baked Eggs, **222**

Crustless Zucchini Quiche, **229**

Leek & Hazelnut Ravioli, **165**

Sweet Potato & Two-Cheese Tarte Tatin, **91**

Zucchini, Chèvre & Walnut Tart, **86**

cheese, halloumi. See also cheese

Greek Halloumi Salad With Herbed Pita Chips, **119**

Halloumi & Quinoa Salad With Sumac-Lime Dressing, **137**

Lentil & Sweet Potato Salad With Halloumi, **132**

Tomato & Vegetable Soup With
Halloumi, **99**
cheese, mozzarella
Creamy Skillet Mushroom Lasagna, 180
Double Mozzarella & Spinach Pita
Pizzas, 200
Grilled Asparagus Pizza, 196
Lazy Skillet Lasagna, 181
Roasted Squash & Spinach Lasagna, 182
cheese, Parmesan
Beet Risotto, **193**
Butternut Squash Risotto, **194**
Cheesy Polenta Squares, **269**
Classic Pesto, **54**
Creamy Kale & Sun-Dried Tomato
Carbonara, **166**
Creamy Tomato Soup With Pesto
Drizzle, **96**
Crispy Polenta With Vegetable
Ragout, **195**
Crunchy Parmesan-Topped Double
Potato Mash, **258**
Crunchy Parmesan-Topped Potato &
Celery Root Mash, **258**
Grilled Parmesan Corn, **265**
Kale & Fennel Salad With Lemon Dill
Dressing, **118**
Olive & Parmesan Crackers, **45**
Ricotta Gnocchi With Sautéed
Beets, **177**
Roasted Cauliflower With Parmesan &
Capers, **274**
Roasted Squash & Spinach Lasagna, **182**
Walnut Pesto Potato Salad, **131**
Zucchini Ribbon & Caper Pasta, **171**
cheese, ricotta
Creamy Skillet Mushroom Lasagna, **180**
Homemade Ricotta, **78**
Lazy Skillet Lasagna, **181**
Ricotta Gnocchi With Sautéed Beets, **177**
Sun-Dried Tomato Agnolotti With
Walnuts & Swiss Chard, **179**
Cheesy Polenta Squares, **269**
chickpeas
Chana Masala, **164** V
Curried Cauliflower & Spinach
Wraps, **154** V
Eggplant Walnut Dip With Za'atar Pita
Chips, **83** V

Mediterranean Stewed Chickpeas, **221** V
Sweet Potato & Cauliflower Tagine, **218** V
Sweet Potato Veggie Burgers, **158** V
Tahini Falafel Lettuce Burgers With
Cucumber Salsa, **153**
Vegetable Tikka Masala Naan
Pizza, **199**
Wheat Berry & Chickpea Salad With
Garam Masala Dressing, **125**
chili
One-Pot Quinoa Chili, **188** V
Chili Garlic Dipping Sauce, **77**
Chili-Lime Sweet Potato Tacos, **157** V
Chipotle Bean Cakes With
Lime Mayo, **72**
Chipotle Vinaigrette, **145**
Chive Mayo, **260**
chocolate
Dairy-Free Chocolate Fondue, **285** V
Dark & Delicious Vegan Chocolate
Cake, **290** V
Fruit & Nut Truffles, **284** V
Pomegranate, Pistachio & Apricot
Bark, **278** V
Chocolate Glaze, **290**
chutney. See salsa & chutney
cilantro
Cilantro Ginger Chutney, **68** V
Cilantro-Jalapeño Grilled Tofu
Salad, **120**
Cilantro-Jalapeño Sauce, **59** V
Cilantro Sour Cream, **266**
Roasted Cilantro Lime
Squash, **242** V
Spicy Cilantro Pesto, **54** V
Thai Green Curry Paste, **62** V
Cilantro Ginger Chutney, **68** V
Cilantro-Jalapeño Grilled Tofu
Salad, **120**
Cilantro-Jalapeño Sauce, **59** V
Cilantro Sour Cream, **266**
Cipollini Onions, **253**
Cinnamon Raisin Sandwich Bread, **40**
Citrus Dressing, **236**
Classic Aioli, **59**
Classic Chili Sauce, **48** V
Classic Pesto, **54**
Clementine Yogurt Smoothie, **14**
Coconut Date Breakfast Cookies, **25**

coconut milk
Curried Cauliflower & Spinach
Wraps, **154** V
Dairy-Free Chocolate Fondue, **285** V
Gluten- & Dairy-Free Maple Carrot
Loaf, **289** V
Sweet & Spicy Thai Oatmeal, **24**
Swiss Chard & Mango Smoothie, **14**
Thai-Style Tofu Curry, **163** V
Tropical Mint Oatmeal, **23**
condiments, dips & sauces. See also
dressings; salsa & chutney
Béchamel Sauce, **182**
Buffalo Sauce, **271**
Chili Garlic Dipping Sauce, **77**
Chive Mayo, **260**
Cilantro Sour Cream, **266**
Cilantro-Jalapeño Sauce, **59** V
Classic Aioli, **59**
Classic Chili Sauce, **48** V
Classic Pesto, **54**
Creamy Dill Dip, **82**
Easy Marinara Sauce, **50** V
Eggplant Walnut Dip, **83** V
Feta Pesto, **155**
Fresh Tomato Sauce, **49** V
Ginger, Hot Pepper & Lime Butter, **61**
Green Onion & Ginger Butter, **60**
Green Tomato Chow Chow, **69** V
Herbed Mustard, **19**
Honey Ketchup, **64**
Lime Mayo, **72**
Mint-Garlic Yogurt Sauce, **248**
No-Cook Peanut Sauce, **216**
Orange Tarragon Garlic Butter, **61**
Paprika Butter, **224**
Pressure Cooker Fresh Tomato
Sauce, **49** V
Quick-Pickled Radishes, **157**
Roasted Garlic Butter, **246**
Sesame Garlic Chili Oil, **62** V
Sherried Shallot Butter, **61**
Spicy Cilantro Pesto, **54** V
Spicy Sesame Dipping Sauce, **76**
Sriracha Aioli, **264**
Sun-Dried Tomato & Almond Pesto, **55** V
Sun-Dried Tomato &
Roasted Red Pepper Cream Sauce, **53**
Sweet & Sour Ketchup, **63** V

Tarragon Chive Mayonnaise, **56**
Thai Green Curry Paste, **62** V
Tomato & Basil Mayonnaise, **56**
Tomato Pear Ketchup, **64** V
Tomato Sauce, **182**
Watercress & Walnut Pesto, **55** V
Wild Mushroom Cream Sauce, **53**
Yogurt Sauce, **224**
Zesty Tomato Jam, **63** V
Corn & Feta Tart With Fresh
Tarragon, **205**
corn
Cauliflower Corn Chowder, **109**
Charred Corn & Tomato Salad, **145**
Corn & Feta Tart With Fresh
Tarragon, **205**
Creamy Leek & Corn Baked Eggs, **222**
Crustless Zucchini Quiche With Grilled
Corn Salad, **229**
Grilled Corn With Sriracha Aioli, **264**
Grilled Garam Masala Corn, **265**
Grilled Parmesan Corn, **265**
Jalapeño Corn Fritters With Cilantro
Sour Cream, **266**
One-Pot Quinoa Chili, **188** V
Cornmeal Pastry, **205**
couscous
Couscous & Cheese–Stuffed
Zucchini, **241**
Mediterranean Stewed Chickpeas, **221** V
Couscous & Cheese–Stuffed
Zucchini, **241**
Cozy Apple Pie Oatmeal, **24**
Creamed Brussels Sprouts, **257**
Creamed Cabbage, **257**
Creamy Dill Dip, **82**
Creamy Kale & Sun-Dried Tomato
Carbonara, **166**
Creamy Leek & Corn Baked Eggs, **222**
Creamy Skillet Mushroom Lasagna, **180**
Creamy Tomato Soup With Pesto
Drizzle, **96**
crispbread
Whole Wheat Sesame Crispbread, **44**
Crispy Polenta With Vegetable
Ragout, **195**
Crispy Tofu & Broccoli With Udon
Noodles, **209** V
Crunchy Curry Rice & Squash, **245** V

Crunchy Parmesan-Topped Double
Potato Mash, **258**
Crunchy Parmesan-Topped Potato &
Celery Root Mash, **258**
Crunchy Peanut Veggie Noodle
Salad, **123** V
Crustless Zucchini Quiche With Grilled
Corn Salad, **229**
Cucumber Salsa, **153**
Curried Cauliflower & Spinach
Wraps, **154** V
Curried Lentil Cashew Burger, **162**
curry
Brown Rice & Baby Kale Salad With
Curry Dressing, **126**
Crunchy Curry Rice & Squash, **245** V
Curried Cauliflower & Spinach
Wraps, **154** V
Curried Lentil Cashew Burger, **162**
Curry Dressing, **126**
Thai Green Curry Paste, **62** V
Thai-Style Tofu Curry, **163** V
Curry Dressing, **126**

D
daikon
Rice Salad With Quick-Pickled Carrot &
Daikon, **127** V
dairy-free
Dairy-Free Chocolate Fondue, **285** V
Dark & Delicious Vegan Chocolate
Cake, **290** V
Gluten- & Dairy-Free Maple Carrot
Loaf, **289** V
Gluten-Free, Dairy-Free Banana
Pancakes, **27**
Dairy-Free Chocolate Fondue, **285** V
Dark & Delicious Vegan Chocolate
Cake, **290** V
dates
Coconut Date Breakfast Cookies, **25**
desserts, **276–291**
dips. See condiments, dips &
sauces
Double Mozzarella & Spinach Pita
Pizzas, **200**
dough
Fresh Pasta Dough, **52**
Grilled Asparagus Pizza, **196**

dressings. See also condiments, dips &
sauces
Chipotle Vinaigrette, **145**
Citrus Dressing, **236**
Curry Dressing, **126**
Garam Masala Dressing, **125**
Garlicky Tahini Dressing, **133**
Ginger Dressing, **127**
Lemon Dill Dressing, **118**
Miso Dressing, **128**, 146
Pesto Drizzle, **96**
Sesame Dressing, **144**
Shallot Vinaigrette, **132**
Sumac-Lime Dressing, **137**
Tarragon Vinaigrette, **138**

E
Easy Cranberry Yogurt Parfaits, **33**
Easy Marinara Sauce, **50** V
Easy No-Knead
White Sandwich
Bread, **38** V
Easy No-Knead Whole Wheat
Sandwich Bread, **39** V
edamame
Edamame Guacamole, **82** V
Edamame Vegetable Soup, **100** V
Vegetarian Watermelon Poke
Bowl, **134**
Edamame Guacamole, **82** V
Edamame Vegetable Soup, **100** V
eggplant
Afghan-Style Baked Eggplant With
Mint-Garlic Yogurt Sauce, **248**
Eggplant Walnut Dip With Za'atar Pita
Chips, **83** V
Slow Cooker Garam Masala
Eggplant, **161**
Thai-Style Tofu Curry, **163** V
Vegetable Saffron Paella, **189** V
Eggplant Walnut Dip With Za'atar Pita
Chips, **83** V
eggs
Baked Phyllo Egg Nests, **223**
Creamy Kale & Sun-Dried Tomato
Carbonara, **166**
Creamy Leek & Corn Baked Eggs, **222**
Crustless Zucchini Quiche With Grilled
Corn Salad, **229**

Eggs Poached in Tomato & Fennel Sauce, **232**
Feta & Dill Scrambled Eggs, **18**
Huevos Rancheros Casserole, **20**
Panzanella With Asparagus & Eggs, **143**
Peanut Butter & Banana French Toast Sandwiches, **26**
Quick Egg & Veggie Fried Rice, **186**
Ramen Noodle Soup, **102**
Roasted Peppers With Eggs, **227**
Spinach & Feta Omelette Soufflé, **228**
Turkish Egg Tartines, **224**
Eggs Poached in Tomato & Fennel Sauce, **232**
endive
  Roasted Leek & Endive With Citrus Dressing, **236**

F
Falafel Burgers, **153**
fennel
  Blood Orange & Fennel Salad, **117**
  Eggs Poached in Tomato & Fennel Sauce, **232**
  Kale & Fennel Salad With Lemon Dill Dressing, **118**
Feta & Dill Scrambled Eggs, **18**
feta cheese. See cheese, feta
Feta Pesto, **155**
focaccia. See bread (as ingredient)
Fresh Pasta Dough, **52**
Fresh Tomato Sauce, **49** V
Fried Tofu With Spicy Sesame Dipping Sauce, **76** V
Frizzled Onions, **240**
Fruit & Nut Truffles, **284** V

G
Garam Masala Dressing, **125**
Garlicky Tahini Dressing, **133**
Ginger Dressing, **127**
Ginger, Hot Pepper & Lime Butter, **61**
Gingery Fruit Salad, **32** V
Gluten- & Dairy-Free Maple Carrot Loaf, **289** V
Gluten-Free, Dairy-Free Banana Pancakes, **27**
gnocchi. See pasta
goat cheese. See cheese, goat

gorgonzola cheese. See cheese
Gouda cheese. See cheese
granola
  Granola Bowls, **31**
  Toasted Almond Granola, **31**
Granola Bowls, **31**
Greek Halloumi Salad With Herbed Pita Chips, **119**
Green Bean & Radish Salad, **140** V
Green Beans With Mustard Seed & Onions, **252** V
Green Onion & Ginger Butter, **60**
green beans. See beans, green
green peas. See peas
greens, mixed baby
  Cilantro-Jalapeño Grilled Tofu Salad, **120**
  Greek Halloumi Salad With Herbed Pita Chips, **119**
  Loaded Cheddar Broccoli Potatoes With Tossed Salad, **231**
Green Tomato Chow Chow, **69** V
Grilled Asparagus Pizza, **196**
Grilled Corn Salad, **229**
Grilled Corn With Sriracha Aioli, **264**
Grilled Garam Masala Corn, **265**
Grilled Parmesan Corn, **265**
Gruyère cheese. See cheese
guacamole. See also salsa & chutney
  Edamame Guacamole, **82** V

H
Halloumi & Quinoa Salad With Sumac-Lime Dressing, **137**
halloumi cheese. See cheese, halloumi
havarti cheese. See cheese
hazelnuts. See nuts
Heirloom Tomato Tabbouleh Salad, **124** V
Herbed Mustard, **19**
Herbed Pita Chips, **119**
Herb Salad, **224**
Homemade Ricotta, **78**
Honey Ketchup, **64**
Honey-Lime Carrots With Cipollini Onions, **253**
Huevos Rancheros Casserole, **20**
Hungarian Potato Soup, **108**

I
Icewine Glaze, **89**

J
Jalapeño Bean Cakes With Lime Mayo, **72**
Jalapeño Corn Fritters With Cilantro Sour Cream, **266**
Japchae, **185** V

K
kale
  Brown Rice & Baby Kale Salad With Curry Dressing, **126**
  Creamy Kale & Sun-Dried Tomato Carbonara, **166**
  Kale & Fennel Salad With Lemon Dill Dressing, **118**
  Sautéed Kale With Raisins, **270** V
  Vegetable Quinoa Soup, **101** V
  Warm Kale & Quinoa Salad, **138**
Kale & Fennel Salad With Lemon Dill Dressing, **118**
kidney beans. See beans

L
lasagna. See pasta
Lazy Skillet Lasagna, **181**
Leek & Hazelnut Ravioli, **165**
leeks
  Broccoli Soup With Cheddar Croutons, **105**
  Corn & Feta Tart, **205**
  Creamy Leek & Corn Baked Eggs, **222**
  Leek & Hazelnut Ravioli, **165**
  Roasted Leek & Endive With Citrus Dressing, **236**
  Slow Cooker French Leek Soup, **106**
  Spiced Cauliflower & Leek Purée, **273**
Lemon Dill Dressing, **118**
lemongrass
  Lemongrass Chili Oil, **242** V
  Thai Green Curry Paste, **62** V
Lemongrass Chili Oil, **242** V
Lemony Ravioli With Sun-Dried Tomatoes, **178**
Lentil & Sweet Potato Salad With Halloumi, **132**

lentils
Brown Rice & Baby Kale Salad With
Curry Dressing, 126
Chili-Lime Sweet Potato Tacos, 157 V
Curried Lentil Cashew Burger, 162
Lentil & Sweet Potato Salad With
Halloumi, 132
Meatless Shepherd's Pie, 206
Slow Cooker Dal, 239
Light Vegetable Stock, 51 V
Lime Mayo, 72
Loaded Cheddar Broccoli Potatoes With
Tossed Salad, 231

M
mains, 148–233
Make-Ahead Butter Sauces, 61
Malt & Yogurt Rye Bread, 42
mango
Black Bean Tostadas With Mango
Avocado Salad, 156
Swiss Chard & Mango Smoothie, 14
Tropical Mint Oatmeal, 23
Tropical Yogurt Parfait, 34
Mango Avocado Salad, 156
Maple Candied Nuts, 263
Marinated White Bean & Vegetable
Salad, 139
Meatless Shepherd's Pie, 206
Mediterranean Baked Peppers, 247
Mediterranean Stewed Chickpeas, 221 V
Mediterranean Vegetable Panini With
Grape Tomatoes & Feta Pesto, 155
Mexican Tortilla Soup, 107 V
Mint-Garlic Yogurt Sauce, 248
Miso Ginger Soba Salad, 128 V
Miso Dressing, 128, 146
mixed baby greens. See greens, mixed
baby
Molasses Teriyaki Sauce, 212 V
Monterey Jack cheese. See cheese
mozzarella cheese. See cheese,
mozzarella
Mushroom & Spinach Sauté, 270
mushrooms
Arugula Mushroom Pizza, 203
Baked Spring Rolls With Chili Garlic
Dipping Sauce, 77
Creamy Skillet Mushroom Lasagna, 180

Crispy Polenta With Vegetable
Ragout, 195
Crispy Tofu & Broccoli With Udon
Noodles, 209 V
Curried Lentil Cashew Burger, 162
Japchae, 185 V
Meatless Shepherd's Pie, 206
Mushroom & Spinach Sauté, 270
Pine Nut, Quinoa & Mushroom
Strudel, 190 V
Portobello & Egg Breakfast
Sandwiches, 17
Quick Egg & Veggie Fried Rice, 186
Ramen Noodle Soup, 102
Vegetable Quinoa Soup, 101 V
Vegetarian Ma Po Tofu, 215 V
Warm Kale & Quinoa Salad, 138
Wild Mushroom Cream Sauce, 53
Mustard-Spiced Nuts, 85 V

N
naan
Vegetable Tikka Masala Naan
Pizza, 199
No-Cook Peanut Sauce, 216
noodles
Crispy Tofu & Broccoli With Udon
Noodles, 209 V
Japchae, 185 V
Miso Ginger Soba Salad, 128 V
Ramen Noodle Soup, 102
Tofu & Chow Mein Noodles, 210 V
Vegetarian Singapore Noodles, 187
nuts
Broccoli & Brown Butter Fusilli With
Toasted Almonds, 173
Classic Pesto, 54
Creamy Tomato Soup With Pesto
Drizzle, 96
Crunchy Peanut Veggie Noodle
Salad, 123 V
Curried Lentil Cashew Burger, 162
Eggplant Walnut Dip With Za'atar Pita
Chips, 83 V
Feta Pesto, 155
Fruit & Nut Truffles, 284 V
Granola Bowls, 31
Leek & Hazelnut Ravioli, 165
Mustard-Spiced Nuts, 85 V

Pine Nut, Quinoa & Mushroom
Strudel, 190 V
Pomegranate, Pistachio & Apricot
Bark, 278 V
Ricotta Gnocchi With Sautéed
Beets, 177
Roasted Winter Vegetables With Maple
Candied Nuts, 263
Sun-Dried Tomato Agnolotti With
Walnuts & Swiss Chard, 179
Sun-Dried Tomato & Almond Pesto, 55 V
Sweet Onion & Gorgonzola Pizza, 201
Toasted Almond Granola, 31
Tofu & Chow Mein Noodles, 210 V
Tropical Yogurt Parfait, 34
Walnut Pesto Potato Salad, 131
Watercress & Walnut Pesto, 55 V
Zucchini, Chèvre & Walnut Tart, 86

O
oats
Coconut Date Breakfast Cookies, 25
Cozy Apple Pie Oatmeal, 24
Granola Bowls, 31
Overnight Steel-Cut Oatmeal, 23
Sweet & Spicy Thai Oatmeal, 24
Toasted Almond Granola, 31
Tropical Mint Oatmeal, 23
Olive & Parmesan Crackers, 45
olives
Greek Halloumi Salad, 119
Mediterranean Stewed Chickpeas, 221 V
Mediterranean Vegetable Panini With
Grape Tomatoes & Feta Pesto, 155
Olive & Parmesan Crackers, 45
Vegetarian Saffron Paella, 189
omelettes
Spinach & Feta Omelette Soufflé, 228
One-Pot Quinoa Chili, 188 V
onions
Classic Chili Sauce, 48 V
Green Beans With Mustard Seed &
Onions, 252 V
Green Onion & Ginger Butter, 60
Honey-Lime Carrots With Cipollini
Onions, 253
Smoky Grilled Cheese With Ale-Braised
Onions, 150
Sweet Onion & Gorgonzola Pizza, 201

Sweet Potato & Cauliflower Tagine, **218** V
Swiss Chard With Frizzled Onions, **240**
Orange Tarragon Garlic Butter, **61**
Oven-Baked Teriyaki Tofu, **212** V
Overnight Steel-Cut Oatmeal, **23**

P
pancakes
Gluten-Free, Dairy-Free Banana
   Pancakes, **27**
   Smoked Cheddar Pancakes With
      Pickled Beets, **75**
   The Perfect Dutch Baby Pancake, **28**
Panzanella With Asparagus & Eggs, **143**
Paprika Butter, **224**
Parmesan & Capers, **274**
Parmesan cheese. See cheese,
   Parmesan
parsnips
   Roasted Winter Vegetables With Maple
      Candied Nuts, **263**
pasta
   Aglio e Olio, **171**
   Broccoli & Brown Butter Fusilli With
      Toasted Almonds, **173**
   Cacio e Pepe, **169**
   Creamy Kale & Sun-Dried Tomato
      Carbonara, **166**
   Creamy Skillet Mushroom
      Lasagna, **180**
   Crunchy Peanut Veggie Noodle
      Salad, **123** V
   Fresh Pasta Dough, **52**
   Lazy Skillet Lasagna, **181**
   Leek & Hazelnut Ravioli, **165**
   Lemony Ravioli With Sun-Dried
      Tomatoes, **178**
   Ricotta Gnocchi With Sautéed Beets, **177**
   Roasted Squash & Spinach
      Lasagna, **182**
   Seared Cherry Tomato Pasta, **172**
   Spinach & Avocado Green Goddess
      Pasta, **174** V
   Sun-Dried Tomato Agnolotti With
      Walnuts & Swiss Chard, **179**
   Zucchini Ribbon & Caper Pasta, **171**
pastry, frozen butter puff
   Apple & Blue Cheese Tartlets With
      Icewine Glaze, **89**

Spinach & Artichoke Pissaladière, **90**
Sweet Potato & Two-Cheese Tarte
   Tatin, **91**
Zucchini, Chèvre & Walnut Tart, **86**
pastry, phyllo
   Baked Phyllo Egg Nests, **223**
   Pine Nut, Quinoa & Mushroom
      Strudel, **190** V
Peach Blackberry Cheesecake Tart, **283**
peaches
   Spiced Peach Chutney, **67** V
   Peach Blackberry Cheesecake
      Tart, **283**
peanut butter
   Broccoli & Broiled Tofu With No-Cook
      Peanut Sauce, **216** V
   Crunchy Peanut Veggie Noodle
      Salad, **123** V
   Peanut Butter & Banana French Toast
      Sandwiches, **26**
   Sweet & Spicy Thai Oatmeal, **24**
Peanut Butter & Banana French Toast
   Sandwiches, **26**
peanuts. See nuts
peas
   Arugula Mushroom Pizza, **203**
   Crunchy Peanut Veggie Noodle
      Salad, **123** V
   Miso Ginger Soba Salad, **128** V
   Sugar Snap Peas & Avocado Salad With
      Sesame Dressing, **144** V
   Sweet Potato & Cauliflower Tagine,
      218 V
   Tofu & Chow Mein Noodles, **210** V
   Twin Peas With Roasted Garlic
      Butter, **246**
   Vegetable Saffron Paella, **189** V
pecans. See nuts
peppers, sweet
   Classic Chili Sauce, **48** V
   Crispy Polenta With Vegetable
      Ragout, **195**
   Mediterranean Baked Peppers, **247**
   Roasted Peppers With Eggs, **227**
   Tempeh & Rice–Stuffed Peppers, **217** V
   Vegetable Saffron Paella, **189** V
pesto. See condiments, dips & sauces
   Pesto Drizzle, **96**
Pickled Beets, **75**

pine nuts. See nuts
Pine Nut, Quinoa & Mushroom
   Strudel, **190** V
pita
   Double Mozzarella & Spinach Pita
      Pizzas, **200**
   Eggplant Walnut Dip With Za'atar Pita
      Chips, **83** V
   Greek Halloumi Salad With Herbed Pita
      Chips, **119**
pizza
   Arugula Mushroom Pizza, **203**
   Double Mozzarella & Spinach Pita
      Pizzas, **200**
   Grilled Asparagus Pizza, **196**
   Sweet Onion & Gorgonzola Pizza, **201**
   Vegetable Tikka Masala Naan
      Pizza, **199**
Poached Eggs & Asparagus With
   Herbed Mustard, **19**
polenta
   Crispy Polenta With Vegetable
      Ragout, **195**
Pomegranate, Pistachio & Apricot
   Bark, **278** V
Portobello & Egg Breakfast
   Sandwiches, **17**
portobello mushrooms. See mushrooms
Potato & Zucchini Mini Latkes, **84**
potatoes
   Beet Borscht, **110** V
   Broccoli Soup With Cheddar
      Croutons, **105**
   Crunchy Parmesan-Topped Double
      Potato Mash, **258**
   Crunchy Parmesan-Topped Potato &
      Celery Root Mash, **258**
   Hungarian Potato Soup, **108**
   Loaded Cheddar Broccoli
      Potatoes, **231**
   Meatless Shepherd's Pie, **206**
   Potato & Zucchini Mini Latkes, **84**
   Walnut Pesto Potato Salad, **131**
potatoes, sweet
   Chili-Lime Sweet Potato Tacos, **157** V
   Crunchy Parmesan-Topped Double
      Potato Mash, **258**
   Lentil & Sweet Potato Salad With
      Halloumi, **132**

Rainbow Root Fries With Chive Mayo, **260**

Sweet Potato & Cauliflower Tagine, **218** V

Sweet Potato & Two-Cheese Tarte Tatin, **91**

Sweet Potato Veggie Burgers, **158** V

Vegetable Quinoa Soup, **101** V

Pressure Cooker Fresh Tomato Sauce, **49** V

Q

quiche

Crustless Zucchini Quiche With Grilled Corn Salad, **229**

Quick Egg & Veggie Fried Rice, **186**

Quick-Pickled Radishes, **157**

quinoa

Halloumi & Quinoa Salad With Sumac-Lime Dressing, **137**

Heirloom Tomato Tabbouleh Salad, **124** V

One-Pot Quinoa Chili, **188** V

Pine Nut, Quinoa & Mushroom Strudel, **190** V

Vegetable Quinoa Soup, **101** V

Warm Kale & Quinoa Salad, **138**

R

radishes

Chili-Lime Sweet Potato Tacos, **157** V

Green Bean & Radish Salad, **140** V

Rainbow Root Fries With Chive Mayo, **260**

ramen. See noodles

Ramen Noodle Soup, **102**

ravioli. See pasta

Red Sauce, **20**

rice

Beet Risotto, **193**

Brown Rice & Baby Kale Salad With Curry Dressing, **126**

Butternut Squash Risotto, **194**

Crunchy Curry Rice & Squash, **245** V

Quick Egg & Veggie Fried Rice, **186**

Rice Salad With Quick-Pickled Carrot & Daikon, **127** V

Tempeh & Rice–Stuffed Peppers, **217** V

Vegetable Saffron Paella, **189** V

Vegetarian Ma Po Tofu, **215** V

Rice Salad With Quick-Pickled Carrot & Daikon, **127** V

ricotta cheese. See cheese, ricotta

Ricotta Gnocchi With Sautéed Beets, **177**

risotto

Beet Risotto, **193**

Butternut Squash Risotto, **194**

Roasted Cabbage Wedges With Buffalo Sauce, **271**

Roasted Cauliflower With Parmesan & Capers, **274**

Roasted Cilantro Lime Squash, **242** V

Roasted Garlic Butter, **246**

Roasted Grape Tomatoes, **155**

Roasted Leek & Endive With Citrus Dressing, **236**

Roasted Peppers With Eggs, **227**

Roasted Squash & Spinach Lasagna, **182**

Roasted Vegetable Stock, **51** V

Roasted Winter Vegetables With Maple Candied Nuts, **263**

Rosé Snow Cones, **280** V

rutabaga

Rainbow Root Fries With Chive Mayo, **260**

Roasted Winter Vegetables With Maple Candied Nuts, **263**

S

salads

Blood Orange & Fennel Salad, **117**

Brown Rice & Baby Kale Salad With Curry Dressing, **126**

Charred Corn & Tomato Salad With Chipotle Vinaigrette, **145**

Cilantro-Jalapeño Grilled Tofu Salad, **120**

Crunchy Peanut Veggie Noodle Salad, **123** V

Gingery Fruit Salad, **32** V

Greek Halloumi Salad With Herbed Pita Chips, **119**

Green Bean & Radish Salad, **140** V

Grilled Corn Salad, **229**

Halloumi & Quinoa Salad With Sumac-Lime Dressing, **137**

Heirloom Tomato Tabbouleh Salad, **124** V

Herb Salad, **224**

Kale & Fennel Salad With Lemon Dill Dressing, **118**

Lentil & Sweet Potato Salad With Halloumi, **132**

Mango Avocado Salad, **156**

Marinated White Bean & Vegetable Salad, **139**

Miso Ginger Soba Salad, **128** V

Panzanella With Asparagus & Eggs, **143**

Rice Salad With Quick-Pickled Carrot & Daikon, **127** V

Shaved Beet & Celery Root Salad With Miso Dressing, **146**

Sugar Snap Peas & Avocado Salad With Sesame Dressing, **144** V

Swiss Chard, Strawberry & Feta Salad, **114**

Tossed Salad, **231**

Vegetarian Watermelon Poke Bowl, **134**

Walnut Pesto Potato Salad, **131**

Warm Kale & Quinoa Salad, **138**

Warm Roasted Cauliflower Salad With Garlicky Tahini Dressing, **133**

Wheat Berry & Chickpea Salad With Garam Masala Dressing, **125**

salsa & chutney. See also condiments, dips & sauces; guacamole

Cilantro Ginger Chutney, **68** V

Cucumber Salsa, **153**

Spiced Peach Chutney, **67** V

sauces. See condiments, dips & sauces

Sautéed Beets, **177**

Sautéed Kale With Raisins, **270** V

Seared Cherry Tomato Pasta, **172**

Sesame Dressing, **144**

Sesame Garlic Chili Oil, **62** V

seaweed

Ramen Noodle Soup, **102**

Shallot Vinaigrette, **132**

Shaved Beet & Celery Root Salad With Miso Dressing, **146**

Sherried Shallot Butter, **61**

sides, **234–275**

Slow Cooker Dal, **239**

Slow Cooker French Leek Soup, **106**

Slow Cooker Garam Masala Eggplant, **161**

Smoked Cheddar Pancakes With Pickled Beets, **75**

Smoked Tomato Bruschetta With Gouda, **92**

Smoky Grilled Cheese With Ale-Braised Onions, **150**

Smooth & Creamy Mashed Potatoes, **259**

smoothies
  Clementine Yogurt Smoothie, **14**
  Swiss Chard & Mango Smoothie, **14**

snacks, **70–93**

soba noodles. See noodles

soups, **94–111**

Southwestern Cauliflower Cakes, **272**

spaghetti. See pasta

Spiced Cauliflower & Leek Purée, **273**

Spiced Peach Chutney, **67** V

Spicy Cilantro Pesto, **54** V

Spicy Green Bean & Tofu Stir-Fry, **211** V

Spicy Sesame Dipping Sauce, **76**

spinach
  Creamy Skillet Mushroom Lasagna, **180**
  Crustless Zucchini Quiche With Grilled Corn Salad, **229**
  Curried Cauliflower & Spinach Wraps, **154** V
  Double Mozzarella & Spinach Pita Pizzas, **200**
  Halloumi & Quinoa Salad With Sumac-Lime Dressing, **137**
  Japchae, **185** V
  Mushroom & Spinach Sauté, **270**
  Roasted Squash & Spinach Lasagna, **182**
  Spinach & Artichoke Pissaladière, **90**
  Spinach & Avocado Green Goddess Pasta, **174** V
  Spinach & Feta Omelette Soufflé, **228**
  Tomato & Vegetable Soup With Halloumi, **99**
  Vegetable Tikka Masala Naan Pizza, **199**
  Vegetarian Watermelon Poke Bowl, **134**

Spinach & Artichoke Pissaladière, **90**

Spinach & Avocado Green Goddess Pasta, **174** V

Spinach & Feta Omelette Soufflé, **228**

Spring Rolls, **77**

squash
  Butternut Squash Risotto, **194**
  Crunchy Curry Rice & Squash, **245** V
  Roasted Cilantro Lime Squash, **242** V
  Roasted Squash & Spinach Lasagna, **182**
  Vegetable Tikka Masala Naan Pizza, **199**

Sriracha Aioli, **264**

Sriracha Mayonnaise, **264**

stir-fry
  Spicy Green Bean & Tofu Stir-Fry, **211** V

stock
  Light Vegetable Stock, **51** V
  Roasted Vegetable Stock, **51** V

strawberries
  Gingery Fruit Salad, **32** V
  Strawberries & Cream Loaf, **286**
  Strawberry Granita, **279** V
  Strawberry Mint Granita, **279**
  Swiss Chard, Strawberry & Feta Salad, **114**

Strawberries & Cream Loaf, **286**

Strawberry Granita, **279** V

Strawberry Mint Granita, **279**

sugar snap peas. See peas

Sugar Snap Peas & Avocado Salad With Sesame Dressing, **144** V

Sumac-Lime Dressing, **137**

Sun-Dried Tomato & Almond Pesto, **55** V

Sun-Dried Tomato & Roasted Red Pepper Cream Sauce, **53**

Sun-Dried Tomato Agnolotti With Walnuts & Swiss Chard, **179**

Sweet & Sour Ketchup, **63** V

Sweet & Spicy Thai Oatmeal, **24**

Sweet Onion & Gorgonzola Pizza, **201**

sweet peppers. See peppers, sweet

Sweet Potato & Cauliflower Tagine, **218** V

Sweet Potato & Two-Cheese Tarte Tatin, **91**

Sweet Potato Tacos, **157**

Sweet Potato Veggie Burgers, **158** V

Swiss chard
  Sun-Dried Tomato Agnolotti With Walnuts & Swiss Chard, **179**
  Swiss Chard & Mango Smoothie, **14**
  Swiss Chard, Strawberry & Feta Salad, **114**
  Swiss Chard With Frizzled Onions, **240**
  Swiss Chard & Mango Smoothie, **14**

Swiss Chard With Frizzled Onions, **240**

Swiss Chard, Strawberry & Feta Salad, **114**

T

tacos
  Chili-Lime Sweet Potato Tacos, **157** V

Tahini Falafel Lettuce Burgers With Cucumber Salsa, **153**

Tarragon Chive Mayonnaise, **56**

Tarragon Vinaigrette, **138**

Tempeh & Rice–Stuffed Peppers, **217** V

Thai Green Curry Paste, **62** V

Thai-Style Tofu Curry, **163** V

The Perfect Dutch Baby Pancake, **28**

Toasted Almonds, **173**

Toasted Almond Granola, **31**

tofu
  Broccoli & Broiled Tofu With No-Cook Peanut Sauce, **216** V
  Cilantro-Jalapeño Grilled Tofu Salad, **120**
  Crispy Tofu & Broccoli With Udon Noodles, **209** V
  Edamame Vegetable Soup, **100** V
  Fried Tofu With Spicy Sesame Dipping Sauce, **76**
  Oven-Baked Teriyaki Tofu, **212** V
  Spicy Green Bean & Tofu Stir-Fry, **211** V
  Thai-Style Tofu Curry, **163** V
  Tofu & Chow Mein Noodles, **210** V
  Vegetarian Ma Po Tofu, **215** V
  Vegetarian Singapore Noodles, **187**

Tofu & Chow Mein Noodles, **210** V

Tomato & Basil Mayonnaise, **56**

Tomato & Vegetable Soup With Halloumi, **99**

tomatoes, bottled strained (passata)
  Crispy Polenta With Vegetable Ragout, **195**
  Double Mozzarella & Spinach Pita Pizzas, **200**
  Huevos Rancheros Casserole, **20**
  Pine Nut, Quinoa & Mushroom Strudel, **190** V
  Sweet & Sour Ketchup, **63** V

tomatoes, canned
  Afghan-Style Baked Eggplant With Mint-Garlic Yogurt Sauce, **248**

Curried Cauliflower & Spinach Wraps, **154** V

Mediterranean Stewed Chickpeas, **221** V

One-Pot Quinoa Chili, **188** V

Roasted Squash & Spinach Lasagna, **182**

Slow Cooker Garam Masala Eggplant, **161**

Tempeh & Rice–Stuffed Peppers, **217** V

Tomato & Vegetable Soup With Halloumi, **99**

tomatoes, fresh

Arugula & Bulgur–Stuffed Tomatoes, **251**

Asparagus & Gruyère Cups, **230**

Charred Corn & Tomato Salad With Chipotle Vinaigrette, **145**

Cilantro-Jalapeño Grilled Tofu Salad, **120**

Classic Chili Sauce, **48** V

Creamy Tomato Soup With Pesto Drizzle, **96**

Crustless Zucchini Quiche With Grilled Corn Salad, **229**

Easy Marinara Sauce, **50** V

Fresh Tomato Sauce, **49** V

Greek Halloumi Salad With Herbed Pita Chips, **119**

Green Tomato Chow Chow, **69** V

Grilled Asparagus Pizza, **196**

Halloumi & Quinoa Salad With Sumac-Lime Dressing, **137**

Heirloom Tomato Tabbouleh Salad, **124** V

Honey Ketchup, **64**

Light Vegetable Stock, **51**

Mediterranean Vegetable Panini With Grape Tomatoes & Feta Pesto, **155**

Mexican Tortilla Soup, **107** V

Panzanella With Asparagus & Eggs, **143**

Pressure Cooker Fresh Tomato Sauce, **49**

Seared Cherry Tomato Pasta, **172**

Slow Cooker Dal, **239**

Smoked Tomato Bruschetta With Gouda, **92**

Sun-Dried Tomato & Roasted Red Pepper Cream Sauce, **53**

Tahini Falafel Lettuce Burgers With Cucumber Salsa, **153**

Tomato Pear Ketchup, **64** V

Zesty Tomato Jam, **63** V

tomatoes, sun-dried

Creamy Kale & Sun-Dried Tomato Carbonara, **166**

Lemony Ravioli With Sun-Dried Tomatoes, **178**

Sun-Dried Tomato Agnolotti With Walnuts & Swiss Chard, **179**

Sun-Dried Tomato & Almond Pesto, **55** V

Tomato Pear Ketchup, **64** V

Tomato Sauce, **182**

tortillas

Black Bean Tostadas With Mango Avocado Salad, **156**

Chili-Lime Sweet Potato Tacos, **157** V

Curried Cauliflower & Spinach Wraps, **154** V

Huevos Rancheros Casserole, **20**

Mexican Tortilla Soup, **107** V

Tossed Salad, **231**

Tropical Mint Oatmeal, **23**

Tropical Yogurt Parfait, **34**

Turkish Egg Tartines, **224**

Twin Peas With Roasted Garlic Butter, **246**

V

Vegetable Panini, **155**

Vegetable Quinoa Soup, **101** V

Vegetable Ragout, **195**

Vegetable Saffron Paella, **189** V

Vegetable Tikka Masala Naan Pizza, **199**

Vegetarian Ma Po Tofu, **215** V

Vegetarian Singapore Noodles, **187**

Vegetarian Watermelon Poke Bowl, **134**

vermicelli. See noodles

W

Walnut Pesto Potato Salad, **131**

walnuts. See nuts

Warm Kale & Quinoa Salad, **138**

Warm Roasted Cauliflower Salad With Garlicky Tahini Dressing, **133**

watercress

Asparagus & Gruyère Cups, **230**

Black Bean Tostadas With Mango Avocado Salad, **156**

Mango Avocado Salad, **156**

Watercress & Walnut Pesto, **55** V

Watercress Salad, **230**

Watercress & Walnut Pesto, **55** V

Watercress Salad, **230**

watermelon

Vegetarian Watermelon Poke Bowl, **134**

Wheat Berry & Chickpea Salad With Garam Masala Dressing, **125**

Whole Wheat Sesame Crispbread, **44**

Wild Mushroom Cream Sauce, **53**

Y

Yeastless Whole Wheat Sesame Thins, **44** V

yogurt

Afghan-Style Baked Eggplant With Mint-Garlic Yogurt Sauce, **248**

Cauliflower & White Bean Dip, **81**

Clementine Yogurt Smoothie, **14**

Easy Cranberry Yogurt Parfaits, **33**

Malt & Yogurt Rye Bread, **42**

Slow Cooker Dal, **239**

Tropical Yogurt Parfait, **34**

Turkish Egg Tartines, **224**

Z

Za'atar Pita Chips, **83**

Zesty Tomato Jam, **63** V

zucchini

Couscous & Cheese–Stuffed Zucchini, **241**

Crunchy Peanut Veggie Noodle Salad, **123**

Crustless Zucchini Quiche With Grilled Corn Salad, **229**

Edamame Vegetable Soup, **100** V

Lazy Skillet Lasagna, **181**

Mediterranean Vegetable Panini With Grape Tomatoes & Feta Pesto, **155**

Potato & Zucchini Mini Latkes, **84**

Tomato & Vegetable Soup With Halloumi, **99**

Vegetable Saffron Paella, **189** V

Zucchini, Chèvre & Walnut Tart, **86**

Zucchini Ribbon & Caper Pasta, **171**

Zucchini, Chèvre & Walnut Tart, **86**

Zucchini Ribbon & Caper Pasta, **171**

CONTRIBUTORS

RECIPES

All recipes were developed and Tested Till Perfect by the Canadian Living Test Kitchen

PHOTOGRAPHY

RYAN BROOK 151, 303

JEFF COULSON 12, 16, 22, 35, 46, 65, 66, 88, 103, 111, 121, 122, 130, 136, 142, 160, 168, 170, 176, 184, 197, 204, 208, 226, 237, 243, 244, 256, 275

YVONNE DUIVENVOORDEN 220

ANGUS FERGUSSON 135

JODI PUDGE 8, 15, 73, 80, 87, 94, 97, 116, 129, 147, 159, 175, 183, 191, 207, 213, 219, 234, 249, 250, 255, 261, 262, 267, 268, 281, 288, 291

STEVE KRUG 74

VIRGINIA MACDONALD 141

RYAN SZULC 93, 202

RONALD TSANG 88, 104, 152, 225, 276, 292

JAMES TSE 21, 29, 30, 36, 41, 57, 70, 112, 167, 214, 233, 238, 287

MAYA VISNEYI 58, 79, 115, 148, 192, 198, 282

FOOD STYLING

ASHLEY DENTON 57, 98, 116, 147, 167, 191, 197, 202, 204, 207, 214, 233, 255, 261, 262, 268, 281

MICHAEL ELLIOTT 15, 58, 70, 73, 79, 80, 94, 97, 104, 115, 135, 152, 183, 192, 213, 219, 234, 238, 249, 250, 267

DAVID GRENIER 12, 16, 22, 35, 103, 121, 142, 148, 151, 176, 198, 226, 237, 243, 256, 275, 276, 282, 288, 291

ADELE HAGAN 111

MIRANDA KEYES 208

LUCIE RICHARD 21, 29, 30, 36, 41, 112, 287

HEATHER SHAW 46

CHRISTOPHER ST. ONGE 88, 122, 136, 168, 225, 292

CLAIRE STUBBS 8, 65, 87, 129, 159, 160, 175, 220, 244

MELANIE STUPARYK 66, 170, 303

SARAH SWEENEY 141

NOAH WITENOFF 74, 130, 184

NICOLE YOUNG 93

PROP STYLING

LAURA BRANSON 8, 15, 21, 29, 30, 36, 41, 46, 97, 104, 111, 112, 129, 152, 159, 175, 202, 208, 287, 303

AURELIE BRYCE 121, 170, 176

ALANNA DAVEY 88, 292

CATHERINE DOHERTY 57, 65, 66, 73, 80, 87, 94, 103, 148, 167, 183, 198, 213, 214, 219, 220, 233, 234, 237, 243, 244, 249, 250, 256, 267, 276, 281, 282

JENNIFER EVANS 58, 70, 79, 74, 115, 141, 147, 192, 207, 238, 255, 261, 288, 291

MADELEINE JOHARI 93, 116, 135, 160, 184, 191, 225, 262, 268

KAREN KIRK 151

SABRINA LINN 130, 226, 275

SASHA SEYMOUR 98, 122, 136, 168, 197, 204

CAROLYN SOUCH 12, 16, 22, 35, 142

GOAT CHEESE & ZUCCHINI CRUSTLESS QUICHE
P 229

Canadian Living

Complete your collection of Tested-Till-Perfect recipes!

The Ultimate Cookbook
The Special Occasions Cookbook
New Slow Cooker Favourites

The Complete Chicken Cookbook
The Complete Chocolate Cookbook
The Complete Preserving Cookbook
The Complete Vegetarian Cookbook

400-Calorie Dinners
Dinner in 30 Minutes or Less
Essential Barbecue
Essential Salads
Fish & Seafood
Healthy Family Meals
Make It Ahead!
Make It Chocolate!
Pasta & Noodles
Sweet & Simple

The Affordable Feasts Collection
The Appetizer Collection
The Barbecue Collection
The International Collection
The One Dish Collection
The Slow Cooker Collection
The Vegetarian Collection

150 Essential Beef, Pork & Lamb Recipes
150 Essential Salads
150 Essential Whole Grain Recipes

canadianliving.com/books